# Captain François: From Valmy, 1792 to Waterloo, 1815

GENERAL BONAPARTE

# Captain François:
# From Valmy, 1792 to
# Waterloo, 1815

The Journal of the Military Career of a French
Soldier of the Napoleonic Age

Charles François

Translated by Robert B. Douglas

**LEONAUR**

Captain François: From Valmy, 1792 to Waterloo, 1815
*The Journal of the Military Career of a French Soldier of the Napoleonic Age*
by Charles François
Translated by Robert B. Douglas

First published under the title

*From Valmy to Waterloo*

Leonaur is an imprint of Oakpast Ltd
Copyright in this form © 2014 Oakpast Ltd

ISBN: 978-1-78282-427-5 (hardcover)
ISBN: 978-1-78282-428-2 (softcover)

**http://www.leonaur.com**

Publisher's Notes

# Contents

# Preface

There is no end to the memoirs and souvenirs of the actors or supernumeraries in the great drama of the Revolution and the Empire. Every day a fresh witness comes forth, like a skeleton starting from the tomb, to relate the heroisms and hardships of the times. When it is not history which evokes this dramatic past, it is fiction, and M. Paul Adam appears to have lived in those far-off days in his admirable *Enfant d'Austerlitz*. But a soldier who—whilst still a soldier—relates what *he has seen*, notes down his halting places and his adventures, and those of his comrades in barracks and battles, is always a lucky find. Thanks to my friend, Georges Cain, who possesses, at the Musée Carnavalet, a copy, which is, perhaps, unique, of the *Memoirs of an Unknown*—an unknown who deserves fame—I one day had that good fortune, and it is to that lucky chance that the present volume is due. This is how it happened.

In a Breton review, the *Lycée Armoricain*, that was printed and published at Nantes, by Mellinet and Malasses (Emile Souvestre began his literary career there) will be found—but it is terribly difficult to meet with the collection—the *Journal of a French Officer*, from 1792 to 1815, by Captain François. And this *Journal* (or rather the analysis of this journal) is most interesting and veracious. In a score of copybooks, of about 100 pages each, this Captain François relates, without any pretentiousness, all his military life, and this humble fighter, this officer lost amidst the crowd of his fellows, fully deserves as much attention and glory as has been given to Thiébault[1] or Marbot[2]. Born in Picardy, June 19th, 1775, at Guinchy, near Péronne, in the Department

1. *Thiébault: Soldier of Napoleon* in 2 volumes by Paul Thiébault is also published by Leonaur.
2. *The Life of the Real Brigadier Gerard* Volume 1 *The Young Hussar* 1782-1807 and Volume 2 *Imperial Aide-De-Camp* 1807-1811 by Jean-Baptiste De Marbot is also published by Leonaur.

of Somme, the son of a brigadier in the "King's farms and salt-tax," the author of this *Journal of a French Officer* was one of the first volunteers who went to defend the threatened frontiers of the Republic.

He enlists at fifteen, and a fortnight later, at Valmy, September 20th, 1792, receives his first bullet. He is at Jemmapes in October; he is present at the taking of Brussels, the siege of Antwerp, and the siege of Namur; and December 3rd, 1793, is promoted to corporal. At Nerwinde he has his second wound. He is appointed quartermaster.

Then follows the campaign in Holland. Then François leaves the army of the North, crosses the Rhine with the army of Sambre-et-Meuse, and fights nearly every day. Every day and every night. One night, for instance, in order that he may make a present of a horse to a young sutler woman, he goes straight to an outpost of the enemy, attacks the horseman, sabres him, brings back the horse and gallantly gives it to the fair one. In '96 he is wounded at Sulzbach, is taken prisoner soon afterwards, escapes, and rejoins, in '97, the 9th half-brigade, which is just starting for Italy.

He belongs to Bernadotte's division. He fights at Tagliamento. Then he forms one of a flying column commanded by Lannes, and when the expedition to Egypt is resolved on, François embarks at Toulon as steward's mate, on board the mortar-boat, *Hirondelle*. What adventures and what memories Egypt has in store for him! It is like a romance in real life, or rather an epopee. Battles against Mamelukes with terrible Damascus blades. François says:

> I have seen many of our cavalry stretched dead on the sand, the head entirely separated from the body; others whose arms and legs had been cut clean off, and even the body of a *chasseur* of the 22nd cloven in two. You may judge from that the temper of the Mamelukes' sabres. I have one, and many times I have cut in two a goat, or sheep, or dog at a single cut, without striking, but by drawing my Damascus blade across the animal's body.

And François, despite his wounds, despite his courage, is still quartermaster. That is because all his comrades show the same devotion, the same heroism. He is in Reynier's division. He relates plainly, with painful precision, the story of the expedition to Syria, deaths from thirst, the soldiers committing suicide on the march, in the sand, to end their troubles. Two brothers of his company killed one another. At last somebody thinks of digging in the sand: they find water. The poor wretches are saved. Water! Water! Then they fight and they sing. "That is the French soldier!" Blood is poured in pints for a drop of water.

François is one of the few eyewitness narrators of the Egyptian expedition. The captain is at St. Jean d'Acre. Nothing could be more terrible than this siege. The assault is furious, it is repelled obstinately, and the wounded and the dead, despatched by the Turks, form a row of trunkless heads along the ramparts. The soldiers, however, quarrel for the honour of forming the storming party, in the attack on the terrible "Square Tower."

I have seen them weep, and heard them say to their colonels, 'Am I not as good a soldier and as brave as so-and-so, who is chosen before me?' The colonels replied, 'Your turn will come!'

I do not reckon the shot wounds and sabre cuts which François received in these night combats, lighted up by fire-pots. When the wounds are healed, he enters the famous corps of "Dromedaries," and wears a white turban on his head, and is clad, when in full uniform, in a tunic of sky-blue cloth with red trimmings. These scouts covered their twenty or thirty leagues a day, and their mounts went as much as six days without drinking, when they were pursuing Mourad Bey.

History, seen closely, is always more dramatic in the realism of "minor facts," and François saw with his own eyes the punishment of the assassin of Kléber. The page on which he describes this punishment is horrifying.

On the 14th June, 1800, at Gizeh, Kléber is walking with the architect Protin, on a long terrace covered with vines. A man presents himself before him, bows as though to kiss his hand, and stabs him with a dagger. "Help, guide, I am wounded!" Kléber cries, seeing an officer of the Guides near. He leans against the terrace wall, and falls. Protin rushes on the murderer, and strikes him with a light cane; he struggles with him, receives six stabs, and falls by the side of the general. The assassin returns to Kléber, stabs him three times, then runs away through the gardens.

François, who has touched the weapon handled by Suliman el Halebi—a kind of cutlass with a curved blade 15 or 16 inches long—was present at the execution of the murderer; whose skeleton is now in a glass case in one of the rooms at the Jardin des Plantes at Paris. He was a fanatic, aged twenty-four, whose religious faith and patriotism had been worked upon by the Ulemas. The Council of War condemned him to have his hand burned off, and be impaled, and his accomplices, three Ulemas, to be beheaded.

François is present at the embalming of Kléber's body. "I saw his entrails taken out." He is present at the funeral, he is present at the punishment. The three condemned Ulemas wept when they were to be executed, and cursed the day they met "the Syrian" (Suliman). He was very calm, and replied that he was ashamed to have such cowards for his accomplices. Their heads were cut off before him. He was unmoved, and waited.

Marks of the terrible punishment he underwent may still be seen on the skeleton. What agony the flesh which clothed this skeleton must have endured!

Reverses befell the army in Egypt, and Ménou could not succeed in saving our conquest. On June 19th, 1801, two envoys, an Englishman and a Turk, summoned the general to surrender Cairo. François is ordered to escort the French envoy who is to take back the reply. He is attacked on the left bank of the Nile, at the village of Hem-Raheb, by a squadron of horse, dismounted from his dromedary, and led into captivity, whilst the Turks cut off the heads of his comrades, whom they had killed.

And it is—cruel retort for the death of—preceded by a Turkish horseman who carries suspended at his saddle-bow the heads of two Frenchmen, that the unfortunate François is marched off with these fearful trophies before his eyes. But, "what is worse," as Goya says, the horseman orders François to carry these heads:

A hole was pierced through the cheek, and a rope passed through the mouth. He put the middle of the cord round my neck, and the two heads hung on my shoulders.

It is thus that, called a "dog," struck, and bruised, the soldier comes to a mosque, where he is relieved of his horrible burden. Then they take him to Damascus, with a gang of convicts being escorted to gaol. He is imprisoned, undergoes fearful sufferings. François, who has learned the language of the country, passes himself off as an Egyptian, and thus gets a little better treated, until one day an *emir*, governor and viceroy of the Pachalik of Antioch, to whom he relates his misfortunes, is touched by the story of his adventures, and takes François into his service. O Fortune! Essed Katif-el-Becker had been ambassador at Versailles in 1787; he had known Louis XVI., and had a great liking for the French. And now François, richly clad in the Turkish fashion, is henceforth one of the military household of the *emir*.

Here his history approaches the marvellous. It is a story of the *"Thousand and one Nights."* François visits Jaffa, Bagdad, Naplouse (Shechem), he holds reviews, he travels in Judea, enters Jerusalem, sees the Black Sea, and leaves there for Constantinople, where he gets a position in the mounted Janissaries, but where he plans to make his escape, and does not have to wait long. He goes straight to the French Embassy, and makes himself known. General Sebastiani gives him European dress and 400 *francs*, and sends him off to Dalmatia. And at Udine, October 2nd, 1803, François rejoins a French regiment. By a miracle, it is his own. It is his old half-brigade—the 9th of the line. His comrades embrace him, they take him to General Boursier, who commands at Udine. François is provided with a letter from Sebastiani, and, the "Dromedaries" having been disbanded and incorporated with the *chasseurs* of the Guard, the old soldier of the 9th is quite happy to re-enter his former regiment. At Landau, his colonel—Colonel Pépin—gives him a banquet, and the band plays, "Where can one be better than in the bosom of his family?" And, as it is a long time since the regiment made a move, they start for Strasbourg.

From Strasbourg they go to the camp at Boulogne, and from Boulogne to the Danube. François is at Jena. There he receives four bullets, of which one makes a bruise on his thigh. He gives us, in passing, the name of the cavalry sergeant who killed Prince Louis of Prussia with a sabre cut. It was "a man named Guindé."

François lived through all the military epopee, and his notes thereon are of deep interest. The wars are depicted to the life. We see the French *voltigeurs* starving, and sadly making a truce with the Cossacks (before Friedland) to get provisions, and even sometimes bartering for potatoes with them, when they had found some. And what heroic deeds are recounted in a few words!

The 19th (May) we saw an English corvette coming up the Vistula; *the grenadiers of the Guard swam out and boarded her.* She was loaded with gunpowder and oats.

Then comes that ill-omened campaign, the war with Spain. François is there and relates the story with his usual truthfulness. The *Dos de Mayo*, the tragic second of May, has here its eyewitness, and the tortures inflicted on the stragglers of the army have a painter who is quite as realistic as he who described the "Horrors of War." Even on the bushes which bordered the roads, our soldiers, when on the march, found shreds of human flesh, fragments of corpses. Men were not only killed but chopped to pieces.

François is at Baylen. Imprisoned at Xeres, he runs the risk of being murdered by the mob. The prisoners prepare to defend themselves with banisters, or razors fastened to sticks. They are thrown on board a vessel, the *Vieille Castille*. There are there 1,157 prisoners, of whom 943 are officers. The prisoners revolt, gag the crew, pass through the English fleet. No hero of Dumas' novels had so many authentic adventures. The account of them ought to be read in this now forgotten *Journal*.

To rest himself he goes to Russia, Wilna, Smolensk, Moscow. There, François is seriously wounded. General Morand notices it; "Captain, you cannot march. Retire to the flag-guard."

"General, the day's work has too many attractions for me. I want to share the glory of the regiment."

General Morand grasps his hand. "I knew you would say that."

This is on the eve of battle, and the next day François nevertheless attacks the great redoubt. This time he will be stretched in the ambulance waggon, by the side of the brave Morand, who has been hit on the chin by a round shot. François is believed to be killed. He goes to Moscow, crossing the battlefield, where the neglected wounded are lodged "in the belly of a horse, of which they eat the flesh, like dogs."

The disastrous retreat, the tragic grandeur of which has been described by Ségur,[3] has never been painted more faithfully than by this soldier, who marches "armed with a crutch, and clad in a pink cloak embroidered with gold, and lined with ermine, and with a hood over his head," across the white plains, and replies to those who are groaning at their hard lot.

Oh, but we might be worse off! Here, at least, we have horse to eat. In Syria we often had nothing. Heat is more terrible than cold. Patience and courage, comrades!

In this deadly frost, fingers break like glass; or putrefy when a fire is approached. Captain Chidor, of the 9th regiment of the line, takes off the rag which binds up his foot; three toes come off with it. He pulls off the great toe of his other foot, without feeling any pain.

François does not state that he was clean-shaved during the retreat as Stendhal was; but he defends his flag against the Cossacks with his crutch. They arrive at last at the Beresina,—and, at the end

---

3. *Napoleon's Russian Campaign* and *Aide-de-Camp to Napoleon* by Philippe Henri de Ségur are also published by Leonaur.

of this dreadful retreat, the grand army of 415,000 men is reduced to 26,000. The 30th regiment of the line, which numbered 4,480 men at the passage of the Niemen, has left only its colonel, its major, 2 *chefs de bataillon*, 11 captains, 16 lieutenants and sub-lieutenants, and 131 non-commissioned officers and privates. But on January 1st, 1814, at Thorn, when the colonel is grieving about having lost his eagle; "Colonel, have you forgotten that it has not left my shoulders since we started from Krasnoe," replies François.

"Can it be possible? My brave François!"

And, the next day, he presents him to Davoust, that the model of marshals may salute the model of soldiers. Then comes Ligny—then Waterloo. The retreat on Paris with Gerard, the plain of Grenelle, where they hope once more to rush on the enemy and devour him, the bivouac at Montrouge, the retreat to the Loire. . . . And that is the end.

François, "the brigand of the Loire," is discharged at Saint Fleur; in 1824 he is pensioned off with the rank of honorary chef *de bataillon*. He is still young; he might fight or serve, but he is never employed, and is content with his lot. He says, smiling:

"I did not enlist to become a Marshal of France!"

Till the end of his life, this brave soldier, resigned, but not worn out, lived at Nantes. He had married a young woman of Rennes. He jotted down his recollections without any attempt to play the literary man. The old Picard volunteer wished to dedicate to Brittany his *Journal of a French Officer*,—the book which ought to have appeared in 1829, "with a portrait of the author and a facsimile of his handwriting," and which has mostly remained unpublished, only some extracts and a full analysis having appeared in the *Lycée Armoricain* of Mellinet and Malassis.

Malassis! The father of the publisher of Banville and Baudelaire. Mellinet, father of the hero of Magenta. With François we are amongst old friends. And I wished, when I examined his Journal, that some publisher would print the work which had, in spite of the prospectus, remained in limbo for seventy-five years. As good luck would have it, my article was seen by the possessor of François' M.S., and at the same time a publisher asked me if I could help him to find these memoirs, which he wished to print. My part in the transaction—a very modest one—was confined to putting M. Foulon, the proprietor of the MS., in communication with the publisher, and thus the *Journal* of François emerged from the *Lycée Armoricain*, where only a few literary searchers knew of its existence. Today it may be said that French military literature, which was already so rich, counts one masterpiece the more. Not that the writer was a great author, but he was essentially a soldier,—a man!—one who did his duty unswervingly, unflinchingly.

Jules Claretie.

# Translator's Preface

When I was first asked, by the editor of the French edition, whether I considered this book suitable for translation, I replied, after a brief examination, that I did not think so. My reason for this verdict was that Captain François never occupied any position which would make his opinion worth having. He knew nothing of statecraft, or politics, and had not the ambition nor the curiosity to become the confidant of men who did know. His history is a story of hard knocks, given or received, but of the reason why he should be called upon to give or receive those knocks he knew nothing, beyond the little he could pick up round the camp fire.

A more careful perusal led me to see that the book had a value of another kind. Some years ago, a French historian calculated that there were fully 200,000 books concerning Napoleon then existing, and the number has considerably increased since then; but, great as the literary output has been, the popular interest in the greatest figure in modern history has kept pace with it, and bids fair to continue to do so for many years to come. Only a few weeks ago, it was stated in a leading literary paper that "never has there been such a boom in Napoleonic literature as there is at the present moment," and the statement is not exaggerated.

We have had numerous *Lives of the Emperor*, in which he has been depicted in every hue from rose-pink to the deepest black; we have also had the *Memoirs* or *Recollections* of many of the marshals who fought for him in the field, and the diplomatists who schemed for him in the council-chamber.

But very little of this huge mass of printed matter has come from the rank and file, or subaltern officers of the Grand Army. This hardly a matter for surprise. The lads, who flocked round the flag when the country was in danger, had little learning, and the few that had found scant leisure for diary-making in the rapidly-succeeding scenes of the world-drama in which they played their part. Very few of the tough old warriors who followed the fortunes of Bonaparte from Arcole to Waterloo had time, inclination, or ability to describe the events which took place before their eyes.

When they did, their diaries—like this of Captain François—possess a grim realism which the library historian very rarely attains. A description of the retreat from Moscow, written by a prosperous, middle-aged gentleman seated in a comfortable armchair, in a well-stocked library, in front of a good fire, could hardly have the graphic force of that of a man who had limped weary miles through the unending snow, and fought with comrades, as famished as himself, for gobbets of raw horseflesh.

In many cases, François relates incidents, or supplies details of which the professional historian probably never heard, or considered beneath his dignity to insert. I will not, however, call the reader's attention to instances of this, for a far abler pen than mine has already dealt pretty fully with the principal events of François' adventurous career, and "the words of Mercury are harsh after the songs of Apollo." Nor need I dwell upon the evidence which François supplies relative to some disputed points in history. For instance, much ink has been spilled concerning the poisoning of the plague-patients at Jaffa, some writers declaring that Bonaparte never ordered the death of a single Frenchman, and others asserting that over 400 perished, after partaking of the "opium broth" he commanded to be prepared for them. According to François, the poison was administered to thirty men, of whom eighteen died, and as he was on the spot, and knew one of the men who took some of the poison (but recovered), his account is possibly correct; for, as he was not troubled with moral scruples himself, and thought every act of Bonaparte to be the wisest and noblest that could be devised, he would not have penned a word of protest in his diary if his beloved general had thought fit to poison three thousand men instead of thirty.

On the other hand, it does not do to accept all his statements unreservedly. The things that happened round him he recorded faithfully enough, but he was somewhat apt to accept hearsay evidence without sifting it. Of a great battle he knew little but what he could see from his own place in the ranks; and his account of the death of Sir Ralph Abercromby at Aboukir was derived from an over-imaginative comrade, and is not in accordance with facts; but, on the whole, he is correct, circumstantial, impartial, and always interesting.

There is one other point on which I would touch before I conclude. François was a thorough-going type of the French soldiers of the Grand Army,—lads who had been carried away by the popular enthusiasm of the Revolution, and had developed into the most perfect war-machine that the world had then seen. They were not particularly noble, or generous, or moral, but they had brute courage and blind fidelity, and, under a leader they loved—if he paid them regularly, or gave them frequent opportunities of plunder—there was nothing they would not dare. Their character has been depicted by scores of novelists of all nations—notably by Charles Lever and Sir Conan Doyle in English literature—but though their psychology is not over complex, and has been well studied, this frankly ingenuous autobiography may be of use to intending novelists.

Robert B. Douglas.

# CHAPTER 1

# 1775—1792

Charles François, the author of these *Memoirs*, was, he tells us in the beginning of his diary, born at Guinchy, in Picardy, June 19th, 1775, and was the second of seven children. His father was employed in the collection of the salt-tax, but lost his post at the outbreak of the Revolution, and retired on a small pension, which he did not long enjoy, for he died in 1795.

Young Charles was sent, as a day-boarder, at the early age of five, to a school at the neighbouring town of Peronne, where his father was then employed. Two years later, he was removed to a Minorite monastery of which his cousin was Prior, and remained there four years. Afterwards he had two years' teaching, at home, from tutors; but he owns he was self-willed, obstinate, and neglected his lessons, and, as his mother was dead, and his father's duties prevented him from looking after the education of his children, Charles and his brothers did not learn much.

The father, Jean Baptiste Joseph François, seems to have been a man of intelligence, and he foresaw that there would shortly be a great national upheaval. He guessed that when this did take place he would lose his post, and, as that was his only source of revenue, he was anxious about the fate of his children. The best thing, he thought, was to give them a good education, and, for that purpose, he took young Charles, early in 1789, to a relative who lived in Paris.

A few months later, the Bastille fell, and the boy, carried away by youthful enthusiasm, joined the patriotic movement. He informed his father that he had determined to be a soldier, and nothing else would suit him. At that time, the National Guard was being formed, and François begged his guardian to let him join. The request rather pleased his relative, who was a bit of a patriot, and he fitted out the

19

boy with uniform, musket, and sabre, and presented him before the section of Saint Méderic where he was immediately registered as "an active citizen," and enrolled in the battalion of *chasseurs*.

Ten days or a fortnight later, the lad mounted guard for the first time, at the Tuileries. The National Guards were drilled by sergeants and old soldiers who had deserted from the royal regiments. François had a natural aptitude for drill, and in a very little time knew as much about it as his instructors.

One day that he was on sentry-go at the Convention, a citizen, remarking his youth, asked if he had any profession. François replied that he had not, and had not thought about any. The citizen was a well-to-do merchant, named Chrétien Raflay. He had taken a liking to François, and called on the lad's guardian, and the result was that the youth entered Raflay's counting-house as the junior clerk of a staff of eleven. The staff was soon reduced, for, early in 1790, two of the clerks enrolled themselves as volunteers, and were sent off to the frontier. François would have liked to have gone too, but as he was not yet fifteen, he was judged to be too young, and the military authorities refused him.

Two years later, "the country was in danger," the Prussians had entered Champagne and seized Verdun. The memorable massacre of August 10th had taken place, and the king was virtually a prisoner in Paris. François, and four of his fellow-clerks offered themselves as volunteers, and this time he was deemed old enough and strong enough to be enrolled. He told his relative he had enlisted, and his guardian—perhaps wisely—said little or nothing, except that he would inform the lad's father, though Charles did not think that necessary, as the officer at the enlistment office had assured him the campaign would not last more than three or four months.

On September 3rd, the volunteers of the section, to the number of 116, some boys, some middle-aged, married men, assembled and elected their officers, sergeants, corporals, and fuglemen. Then they were reviewed, and—it is hardly necessary to say—harangued. The company was to form part of the 5th battalion of Paris, which numbered 1,143 men, and was commanded by Citizen Chopplet, late of the king's household. About three-fourths of the men in the company were armed and equipped at their own expense; the others were provided with arms and uniform at the cost of the section, or by "patriotic gifts."

After the review the men were informed they were to start for the frontier on the 5th, and were then dismissed, crying "*Vive la Nation!*" Each captain received 400 *francs* in cash, and 8,000 in paper for preliminary expenses: for pay, at the rate of fifteen *sous* a day, was to begin on the 5th. More speeches were made before the company was dismissed. François passed the next day and night in arranging his affairs, saying farewell to his friends, and in "running about, drinking, singing, loving and weeping."

Of course he assured his friends and relatives that he would soon be back, and promised to write frequently, and, all the leave-takings being finished, he duly turned up at the meeting-place of the section at five o'clock on the morning of the 5th, with knapsack on back, and musket on shoulder, and accompanied by hosts of friends. When all the company had assembled, they were marched to the Place de Grève, where the battalion was formed, amidst cries of "Long live the Nation!"

At 7.0 a.m. the battalion marched out of Paris, followed by a crowd, "some singing, others weeping." Passing through Meaux, La Ferté-sous-Jouarre, and Château Thierry, at all of which places they were well received, they arrived in a week at Chalons-sur-Marne, near which town was a camp, where the volunteers from the departments were assembled, under the command of General Arthur Dillon. Three days later, the battalion was ordered to Suippes, and from there to the camp at Grandpré. When within a league of the camp, they met some runaways, who told them the camp was broken up, and, a little later, they saw the French army beating a disordered retreat, but they could hear no cannon or musketry. The men were already fatigued, but the colonel ordered them to march back to Chalons.

Very soon the Prussian cavalry appeared. The colonel called a halt, and prepared to fight, but the Prussians did not molest them, though they came near enough to call out insults in French and German. Some of the men, worn out with fatigue, threw away their knapsacks, and a few were made prisoners by the Prussians. At length, after a forced march of at least eighteen leagues, the regiment arrived at Chalons, and bivouacked in the Place d'Armes, with other battalions which had come from Grandpré. François, in spite of his fatigue, was overcome with rage and indignation, at seeing the French driven back to Chalons by men who did not dare to attack them. The next day, a Prussian spy was caught in the town, and had his head chopped off in the Place d'Armes.

François did not have to wait long for his revenge. The regiment moved to Saint Menehould, where an army, said to consist of 103,000 men, was collected, under the command of Generals Dumouriez, Luckner, Clarembeau, Lafayette, and Kellermann. At six in the morning of September 20th, the Prussian advance guard made an attack, and the French took up a position with its right on the Aisne and the village of Maffrecourt, and the centre on the road from Chalons to Saint Menehould. The advanced guard was near the village of Valmy, with its right on the heights of Valmy and its left at Villemont.

The Prussian advance guard, commanded by Prince Hohenlohe Kirkberg, drove back the French, who retired in good order on the main body. But a part of the reserve, under General Valence, checked the advance of the enemy, and established a battery of eighteen guns near the windmill at Valmy. Then a general advance was ordered by Dumouriez. The division to which François belonged had instructions to turn the enemy's flank, by crossing the Bienne, but to keep as near the camp as possible, so as to be useful when the attack became general.

François says:

Whilst we were executing these movements, the enemy deployed on the heights of the Lune, and placed at least fifty cannon at four different points. I learned these details afterwards, for I could not observe most of them, as a thick fog enveloped everything. It was about seven in the morning when the two armies were opposed.

The battle began about 8 o'clock, and was fought obstinately on both sides up to 9 o'clock. At that moment, the enemy having unmasked a fresh battery near the houses on the Lune, General Kellermann brought up his artillery, and the cannonade recommenced. That of the enemy did us great damage, Kellermann had his horse killed under him by a cannon ball, and his *aide-de-camp* was mortally wounded. At ten, several of our ammunition waggons blew up, which caused some disorder in our ranks. Our light artillery was then placed near the mills, and opened fire; more ammunition arrived and we regained our positions.

We manoeuvred in close columns by battalions. Three Prussian columns moved forward, and marched towards the mill. General Kellermann galloped up, and ordered us to extend in line. 'Comrades!' he cried, 'victory is ours. Let the enemy come without our firing a single shot. Long live the Nation!' These words electrified us; we raised our hats on our bayonets, and cried, 'Long live the Nation!' The enemy advanced nearer and nearer, as steadily as though on parade. At this moment, the mist cleared, and we gave them a terrible volley, which knocked over the front ranks of the Prussians. The others crushed one another in their anxiety to bolt, and their officers had immense trouble to rally them.

General Clerfayt, who had crossed the Bionne to attack the camp at Sainte Menehould, was beaten and driven back by General Beurnonville, which prevented us from being surrounded, and completed the victory. This first success redoubled our ardour.

We of the volunteer battalion, although in line with veterans, lost few men. We manoeuvred like our comrades, and did some shooting, which much amused us, and made us wish the enemy would take his revenge. He did not fail to try. About 4 o'clock in the afternoon, having received reinforcements, he came on in the same order as in the morning, but was received with such a hot fusillade that he was obliged to retreat with heavy loss. A battery of twenty-four guns—eight and twelve pounders—at the Valmy mill, crushed them, and completed the victory. Firing ceased about nine in the evening, when the Prussians were in full retreat, which was difficult for them, for they were shut in to such a degree that some of them had to lay down their arms, and we nearly captured the king.

I do not know why we did not profit by our success, pursue them, and capture their train. The enemy was beaten, and surrounded on every side; it was said that we might have made the King of Prussia sign a peace. Instead of pursuing them, we remained on the field of battle, which was covered with dead and wounded. The battalion to which I belonged had twenty-seven killed and sixty-seven wounded. We of the 5th Paris battalion afterwards returned to the camp at Sainte Menehould; but there were absolutely no provisions for us. I even had to pay five *francs* in cash for a loaf of bad army bread.

I received a ball just above the right ear, which, however, only just grazed the skin and went clean through my hat. I was very proud of that hat, and kept it for a long time. Thus, after serving only sixteen days, we were amongst the victors of Valmy.

The next month was spent in following up the Prussians, who retired through Verdun and Longwy, and finally made a stand at Jemmapes, near Mons, where they had a naturally strong and well fortified position. On October 24th, General Dumouriez arrived from Paris to take the chief command of the French army, and the next day he ordered an advance. General Bernouville attacked the village of Bour, and was repulsed, but General Dampierre afterwards took that village and another at the point of the bayonet, whilst a division seized the wood of Sars, but nightfall prevented any further success. The battalion to which François belonged arrived at 2.0 a.m., and the enemy was attacked at all points at 8.0 a.m.

The artillery and musketry fire were terrible. Several redoubts were taken at the point of the bayonet. General Ferrand, who was seventy-one years old, captured the village of Jemmapes. He had a horse killed under him, and was wounded in the leg, but courageously kept the field. General Bernouville was driven out of Cuesmes, but Valence's division (in which François was) commanded by General Dampierre, recaptured it. The enemy, driven back on all sides, fled, and a fearful carnage ensued.

François owns that he was rather horrified at finding himself in the midst of such a slaughter, and hearing his wounded comrades crying for help, but the victory had to be followed up, and the regiment charged over the dead and wounded, calling out to the latter to have a little patience. The Prussians were pursued as far as Mons, the inhabitants of which came out to welcome the French, and put a laurel wreath on the head of brave General Dampierre.

The other wing did not prosper quite so well. General Dumouriez had said to his men:

Soldiers! there are the heights of Jemmapes, where the enemy is. Nothing but the sabre and bayonet will get them out and win the victory!

Battalions were mown down on both sides by shot and shell, but others took their place. One of the French regiments lost all its officers, and fell into disorder, but a soldier of the 3rd Paris battalion rallied them, and contributed in no small degree to win the victory. The Prussians lost at least 10,000 men, François thinks, in killed and wounded, and all the guns and ammunition in the redoubts. The French loss he puts at 4,000. His own battalion, though in the thick of the fighting, only lost 29 killed and 63 wounded. General Valence was wounded whilst capturing a redoubt defended by some "big devils of Hungarians," who were taken prisoners. The Prussians retired on Mons, but finding that town already in the possession of the French, withdrew towards Antwerp and Brussels.

The latter city surrendered speedily, but Antwerp gave a little more trouble. The inhabitants threw open the gates to the French, but the garrison retired into the citadel and refused to surrender. General Miranda (a Spaniard, born in Peru), who commanded the French artillery, laid siege to the place, and his shells were so well directed that they set the citadel on fire in several places. Then the commander offered to capitulate if he might go out with all the honours of war. This was granted, and the garrison of 1,200 men marched out and joined the army of the Duke of Saxe-Teschen. The French found in the citadel 200 cannon, 97 mortars and howitzers, and a large quantity of small arms, ammunition and provisions. Not a single Frenchman was wounded.

The day after the fall of Antwerp, the French laid siege to Namur, which was held by 8,000 Austrians, commanded by Generals Beaulieu and Schroeder. The Austrians had shut themselves up in the citadel, as the *burghers* threw open the gates as soon as the French appeared. The French had marched so rapidly that the siege artillery could not be brought up in time, and they had to wait three days for the guns. At last they came, and soon made a breach in the citadel walls, but General Valence was afraid to order an assault, as the townspeople assured him that the fort of la Villette, which defended the citadel, was mined. His men were quite ready to make the assault, mines or no mines, and François owns that he would have liked to be of the storming party, for he thought himself "invincible," and was not afraid of death, having escaped the carnage at Jemmapes without a scratch, though he had crossed bayonets with men twice as strong as himself.

Deserters—Belgians and Liegeois—joined the French every day. One of them offered to conduct General Le Veneur to the mine. The general selected 1,200 men—some old soldiers, some volunteers (François was not amongst them), and they marched silently in the dead of the night to the citadel, guided by the deserter. They climbed one palisade, and then they came to another they could not climb, and the enemy discovered them, and began to fire. "Throw me over!" said General Le Veneur to the officer nearest to him. The officer hoisted him over the palisades and the men managed to follow, in spite of the difficulties and the enemy's fire.

25

The general found an Austrian officer, put a pistol to his head, and said, "Take me to the mine, or you are a dead man!" The officer thought it best to comply, and Le Veneur tore away the slow match, whilst his men seized the fort. This gallant action led to the surrender of the citadel. The 8,000 Austrians were made prisoners and sent to France, and the two generals sent home on parole. The French losses were very trifling.

No military operations were carried on during the winter, and the troops were quartered in the villages. François was in the house of a cloth-merchant, who employed a number of workgirls. They could speak no French, and François and his comrades could not talk the German *patois* used in the district, but there is a language more universal and better understood by young soldiers of seventeen and amorous damsels. François says:

> The German girls made us understand by signs that they loved us very much, and I was not the only one who had a sweetheart. After a few days I had quite forgotten all the dangers and hardships of the campaign.

There were plenty of provisions, and all the soldiers had money, for some were rich, and the poor ones had what they had taken from the slain and the prisoners. Balls and dinners were frequently given, and, at these gatherings, officers, non-coms., and privates were all equal. Carra, one of the representatives of the people, sent to watch the campaign, often deigned to be present at these entertainments.

# CHAPTER 2

# 1793—1795

Early in January, 1793, François was elected corporal by his comrades, and celebrated his promotion by spending a week in Liege, where he enjoyed himself hugely, for the ladies were "as light as the name of the city." On January 25th, he read a proclamation, issued by the representatives of the people, to announce that Louis XVI. had been guillotined four days before.

In the beginning of March, fighting began again, and François' company went to Maestricht, which was being besieged by General Miranda. But everything was in a disorganised state. Regiments were ordered to advance by forced marches, and then sent as hurriedly back again. In one of these hurried retreats, François' regiment had to cross a bridge of boats over the Meuse, and there was such confusion and disorder that several of the officers were trampled under foot, and some of the men drowned. At Maestricht, batteries of 24-pounders were supplied with 18-lb. balls, and *vice versa*.

Dumouriez was accused of being a traitor, and, perhaps, that made him one, but he does not seem to have been wholly to blame, for some of the blunders were due to the stupidity of his subordinates. One general lost himself and all his division in the woods, for two days. On the other hand, Dumouriez ought to have known that the Austrians had been reinforced by 30,000 men before he attacked then at Tirlemont, where the French were defeated (March 16th). In this engagement, François had another graze—two balls through his hat, and two through his coat. An attempt to take the village of Nerwinde was unsuccessful. An Austrian dragoon captured the colours of François' regiment, but he was killed whilst making off with them, and the colours recovered.

The French retreated towards Brussels. Provisions were scarce, and

François, who was temporarily acting as quartermaster, was sent with an escort into the city to obtain supplies. He found Austrians, French, and the inhabitants pillaging the shops, and making off with the spoil. As they returned, the convoy was attacked, just outside the walls of Brussels, by Hungarian hussars. The waggons were captured, and the drivers, and some of the escort, made prisoners. François and a few of his comrades managed to get into the woods, and after some trouble and anxiety rejoined the army.

In the first days of April, there was much excitement in the camp, caused by the proclamations of Dumouriez, who invited the army to march on Paris and demand a king, "without which," he said, "we shall never have peace." On April 4th, Dumouriez, followed by his staff, a strong escort of infantry and cavalry, four guns, the La Tour regiment of Austrian dragoons, and a number of Austrian officers, went through the camp. He harangued the troops, and invited them to follow him, saying: "My children, I am your father, I give you till tomorrow to make up your minds." The only effect of this speech was to cause a good many soldiers to desert. The following day, Dumouriez went over to the enemy, with all his staff, several battalions of the line, a regiment of hussars, a battery of artillery, and the treasure chest. The remainder of the army, deserted by its officers, did not know what to do, but some of them raised the cry, "Let us retreat to Valenciennes," and this advice was followed. Most of the soldiers who followed Dumouriez returned the next day, having, they said, no faith in his promises.

General Dampierre assumed the command of the army some days later, and, on May 1st, François was again fighting against the Austrians, who were assisted by French *émigrés*. The account of this day's work is best given in the grim *naïveté* of François' own words.

The Austrians and the *emigres* attacked us in the wood of Bonne Esperance. There was a smart fusillade, and my battalion suffered a good deal. By an incredible mistake, we fired on one another, French against French, almost at close quarters, through the thick foliage of the wood, which prevented us seeing each other. We took the monastery of Pacougne, and several redoubts, two of them at the point of the bayonet. These expeditions were made by men who volunteered; I frankly own I was not the last to come forward, danger being a thing unknown to me, and I never thought for a moment that I might happen to get killed. Today, about 11 o'clock, led by Major Grandjean, we took a redoubt with the bayonet. I was one of the first to get up; an *émigré* seized hold of me, but my comrades came up as we were grappling together. He could not wrest my gun from me, and fled; we ran after him, and just as he was jumping a hedge, I shoved my bayonet into his body; he fell, and I settled him, and took his boots, and also his purse, which contained fifty-three *sous*.

Nothing of importance occurred during the next three months, but, on August 17th, the French were attacked by the Duke of York, and Prince of Orange, and lost twelve guns, though they inflicted heavy losses on the enemy. September the 5th to 9th, the French had their revenge at Hondschoote, where the English General Freytag, and Prince Adolphe, were badly wounded and taken prisoners, but the English cavalry (dragoons) rescued Prince Adolphe. The French grumbled that the Duke of York had escaped, and accused their commander (Houchard) of treason, because he had not taken full advantage of the victory. It seemed "inconceivable" to François, that an experienced general, who had received more than fifty wounds in the service of his country, could be accused of treason. Hoche was promoted to be brigadier-general for his services in this battle. François heard an extraordinary story of a cavalry man who was ordered to carry cartridges to the infantry. He stumbled by chance into a regiment of the enemy, threw down the cartridges, and whilst the men were stooping to pick them up, he killed several of them, and made off with the standard, and the officer who bore it.

Four days later, at the taking of Lannoy, François saw:

A young drummer of a battalion of volunteers, only fourteen or fifteen years old, bring in seven English prisoners, one of whom was a drum-major.

He also heard that when the commander-in-chief visited the wounded, one of them asked if Lannoy was taken, "Yes," replied the general.

"Then I do not regret the loss of my leg," said the man.

Another, who had an arm amputated, said, "I have still one left to exterminate the foe with."

General Houchard defeated the Dutch at Werwicq, and took forty-two guns. The Prince of Orange was seriously wounded. This feat did not wipe out the previous suspicion of treason, and Houchard was soon afterwards arrested, sent back to Paris, and guillotined. He was succeeded by Pichegru.

François' battalion, which had suffered severely, was sent back to Cambrai, to receive fresh recruits, and had a month's rest there, but, on the night of October 14, the alarm was sounded, and 3,000 men, many of them unequipped, were sent off to Wattignies, where Jourdan was being attacked by the Austrians. Help was certainly much needed, for the army there was worn out with fighting, had scarcely any provisions, and the hospital was full of sick and wounded. Some of them told François that when they asked General Chancel to allow them a little rest and more food, he replied:

> Comrades, what merit and what glory would you have if you left a good table and a comfortable lodging to go out and fight? Learn that it is only by long labours and privations that you can purchase the honour of dying for your country!

It is to be hoped they appreciated the logic of this argument.

The Austrians were strongly entrenched, and Coburg felt so sure of his position that he said he would turn Republican, if the Republicans could drive him out of his trenches. The French swore they would, and did, but the victory cost them dear, for the French lost at least 3,000 killed and wounded. François' battalion lost 11 officers and 287 men, and was sent back to Cambrai to pass the winter.

Early in 1794 François was appointed quartermaster; he had been performing the duties for a year. A day or two later, he was named adjutant, but the town was besieged, and he would have had too much work and not been able to take part in the sorties, so he asked to be allowed to remain quartermaster for the present. The regiment had moved from Cambrai to Bouchain. The town was commanded by General Cornu, an old man of seventy, with a young wife. He was a martinet, and always inflicted seventeen days' imprisonment on the soldiers he punished, because he had been seventeen years a corporal.

There were a good many sorties, and the Austrians were obliged to raise the siege. Victory was not always to the French; in one of these sorties a panic seized the French cavalry, and spread to the infantry, and they all bolted back to Cambrai and Bouchain, in abominable disorder. Seven hussars, who were supposed to have begun the panic, were guillotined by order of Pichegru. In another sortie, the English dragoons captured the guns, and killed all the musicians.

This did not complete the disasters, for the garrison joined the army of the North under Chapuy, and was crushed by the English artillery and cavalry. The French lost 35 guns, 8,000 men killed and wounded, and Chapuy, with his staff, were made prisoners.

At Turcoing (May 18th) victory again inclined to the French. There was more fighting four or five days later, and some villages were taken and retaken, but the French were thrown into confusion by the explosion of some of their ammunition waggons, which killed many of the men. The Committee of Public Safety had declared that it was "war to the knife," and no prisoners were to be taken, but the soldiers never obeyed this barbarous order. Sometimes, however, the English and Hessian soldiers were rude to their captors, whom they called "paper soldiers," and suffered for their insolence. François relates that he had taken nine men in a redoubt, and was leading them to the rear, when one of them insulted him, he coolly says.

I passed my bayonet through his body, and left him dying. The other soldiers finished him.

But, unless they were insulted, the French soldiers refused to kill prisoners in cold blood, they said:

Send the prisoners to the representatives of the people, and let them kill them and eat them, too, if they like; that is not our affair.

The account given by François of the Battle of Fleurus, June 26th, does not quite tally with that of the historians. They put the French force at 89,000, and that of the allies at rather less, and say the latter lost through the Prince of Saxe-Coburg ordering a retreat at the moment of victory. François does not give the number of the French but puts the Austrians at 111,000. He says that Jourdan was asked to retreat by his officers, but answered, "No retreat whilst we can fight and win," and the men, electrified by these words, rushed on the foe with renewed ardour. It is interesting to note that:

A balloon hovered over us, governed by means of ropes. Two officers occupied it, and made known by signals the movements of the enemy. We took a battery of eight guns, and found some of them loaded and pointed at the balloon, which had contributed greatly to win the battle.

There was a good deal more fighting in July, but nothing of great importance. The allies retreated to Breda, and might have been cut off if the French had not been so slow. Of course, the French generals were accused of treason, particularly Pichegru, who was not liked because he was very severe, and had marauders and pillagers shot. François, who was one of the besiegers of Antwerp, received a visit from his brother-in-law, who came with a convoy of provisions and forage, and gave François some ready money, which was very acceptable, for the *assignats* of the Republic were at an alarming discount. The young soldier was able to buy some much-needed clothes, and gave the rest to a *vivandière*, who did his washing for him, "and was not cruel in other respects."

The English and Hessians were beaten at Boxtael, and the Duke of York might have been taken, or at least pursued, if Pichegru had shown any energy, the French soldiers thought. Bois-le-Duc and Crevecoeur were captured, and the English defeated again at Nimeguen, though François saw little of this engagement, the enemy being routed before his division arrived. An entire regiment was taken prisoner, and François thinks it must have formed part of Rohan's legion, as nearly all the men spoke French. Sixty-three *émigrés* were taken and shot.

In November, the French besieged Nimeguen, one of the strongest places in Europe, and defended by 38,000 or 40,000 of the allied troops—English and Dutch. Perhaps ammunition was scarce in the town, for the besieged fired off penny pieces instead of grape-shot. The French had only paper money, and were grateful to the English for this new kind of projectile. The soldiers used to run about the common on purpose to draw the enemy's fire, and then pick up the pennies. François picked up 287, which came in very useful afterwards. He says though, that when a man did get hit with one of these monetary missiles he was pretty sure to die of the wound.

The bridge of boats being destroyed by the French fire, the English evacuated the town whilst there was yet time, deserting their allies (François says), who were either drowned in trying to rejoin the English, or killed or made prisoners by the French, who took the town and citadel. But, in spite of their successes, the French army was in a deplorable condition. Their clothes were worn, and they were almost barefooted, though the weather was very cold.

We were covered with glory, but dying of hunger, and sleeping in a marsh. The nine days we were besieging Nimeguen, we had no rations served us but a glass of brandy a day. Meat we had to forage for, and burn the fat to roast the lean with, and, as may be guessed, there were lots of sick.

It was quite a relief to be ordered to Cleves, where François was quartered on an old bachelor who liked the French, and who had a rather pretty housekeeper, who also seems to have liked the French, and whom François unselfishly introduced to his sergeant. When the regiment left she gave him a sack full of provisions, which he shared with his comrades. He returned to Cleves several times in the course of the next few weeks, for the weather was so terribly cold that the troops were relieved every few days. The Rhine was frozen over, and in many places could be crossed on foot. Sentinels were often frozen to death, although they were changed every hour; and many men were crippled by frost-bite. There was not much fighting, but the losses on both sides were rather serious, for any man who was wounded was sure to die of the cold. The frost lasted till nearly the end of January, 1795, and no doubt both sides suffered severely, the French being often without fire. Nevertheless, they maintained strict discipline, and any soldier caught pillaging was shot, which had a good effect on the Dutch, who looked upon the French as their liberators, and treated them like brothers.

The allies were thoroughly discouraged by the repeated successes of the French. The Duke of York returned home; his tactics, the Republican soldiers said, consisted in making his men fly at their approach. General Wollmoden, who succeeded him, did not hope to beat the French, but trusted that cold, hardships, and disease would reduce them.

The advanced guard of the French Army was quartered at Utrecht (January 19th, 1795), and François was in the house of a Herr Van Blekman, a rich merchant. He had a niece, young and pretty, and the daughter of a judge. She fell in love with François, and the young man returned her passion. Her uncle loved the French, and determined to marry his niece to the young soldier. He called a family gathering, at which the girl, her father, and other relatives were present, and pointedly asked Mlle. Eugenie if she loved the French? She replied, "Uncle, it is to them we owe the happiness of seeing you, and I shall always love them?"

"The uncle then asked, "Would you like to marry one of my liberators?"

The damsel, looking shyly at François answered, "But, uncle, I do not know any of them;" which drove the old man out of generalities, and he asked her, "Could you love quartermaster Carle?"

She blushed, but said nothing, and her uncle continued, "He is the first I have had the honour of lodging. I have confidence in him. He is a young, sensible, honest man. If you will marry him, I and my sisters will adopt him as our son, and leave him all our money."

Whereupon the young woman's father said, "I do not know the citizen, but if my daughter thinks him worthy of her, I consent."

"Very well, then," said the uncle; "niece, would you like Carle for a husband?"

The girl blushed still more, and whispered, "Yes."

François could hardly believe in his happiness. He did not sleep all night, and in the morning told his officers, who all greatly esteemed him. Some of them envied his good luck, others made objections, "but at nineteen one does not listen to such things." But he had to procure his papers, and get his father's consent, before he could be married, and, before they arrived, the advance guard was ordered to Zutphen. There was a struggle in his mind between love and duty, but duty won. The family was inconsolable, and the disappointment made Eugenie so ill that she had to take to her bed. François, of course, swore that he would come back, and never leave her again. They exchanged portraits, promised to write to each other, and actually did for a few months, until he was ordered to Egypt. And so François missed getting a young and pretty wife, with a fortune of 16,000 florins a year, but, as he patriotically and philosophically adds, "before I could enjoy such a fortune, I must pay the tribute I owed to my country."

He seems to have quickly consoled himself; for at Zutphen he was secretary to the commander, made some valuable acquaintances, and took his pleasure. He had some intrigues, as was natural for a young soldier who was not shy before women. His acquaintances were valuable to him in a literal sense, for he received many presents from his mistresses, and deceived them all, which did not prevent him from feeling regret when he left them. When he quitted Zutphen, he had in his pocket 140 *ducats*, worth 12 *francs* each.

This method of raising money, though immoral, was not exactly dishonest, but the same cannot be said about François' other transactions. Whilst in garrison at Juliers, he was employed, in his spare time, in the commissariat department, and, having made the acquaintance of the paymaster of one of the divisions, these two worthies invented phantom regiments and detachments, which were supposed to be moving about the country, on duty. François sold the provisions forwarded for these imaginary bodies of men, and in a couple of months found himself quite rich in paper,—though to be sure that was not worth much.

He was the richest man in the half-brigade, he says, and amused himself in all sorts of ways. But he lent a good deal of the money to his officers, who, knowing how it had been obtained, never paid him back. He supposes they could not, as they only received eight *francs* a day in paper money, which was almost worthless. So valueless was it, that, at Aix-la-Chapelle, the troops mutinied, because the general and the Representative of the People were unable to promise that the *assignats* should be made convertible into cash at their full face-value; but eighteen of the ringleaders were arrested, six of them shot, and the others condemned to two years in irons.

François went to Aix-la-Chapelle in August, and liked the town very well—partly because he was able to turn the 3,000 *francs* he had nefariously made into cash (at a loss of only 50 *per cent.*) and also because he learned German of the daughter of his host; who was pretty, liked the French, and was only nineteen.

He appears to have had nothing to do for four months, for there is a break in his diary from April 30th to September 5th. He notes then, that General Pichegru was besieging Mayence in a very desultory kind of way. He was moody, taciturn, and suspected of Royalist tendencies; for emissaries from England, Austria, and Germany were at his headquarters every day. The French crossed the Rhine, came up to the Austrians by rapid marches, and had several smart engagements with them, in which the Republican army was always successful. The men were often without food, as the convoys of provisions could not keep up with them. In fact, the gallant army of the Sambre et Meuse did much, and would have done still more, if it had not been prevented by the treasonable inaction of Pichegru, who refused to co-operate with Jourdan.

But, internally, the army was in a dangerously disorganized condition. It was operating in a district from which the enemy had carried off everything. Supplies did not arrive, and the men, pressed by hunger, pillaged and were mutinous. The government, when appealed to by the generals, replied, "Execute the laws." This reply only further incensed the soldiers, several riots took place, and the men would have turned their arms against their leaders, but for the respect they felt for them, and the knowledge that the state of affairs was not due to them, but to the treason of Pichegru. But, in December, an armistice was signed. The half brigade, to which François was attached, was quartered at Dormagen, between Neuss and Cologne, and enjoyed plenty of bacon and *sauerkraut*, beer, and *schnapps*.

# CHAPTER 3

# 1796—1797

The half-brigade remained at Dormagen till nearly the end of March, 1796, and was then sent to Aix-la-Chapelle. François took care to return to his old quarters, for his host had a young and pretty wife. When the regiment left, she gave him a bracelet, with which he never parted.

The armistice came to an end, and hostilities were renewed. The French Army marched so rapidly that it was often without provisions, and the soldiers pillaged the farms and cottages.

The officers shut their eyes to these proceedings, provided we beat the enemy.

François relates a little episode which throws such light on the military manners and morals of the time that it deserves to be given in full.

I forgot to mention that when the 161st half-brigade was incorporated with us, I arranged to get into my company, a young laundress, who belonged to that half-brigade. She was seventeen or eighteen years old, very nice, and married to an old German sergeant, who had belonged to the Swedish regiment. This young woman chose me for her friend. She was not very rich, but I had still a few *sous* left from the little business I carried on at Juliers, when I sent about flying columns and appropriated their pay and provisions; following the example of the war-commissaries. I procured for this little princess the means to get a small barrel of spirits, to hang across her shoulders, a funnel, and some glasses, and asked the captain of the 2nd battalion to appoint her *vivandière*. She looked as pretty as a cupid following the heroes of Mars.

I undertook to fit her out according to her rank and new title. I procured for her one of those carts called a *char-à-banc* in Germany, with two horses, which had been commandeered from a rich peasant. She could then purchase wholesale. Her husband was pleased at seeing the prosperity of his dear better-half; he liked me very much, and knowing that it was to me she owed her splendour, he often said to me, 'Quartermaster, my wife is at your service.' Finally wishing to make my princess happier, and spare her fatigue on the marches, I went into partnership with one of Chamborand's hussars.

When he was on outpost duty at night, I went out to see him. He was watching an Austrian sentinel. He gave me his pistol, and I made a wide circuit, came on the enemy's sentinel, blew out his brains, and took his horse. The first expedition succeeded—at that time the government paid 400 *francs*, in paper, for every horse captured. My hussar, who had helped me to get the horse, claimed 200 *francs*, which I could not give him, but I promised that I would get him a horse for himself by the same means within a fortnight, with his help; but it was not until my fourth expedition that I could secure the horse and man—one of Banko's dragoons.

I gave the first horse to the little *vivandière*. As it was marked, it was noticed that it was a captured charger, and she was ordered to say where she got it. She said I gave it her, but did not know how I had obtained it. I was sent for, and went to the headquarters of the division. I related the story of my feat, and, thanks to the bravery with which I had obtained these horses, I was allowed to keep them, and was mentioned in the orders of the day.

There were a good many lively skirmishes, but no pitched battle—unless that title can be given to the affair at Fischback, where the French did not get much the best of it. François' division was exposed to artillery from the front and the right, and he saw several of his comrades killed by the cannon balls which passed close in front of them from the right flank. It was the first time he had seen men killed without being wounded, or even touched. The corn was so high that often the troops were within fifty yards of the enemy. The loss was heavy on both sides, but the French claimed the victory, because they bivouacked on the field of battle, and pursued the enemy next day. In doing so, they passed through a village where they found 4,000 oxen, which had been poisoned to prevent them falling into the hands of the French.

Frankfort fell, and the city had to pay an indemnity of eight million *francs*. Two of these millions were to go to equip the army; which was almost barefooted, and in rags. The men were also discontented, because they learned from the newspapers and bulletins that their comrades of the army of Italy were paid in cash, and were better off in every other respect. The commander-in-chief was cordially hated; because he had ordered the troops not to enter any city without his written permission, and had also intimated that the natives were quite at liberty to refuse or accept the French paper money (which was almost valueless) as they saw fit. The soldiers could not compel the natives to take the money, but they could set the other order at defiance, and whole squads of them entered the towns, in spite of the guards set to prevent them. François did not approve of this insubordination, but he thought the generals were not sufficiently mindful of the men to whom they owed their glory, and who were actually without straw to lie on; and he also considered that the inhabitants of a conquered country should be forced to take French paper money at its full value.

On August 17th, the French, under Ney, inflicted a smart defeat on the enemy, near Sulzbach. François was wounded by a sabre cut, which sliced off his right eyebrow, and very nearly cost him an eye. Six days later, the enemy cut off and surrounded the advance guard, and finding that cavalry made no impression on the French square, brought artillery to bear, killing 500 out of the 700, and wounding nearly all the others, or making them prisoners. François was wounded and taken prisoner; but his hurts were not serious. The prisoners were taken to Bamberg—three days' march—and many of them died of hunger and fatigue on the road. The regimental surgeon, paymaster, and quartermasters were, however, regarded as non-combatants; and François being amongst the latter, he was released a few days later, escorted to the outposts, and rejoined the army after a captivity of nine days. The day he returned. General Kléber left the army—ostensibly on account of sickness, but really, François thought, because he was sick of seeing everything going to the devil.

This may have been the right reason, for matters were growing worse every day. General Benneau was killed in September, and in the same month the division of General Marceau overwhelmed by numbers, and that promising young soldier mortally wounded. His last words were, "I am happy, for I die for my country!" His body was sent back to the army of Sambre-et-Meuse with a funeral escort, and the officers, surgeons, and orderlies, who were with Marceau during his last moments, were released without exchange.

The remainder of the year passed in desultory fighting, in which the French sometimes won and sometimes lost; as on October 10th, when they were compelled to beat a precipitate retreat across the Moselle, and many of their men were drowned. On January 8th, 1797, Bernadotte's division, to which François' regiment belonged, was ordered to Italy. The following month, his division crossed Mont Cenis, and lodged at Susa, in Piedmont. The men must have liked the change, for the Piedmontese Government allowed them two pounds of bread, half a pound of meat, a bottle of wine and four ounces of rice per man, per day.

At Susa, François lodged in the posting-house, which was kept by two young women who were pretty, and inspired, the French officers with a desire to be better acquainted with the Italians. François thought of his German sweethearts, and philosophically reflected that women are weak all over the world. As usual, when he left, his hostess gave him a week's provisions, which he shared with his comrades. At Milan, too, he found no dearth of female society, thanks to the priests; but he lodged in a monastery, and never had so many fleas in all his life.

On March 16th, the French first came in touch with the enemy, and had a smart brush on the banks of the Tagliamento. Bernadotte told his men to show themselves worthy of the Army of Italy—and they did. The Austrians lost a general, several superior officers, 500 prisoners, and six guns, besides a large number of killed and wounded; whilst the total on the French side was less than 400. That night, Bonaparte came to their bivouac, and complimented Bernadotte on the bravery of his division. The men cried, "*Vive Bonaparte!*" and François says there was not a man in the army, from the general down to the last recruit, who would not have died for the "Little Corporal."

The Austrians, afraid of seeing Bonaparte swoop down on Vienna, made peace, but the country was still in a very disturbed condition. François' brigade formed part of a flying column, sent under General Lannes, to quell a revolt which had broken out in Genoa. As soon as they arrived, they took sixty prisoners, many of whom were priests, and one was a bishop. They were sent to the headquarters of General Lannes, who had them all shot. The column returned to Milan, and François took part in a grand banquet, given by the city to the French officers on July 14th. He also visited other cities, but, in September, the flying column to which he belonged was sent to Alexandria. General Lespinoy, "a hard, severe man," commanded there, and reviewed the troops when they arrived, but Lannes did not appear at the review, for he was devoted to Bonaparte, and knew that Bonaparte had a supreme contempt for Lespinoy. The column left next day, and François learned they were to enter France and put down the "Chauffeurs."

They passed through Nice, Cannes, and Toulon, were well received at all three places, and (October 9th) arrived at Aubagne, which was the headquarters of some of the royalist associations whom François calls "the cut-throats of the south," but who called themselves "the company of Jehu." They were said to have hanged Bonaparte in effigy, which made the soldiers long to take vengeance on them. Some of the "company of Jehu" did a little "sniping" as the soldiers approached the town, but those who were caught at it were shot. The inhabitants of Aubagne had deserted the town in a body, and the soldiers took possession of their houses, and drank their wine.

General Lannes had received full powers from Bonaparte to put down these political associations, and he certainly did not act in any spirit of conciliation, as the last sentence of his proclamation on arriving in France was:

I arrive today, and tomorrow you will be dead.

The following day, the column entered Marseille. The cannon were loaded, and an artillery-man, with a lighted match, marched beside each gun. The authorities advanced to meet General Lannes, but he received them coldly, ordered several of them to be arrested, and declared the city in a state of siege. This was perhaps needful, for the inhabitants were not well affected towards the Republic. The town was infested with royalists, who were easily known by their high collars, long hair, queues, and pointed shoes. The military commander, General Pill, was not a Republican,—or at best but a lukewarm one,—and his predecessors. Generals Willat and Chaquet had been ardent Royalists. Three-fourths of the 34th half brigade, which was in garrison there, was composed of members of the company of Jehu.

The consequences may well be guessed. Duels took place all night, and several hundred soldiers were killed or wounded. François, for his part, killed two royalists, and wounded three, one of them severely. His duels were fought with the sabre; a weapon with which he was very skilful, and very lucky. The fighting occurred in a low *café* behind the theatre. Three of François comrades were killed there, but he and ten others killed nine, and wounded fourteen, of the companions of Jehu,—François doing, as we have seen, considerably more than his share of the work. The whole night was spent in hunting out and killing Jehus. There were strong patrols of police and military to prevent these conflicts, but they had a strange idea of their duties, for they informed the soldiers where the royalists were to be found, and even accompanied them to the doors. When the roll was called in the morning, twenty-seven men did not answer to their names, and it was rumoured in the ranks that 200 for the garrison and citizens were killed or wounded.

The column remained four days at Marseille, but there does not seem to have been any more fighting in *cafés*—probably Lannes thought it too expensive. But there were:

Plenty of arrests, and many people were shot in the old town.
The prisons were full and the citizens frightened.

After making some arrests at Aix, and shooting a few peasants at Saint Maximin, the column returned through Nice, and Mentone, to Genoa, early in November, and, on December 17th, the half brigade was reviewed by General Soret, and the men were informed that they must hold themselves in readiness to proceed to the Papal States immediately; but counter orders were received, and the regiment did not leave Genoa till February 2nd, 1798, and then went to Bologna, where an army was being rapidly assembled, under the command of General Berthier, with orders to advance on Rome, which was in a state of revolution.

# Chapter 4

# 1798—1799

On February 10th, 1798, the French Army arrived outside the walls of Rome, and the advanced guard took possession of the castle of Saint Angelo. The next day, the troops entered the city without firing a shot. François sarcastically suggests that the Papal Guards were afraid of the rain spoiling their uniforms. The Pope—the citizen Pope, as the French called him—was not even made aware that Berthier's army had entered Rome, till General Servoni informed him that the Papal Government was abolished. He, and a few followers, obtained permission to retire into Tuscany.

Bonaparte had hastened back to Paris, and Berthier followed him, leaving the command to Masséna, who reduced the army of occupation at Rome to 3,000 men. When Masséna also started for France, the soldiers began to suspect that some important expedition was in the wind,—probably a war with England—and François and his comrades longed to punish the proud Britons, whose perfidy and tyrannical maritime rule were a misfortune to Europe.

François regiment was ordered to Nice, and then to Avignon; at which latter place the 2nd half brigade was already quartered. Differences arose between the two regiments, and after the fencing-master of François' company had been found dead in the street—murdered by some of the men of the 2nd, it was said—there would have been sanguinary quarrels, if the military authorities had not promptly removed the 2nd light infantry.

Early in May, the volunteers were sent to Marseille, and learned from the inhabitants they were to be sent on an expedition, the object of which was not known. The men who had been wounded were to stay behind, but François refused to take advantage of the permission, as he wanted to see strange countries and "extraordinary things." On

May 6th, the men heard that Bonaparte was coming, and the news of his much-desired advent, the diarist says:

> Filled us with gladness and hope. The soldiers went through the streets crying, 'Long live Bonaparte, long live our father!' Our excitement knew no bounds. We would have followed our general to the end of the world; I and my comrades-in-arms longed to see him and leave with him.

A few days later, the forces sailed for Toulon, and on May 15th started to attack some as yet unknown antagonist. The troop-ships passed Elba and Sicily, and the captain of the ship on which François was, stated that an English brig, belonging to Nelson's squadron, had been captured, and that admiral was pursuing them, and was not far off. Next day, the transports formed in line of battle, for it was rumoured that the British Fleet had been sighted; but the report turned out to be unfounded, and the ships arrived safely at Malta. The French Consul came on board, and informed Bonaparte there would be little or no resistance to his taking the island, as fully 4,000 of the Knights of Malta were on the side of the French.

Nevertheless, when the troops attempted to land, they were received with a hot fire, which sank many of the boats, though but few men were lost. François and his regiment landed on the island of Gozzo, skipped up the rocks like goats, and seized a fort armed with seventy-two guns, but the carriages were so rotten that they fell to pieces at the first blow. Five hundred loaded muskets were ranged along the parapet, but there was no one to fire them. By five in the afternoon, the whole island was in possession of the French, who pillaged the houses, the inhabitants having all fled to the larger island.

Malta had meanwhile been secured by Bonaparte almost without firing a shot. Most of the Knights were taken prisoner, and brought before Bonaparte, who said to them:

> How could you imagine it was possible for you to defend yourselves, with a few wretched peasants, against troops which had conquered and subdued Europe?

The loot was very considerable, and consisted of 30,000 muskets and 1,200 barrels of powder, six months' provisions for 10,000 men, a frigate, three galleys, and the treasure of the church of St. John, valued at three million *francs*.

After staying only a week at Malta, the troops left for Egypt—all the more hurriedly because Nelson and Lord St.Vincent were reported to be looking for them—and, after a very rough passage, arrived off Alexandria, July 1st. A soldier who was on board the ship with François, jumped overboard, swam to shore, and planted the tricolour on the summit of the Arabs' tower. The troops landed about three leagues from Alexandria, and after camping all night on the shore, marched on the city next day, harassed somewhat by the Bedouins, who picked up a good few stragglers, but afterwards gave them up, Bonaparte paying a ransom of a sheep or a goat for each man.

Alexandria was captured by a bayonet charge, none of the three divisions having any artillery. There was a good bit of street fighting also, and Bonaparte narrowly escaped being killed in one of the narrow streets. Very soon after the fall of the city, the troops were ordered to Rosetta. They were to take four days' provisions—which consisted of dry biscuits!—and every man was to provide himself with a water-bottle, but very few could get them.

The advanced guard, under General Desaix, started at 2 o'clock in the morning. The march lay through the desert, and the few wells met with had been filled with earth and stones by the Arabs, but General Desaix had them cleaned. The division to which François belonged started two hours later. The heat was insupportable, and the men soon consumed the little water they had brought with them. When they reached the wells, the men rushed to the water so frantically that more than thirty were suffocated or trodden under foot. Several others committed suicide because they could not get to the water. The troops camped at El-Arich, and in the night there was an alarm, and the cry was raised that the Arabs were in the camp. There were no Arabs, but the horses, wild with thirst, had stampeded. François says:

We laughed about it afterwards, but we lost several men, killed or wounded, and eighty horses.

At Damanhoor, they were allowed to purchase provisions, but the natives would not take foreign gold. They preferred the white metal buttons on the tunics of the light infantry; the consequence being that, when the troops arrived at Cairo, there was not a light infantryman with a button on his coat.

The march to Damanhoor gave the French a foretaste of some of the hardships they were to undergo. There was not a cloud in the sky to temper the heat of the sun; not a tree to give shade. The hot sand burned the men's feet; few of the soldiers had brought water-bottles, and those who had, drank their supply the first day. The pangs of hunger were added to those of thirst, for the men threw away the dry biscuits which they had brought from Alexandria, and many—François included—also cast off coat, vest, and shirt. Even night brought little relief, for they could not sleep on the burning sand. At every village, the wells were roiled, and the *fellahs* had hidden what water they had; some of them sold their little store. François paid six *francs* for a good draught of water; his only consolation was that the man who sold it to him would probably have given four times as much for it a few hours later.

The division stayed some days at Damanhoor, and Bonaparte joined them there. On leaving the town, he was in the rear of the troops, and was almost captured by the Arabs.

> But this great general, who is known to be somewhat of a fatalist, joked about the incident, and said it was not written on high that he was to be taken by the Arabs.

Three officers, less fortunate, were captured by the Arabs. Bonaparte sent an interpreter with 500 *piastres*, as their ransom. Some of the tribe were for accepting this ransom, others were against it, and the two parties nearly came to blows. Finally, the *sheik* seized a pistol, and blew out the brains of the prisoner in whom Bonaparte was most interested. The *sheik* then handed the money back to the interpreter, saying he could not keep a ransom which was now useless. The fate of the other two unfortunate men was never known.

Bonaparte determined to give the Bedouins a sharp lesson. At the village of Schum[1] the natives refused to sell any provisions to the French. The village was taken at the point of the bayonet, and after all the animals had been carried off—camels, horses, donkeys, cattle, and sheep—the huts were fired, and the whole population, men, women, and children, perished in the flames. This terrible example caused many of the *sheiks* to surrender, and even offer their services; which were accepted.

The route followed by the French Army lay partly along the left bank of the Nile, and the men did not suffer so severely there, though some perished of heat or thirst every day. Bonaparte had sent a flotilla up the river, which kept level with the forces, and came in handy when there was a brush with the Mamelukes.

On the morning of July 22nd, the army marched forward at 2

---

1. Probably Kom Hamada, 25 miles from Damanhoor.—Trans.

o'clock, Desaix's division a little in front, and Reynier's (to which François' regiment was attached) following. When the sun rose, the French saw before them the Pyramids, and also an army of Mamelukes. It was then that Bonaparte made the memorable speech about forty centuries looking down on them from the summit of the Pyramids.

The famous battle need not be described. François owns that he had never seen more brave and determined men. The Arabs failed to break the French squares, and then attacked the village of Belbeis, which was occupied by a small party of French cavalry, who had been sent out foraging, and a few companies of infantry sent as support. The Arabs stormed the village, and the French bolted back to rejoin their squares. A dragoon of the 15th regiment was attacked by a Mameluke midway between the two French divisions, and orders were given to cease firing whilst this single combat endured. The dragoon finally killed his adversary, and returned to the square; after having taken the Arab's scimitar (which had a heavy silver scabbard), his dagger, and pistol.

Three thousand Arabs perished on the battlefield, and as, according to custom, they wore their richest costumes, and carried their choicest weapons and riches when they went out to fight, the French soldiers had a rich spoil, for some of the Mamelukes had as much as 10,000 *francs* in their belts. François, for his part, picked up a fine scimitar with a damascened blade and a silver-gilt scabbard, a pair of pistols inlaid with silver, three cashmere turbans, and a belt which contained 460 pieces of gold, worth nearly 3,000 *francs*. He does not give much account of the battle, for words would fail, he says, to describe the conduct of the soldiers. Bonaparte flew from square to square, and often risked getting killed.

After the battle Bonaparte sent off three companies, under General Dupuy, to take possession of Cairo; a rather risky act considering the size of the city and the small force sent, but the natives were too frightened to molest them. The main army followed a few hours later. The men were billeted on the inhabitants of the European quarter; François lodged with an Italian druggist, who showed him all the sights of the city and neighbourhood, even including a trip to the Pyramids.

Early in August, the troops were ordered to Lower Egypt, an advanced guard from Reynier's division being sent off under General Leclerc. The main body followed, and near their first halting place found General Leclerc engaged with a body of Arabs and armed peasants, who fled when they saw the troops coming, leaving eighty killed or wounded on the ground. The latter were "finished off" by the soldiers. The next morning they met several caravans, which had been robbed by the Arabs. The French, soon afterwards, came upon the Arabs dividing the spoil, and, having driven off the marauders, they appropriated the booty. François got 67 cashmere shawls, perhaps worth from 60 to 100 *louis* each, but which he was compelled to sell to his comrades, or the Jews of Belbeis at from 5 to 12 *francs* each.

No Mamelukes were found at Belbeis, and the division camped in gardens, which, being surrounded by mud walls, no sentinels were set. In the night, naked Arabs crept over the walls and stole twenty-seven knapsacks from under the men's heads, and some of the muskets from between their legs. One of the soldiers, however, woke when his knapsack was taken, and called out "Dogs!" and this aroused the other sleepers. Two of the thieves were caught and shot.

On August 14th, Bonaparte received a letter from General Kléber, enclosing the report of Admiral Gantheaume on the Battle of Aboukir. François was quartered in the village which Bonaparte was passing through on his way back to Cairo, he says:

> We saw him, with his hands behind his back, listening to the report which the *aide-de-camp* was reading, and apparently calm. The bad news was soon known. Bonaparte, as he passed before our ranks, told Captain Grandjean of our battalion. The quiet coolness of our commander-in-chief, and the inspired tone which he so well knew how to put on, made us hope for future glory, and drove away all sad thoughts. He had replied, it was said, to the bearer of these sad tidings: 'Well! we must either remain in these countries, or go out as the ancients did!' Yet, in spite of the confidence with which Bonaparte inspired us, sadness was depicted on all our faces. The loss of our fleet overcame us. Our eyes were turned towards our country. We were without hope of ever returning there.

At Cairo, too, there was considerable consternation on hearing the ill news, but the presence of the commander restored calmness, confidence, and hope.

Reynier's division camped near Belbeis, and remained there some time. The soldiers made bricks, which they dried in the sun, and built houses, each of which would hold a squad. Some of the houses had gardens, and even dovecots in them. Water was abundant, and provisions of all sorts plentiful.

To propitiate the natives, Bonaparte celebrated the birth of Mahomet, and also the overflowing of the Nile, with Oriental pomp and
magnificence. He sent a letter to the Sheikh of Mecca to assure him
that the French were the friends of "all true believers," and a letter was
also sent to Pacha Achmet-Djezzar, commanding at St. Jean d'Acre. In
addition to the usual protestations of friendship, the *pacha* was reminded that Bonaparte had released 2,000 Turks at Malta, who had groaned
in slavery for many years; had proved a good friend to Egypt, and had
celebrated the Prophet's festival with a splendour never before seen,
etc. The epistle concluded with:

> The officer who brings this letter will communicate my in-
> structions verbally.

Pacha Achmet-Djezzar was not, however, to be carneyed or bluffed,
and refused to see the staff-officer who carried the letter.

Bonaparte's position was becoming more hazardous every day. The
French could receive no reinforcements, and were a mere handful in
comparison to the population. Many of the men suffered from ophthalmia. The heavy taxation imposed by the French caused discontent-
ment amongst the natives, which was fomented by religious fanatics.
On October 21st a revolt broke out in Cairo, and but for the energetic
measures taken by Bonaparte, all the French would have been massa-
cred. A good many did perish, amongst them General Dupuy—killed
by a lance-thrust whilst charging the mob—and Sulkowski, one of
Bonaparte's *aides-de-camp*. The insurgents took refuge in the Grand
Mosque, but it was bombarded so effectively that they were obliged
to ask quarter. Bonaparte replied:

> You refused my clemency when I offered it. The hour of venge-
> ance has sounded. You began and I will finish.

He eventually granted them quarter, but it was estimated that fully 4,000 Egyptians had perished in the two days of the revolt. The
French lost 283 men, killed or wounded, which, considering their
small number, was very serious.

After the revolt was put down, "confidence was soon restored," and
the troops could indulge in a little amusement. Gambling dens, *cafés*
and restaurants were established. There were reading rooms, billiard
rooms, fireworks, and a theatre, and two newspapers in French were
published by the members of the Institute.

François formed part of an expedition sent to punish a robber-chief who lived in a strong castle in the Delta. The castle was attacked, the chief of the brigands and thirty of his men slain, and a large quantity of stolen property recovered. Five of the French were slightly wounded. The whole of the plunder was sent to Bonaparte.

A few days later his colonel proposed to promote François to be sergeant. François ventured to reply that he preferred to remain quarter-master. The colonel remarked that this was the fourth time he had refused the grade, and as he intended to make François sergeant-major at the next opportunity, and he must be a sergeant first, he had better accept this time. Then he invited the young man to lunch with him, and François accepted both the invitation and the promotion, which latter he had several times declined for the not very obvious reason that he had an intrigue with the wife of a sergeant—presumably "the princess" for whom he had procured a horse, as already mentioned.

He had just previously rejoined his regiment at Belbeis, and as the camp there was strongly entrenched, and not likely to be attacked, the men had nothing to do, and amused themselves in various ways. They had been without pay for a long time, but nearly all of them had money they had taken from the dead or the living in various battles, more especially the battle of the Pyramids. The canteens in the camp sold all sorts of eatables, even pastry, and—in the way of drinks—date wine, lemonade, and burnt brandy. There were frequent fencing tournaments, in which François was often the winner, and the men hunted, and occasionally killed, gazelles and ostriches. The favourite quarry, however, was the native. After breakfast was over, the soldiers used to make up parties to go Arab hunting. They went out as skirmishers, and blazed at the foe until the Arabs were provoked into charging them, when (François says):

At a given signal we formed in square, and though surrounded by the Arabs, we disdained them, and not a day passed that we did not massacre some of them.

A small expedition sent to Suez, captured the town without difficulty. Bonaparte was anxious to get possession of Suez:

As he wished to see whether it would be practicable to construct a canal between the Mediterranean and the Red Sea.

On the last day of the year, François notes that the army was informed that Turkey had declared war on France. Two-thirds of the

French troops had ophthalmia, and many were blind. Several cases of plague had recently occurred; also measles, which in that hot climate was a very painful disease.

CHAPTER 5

# 1799

Early in January, 1799, Bonaparte, accompanied by the scientific men of the expedition—Monge, Bertholet, Casteux and Bourrienne[1]—paid a visit to Suez, and whilst seeking traces of the canal between the two seas, said to have been constructed by the Egyptians many centuries ago, he narrowly escaped the fate of Pharaoh. The party crossed an arm of the Red Sea, and, on the return journey, the Arab guide miscalculated the tide, and Bonaparte would probably have been drowned if one of the escort had not carried him on his shoulders.

The news of the hostile attitude of the Turks, and of Bonaparte's intention to make a campaign in Palestine caused great excitement amongst the troops, for the men were anxious to see such a celebrated country, and all rejoiced when the marching orders came. Reynier's division was to form the advance guard. All the generals were ordered to see that a good supply of water was carried, and that all the men were provided with water-bottles; but the troops were encamped on the edge of the desert, and the order was given too late, so very few of the men had bottles. At the end of the first day's march, the advance guard had consumed all the water carried by the camels, and could not find any wells. Luckily, the Arabs did not prove troublesome, but fled at the approach of the troops.

Before starting, the men and non-commissioned officers had each been supplied with a new weapon. This was a lance, about five feet long, with two chains hanging from the head. It was intended, in case of a cavalry charge or a night attack, that each soldier should affix the

---

1. *Memoirs of Napoleon Bonaparte:*Volume 1—1769-1802,Volume 2—1802-1813 and Volume 3—1813-1821 by Louis Antoine Fauvelet de Bourrienne are also published by Leonaur.

end of one of the chains to the chain of his right-hand man, thus making a sort of chain-fence. But the lance proved useless in action, and troublesome on the march, and François says:

> We ended by burning them, for they caused the death of a good many men.

The second day, there was not a drop of water with the column, and, to make matters worse, they had to cross shifting sand in some places, over which the artillery had to be carried. The next day they came to Katiel. Most of the cisterns had been roiled, but they found one that had not been touched and which contained enough water for all the division. They stayed there some days, until Bonaparte arrived. His resourceful mind mitigated the great difficulty of the march, for he gave orders that every man that was not provided with a bottle, must carry a sheep's or goat's bladder filled with water, but even that, and the water carried by the camels, was insufficient, and some of the men died of thirst, others blew out their brains.

The next day they came to the sea; many of the soldiers rushed into the water, some were drowned, and others drank such large quantities of sea-water that they went mad, and committed suicide. Two brothers in François' company blew out their brains at the same moment. About noon, the division arrived at a well strongly guarded by Arabs, but the advance guard (in which François was) rendered desperate by their sufferings, rushed to the water and drove off the Arabs. François was one of the first to get to the well, and says he must have drunk four or six bottles of the brackish water. One man was killed and three wounded in the scuffle. The wounded, finding themselves unable to crawl to the water, shot themselves.

When the main body of the division arrived, the men fought so viciously to get to the well, that more than thirty of them were suffocated, and in a few seconds the water was muddied and undrinkable. The soldiers, mad with disappointment, called on the general to resume the march; but they had thrown themselves on the burning sand, and, when he gave the order they desired, not a man could rise. The general begged them to take courage, and try to reach a clump of date-palms, about two leagues distant, but not a man rose. General Reynier dug with his hands in the sand, and found a little water. He told the soldiers to do the same, and soon every man had a little puddle of brackish water.

When the men were refreshed, the general gave orders to resume the march, but more than a hundred had obeyed their last command. Having buried these poor wretches, the troops marched to a wood of date-palms at the mouth of the River Torrint. There they found plenty of water—though brackish—but were without food, having consumed their last biscuit. But necessity is the mother of invention; the men cut down the palm trees, and eat the pith and young leaves at the summit of the stem ("palm cabbage") raw or boiled.

The next day they stormed the village of El-Arish at the point of the bayonet. It was no easy work, for the Syrians fought desperately, and the French lost heavily in the narrow streets and alleys. Forty of the defenders took refuge in a cistern, and refused to surrender until the French threatened to burn them alive. They afterwards enlisted in the French Army, and fought well, but they had to be taught not to cut off the heads of the Turks they slew.

The French had 160 killed, and 240 wounded—a very heavy "butcher's bill," considering their number. General Reynier, in his report, recommended many officers and privates for promotion or reward. François was put down for "a musket of honour," but very few of the soldiers ever received their rewards and he was one of those forgotten. He learned afterwards, that Reynier had bitterly complained to Bonaparte that no notice had been taken of his recommendations, but the commander-in-chief received him coldly, and this coolness continued until Bonaparte returned to France; much to the detriment of the division in general, and François in particular.

The fort had to be bombarded, but there were only two 8-pounders with the division, and they exhausted their ammunition in one morning, without making any impression on the walls; so Reynier had to wait till the siege-train arrived.

The division camped in the village and on the sand-hills, not far from the sea. A day or two later, a sloop, flying the French colours, was seen near the shore. The captain landed, and François' company was sent to escort him to camp. The escort had a smart brush with the enemy, lost 11 men, and would have lost more if another company had not been sent to its aid. The captain informed General Reynier that a French fleet would arrive in a few hours, bringing food and ammunition. The soldiers rejoiced to hear this, for both were much needed, but the poor fellows were again doomed to disappointment. A storm came on that night, the fleet was scattered, and the sloop wrecked.

The situation was serious; all the date-palms had been felled, and the men had no food except the carcases of the horses and camels, which had perished from want of fodder. Kléber's division arrived on February 13th, but it also was not well provisioned, and all it could spare to Reynier's division was four ounces of biscuit per man.

Kléber called a council of war, and it was determined to make a night attack on a large body of the enemy, which was encamped in a strong position in a ravine near the fort. The attack succeeded admirably, for the Turks (says François):

> Believe that when the sun has set, everything that lives must be at rest, whilst, for us, all the twenty-four hours were hours of fighting and glory.

The Turks lost 3,000 men. One of their leaders, Gazy Bey, fell and broke his neck, while running away. The sergeant of the 9th Regiment who found his body, made a good haul, for there were 1,100 pieces of gold (worth some 7,000 *francs*) in his belt. François had a not unprofitable adventure, which we will let him narrate in his own words:

> Towards daybreak, I saw a Mameluke, crouched on his horse, galloping hard, and trying to escape. I chanced to be near him. He fired a pistol at me when he was only six paces off and missed me. I stopped the horse with a bayonet thrust in the right flank, and caught it by the bridle. The rider was quite dazed, could not defend himself, and begged for his life. This I granted him. He got off his horse and gave me his arms, consisting of a pair of pistols, ornamented with silver, two daggers, a big one and a little one, and his sabre, a genuine Damascus blade, with a heavy scabbard of solid silver-gilt. I conducted my prisoner to General Reynier.
>
> The Mameluke asked to serve in our ranks. The general acceded to his request, and the prisoner, weeping, gave me his belt, which I refused. He begged me, however, to accept 100 pieces of gold, representing a value of about 700 *francs*. General Reynier told me to take them, and noted me for a reward. I sold the horse and the pistols to Captain Louis, General Reynier's *aide-de-camp*, for 20 *louis*. So my prizes in this expedition brought me in nearly 1,200 *francs*, not including the sabre, which was worth as much again.

Not the worst part of the plunder was a good stock of provisions, for the army was starving. The next day Bonaparte arrived with two other divisions. There was great joy in the camp, and the soldiers cried,

"Long live the commander-in-chief. Lead us to battle, and let us take the fort by storm!"

Bonaparte, however, was not inclined to risk anything. He could not afford to lose men, and was short of ammunition and stores, and, after a good deal of parleying, the fort surrendered. The garrison was to come out with the honours of war, but the men had to swear not to serve in the forces of Djezzar Pacha for a year to come. When they left the fort, they bivouacked in the French lines, and the soldiers were particularly warned not to insult them. Some three hundred of them joined the French forces, and the remainder—in spite of the terms of the surrender—were disarmed and sent home.

On February 22nd, General Kléber's division, reinforced by two battalions of the 9th half brigade, left El-Arish. Not being on a caravan track, they found no wells, and the only food they had was one biscuit per man. They, naturally, suffered terribly from hunger and thirst. General Kléber attributed all their misfortunes to the treachery of the guide, and had him shot, the consequence being that his division lost its road worse than ever, and wandered aimlessly about the desert for 48 hours.

Bonaparte had arranged to meet the division at a village called Kan-Yonnes, but when he arrived he found only the remnant of a corps of Mamelukes who had retreated there after the battle of El-Arish. Bonaparte was only accompanied by his staff, and 30 men of the Dromedary Corps, and he was rather afraid that the Mamelukes, when they saw such a small escort, would fall upon him and take him prisoner.

Several of his staff advised him to return to El-Arish, where part of Reynier's division was still left, but Bonaparte trusted in his luck, and knew that a retreat would be sure to bring the Mamelukes down on him. Only a bold step could save him. Mounted on a swift Arab steed, he put himself at the head of his small force and dashed into the village. The Mamelukes imagined this was the advance guard of the French Army, and without firing a shot, they fell back on Abdallah Pacha's camp, which was only half a league distant, on the Gaza road.

The enemy was too near to be pleasant, and Bonaparte and his men made for a tomb situated in the desert, about three leagues from the village. There they found an officer, with a small detachment, which had been sent in advance by General Kléber. The main body arrived at two in the morning; the men worn out with hunger, thirst, and fatigue, having wandered about the desert for two whole days. In a moment, the well was trodden into a mud-hole, and the men had to scrape in the sand to procure a few drops of muddy water. Many died, but in spite of their present sufferings and the black outlook as to the future, not a complaint was heard.

> Bonaparte was there, and his presence sufficed to make us forget past misfortunes. Accustomed to calamities, we were not discouraged. We were as ready to struggle against the forces of nature as we were to fight our enemies.

After only a few hours' rest, General Kléber's forces were ordered to attack the enemy, but the *pacha* abandoned his camp—in which the French found some provisions, of which they had much need—and retired on Gaza. He took up a position on a hill covered with olive-trees, just outside the town, which, the French officers told their men, was the identical hill to which Samson carried the gates of Gaza.

The French marched along, singing gaily, for the men were refreshed by the food they had found in the camp, and by a pleasant shower of rain which fell that afternoon. Besides, they were now on the fertile plains of Syria, not in the sandy, sultry, desert. The Turks,—after making a charge, which was easily repelled,—broke and fled, pursued by Murat's cavalry, which chased them through the town of Gaza and a league beyond. So precipitate was their retreat, that they did not even stop to garrison the fort; in which the French found 10,000 rations of "very black biscuit," and a quantity of rice and barley. This came in handy, for no supplies had been sent, and when the soldiers asked Bonaparte for bread, he said, in his usual calm manner; "Friends! there is some in such and such a place; you must take it!"

To which some of the soldiers replied, "Very well! lead us on!" and others cried, "Long live Bonaparte."

The march from Gaza to Jaffa was difficult, for it was through a plain of soft sand in which the wheels of the gun-carriages sank, and not a drop of water was to be procured the first day, and very little the second, but at Ramleh,—which the enemy abandoned at the approach of the French,—they found food and ammunition. On March 3rd, the army encamped under the walls of Jaffa, but Kléber's division was the next day ordered to a village near St. Jean d'Acre. François saw nothing therefore of the siege of Jaffa, but he heard all particulars of it from his comrades. The place, no doubt, would have fallen in the long run, but its capture was really due to an accident.

Some soldiers of Bon's division found a breach in the wall, near the sea, and boldly entered the town. They were set upon by the towns-people and some of them killed, but the others escaped the way they came, and informed their comrades of their discovery. Whilst Bonaparte engaged the attention of the garrison by a feigned attack, Bon's division penetrated into the town, and the news of this having reached the men of Lannes' division, they stormed the walls. The soldiers did not cease slaughtering the garrison and townsfolk until they were tired of killing, and the pillage of the town lasted four days.

The result of this carnage was that the plague broke out amongst the French, and many of the soldiers died within twenty-four hours of being attacked. The disease spread to Kléber's division, which was stationed fifteen leagues away—the contagion being probably brought by a detachment sent over with orders from headquarters. Kléber took energetic quarantine measures. Every man who complained of fever was sent to a special camp, placed 400 yards from the main body, with a line of sentries between, who had orders to shoot any sound person who might endeavour to go and nurse the sick. The rations for the sick men were placed a hundred yards from their camp, and those who were strong enough to crawl out and fetch them did so—those who were not strong enough were left to die. Many of the generals and superior officers, both at Jaffa and Miski, shut themselves up in their houses, and gave their orders through a small trap cut in the door. Some had palisades erected round their houses at a distance of twenty-five paces, and would not receive any paper unless it was steeped in vinegar. But, in spite of these precautions, many of them caught the disease, and died.

General Grizien, of the staff, took more elaborate precautions than any one else, but he was dead in twenty-four hours, and his death did a lot of good, François says, for the soldiers saw there was no means of stopping the pestilence, and their gaiety returned, for there was no good dreading an evil which could not be avoided. He himself took no precautions, on the contrary, he often helped those who were attacked, led them to the sick camp, embraced them when he left, and often inherited their money and effects, he writes:

> Many of my comrades followed my example for we were indifferent as to our fate, and had little hope of ever seeing our native land again.

General Ménou was named by Bonaparte, Governor of Palestine, but he never took possession of the post. He had fallen in love—

despite his sixty-six years—with the daughter of a bath-keeper at Rosetta, and, for her sake, turned Mussulman, and married her. He bestowed on her a wedding-portion of a million *francs* in cash, and jewellery to a like amount. But even the Turks laughed at him for changing his religion for the sake of a woman, when, as they said, he might have gone to the bazaar and bought as many as he liked, of all ages and all colours.

There was a night-alarm at Kléber's camp on March 9th, but the Arabs came to steal, not to fight. Several were captured, and amongst them four Sheikhs. Kléber examined these four men the next morning, and then called for dice and a drum to be brought. The four Arabs threw the dice on the drum-head, and the one who threw the highest number was immediately shot. The other three were let go, after promising to send six oxen a piece to the camp, but whether they ever kept their promise François did not know. It is to be hoped they did, for the division had no provisions except what they could procure from the Arabs.

Bonaparte was anxious to advance at once on Acre, but did not know what to do with the large number of prisoners he had taken at Jaffa and other places. He was not strong enough to divide his army, and if he had released the prisoners, with or without parole, they would probably have joined the garrisons at Acre, Damascus, or Aleppo. The difficulty of procuring provisions for his own men, made it impossible for him to burden the army with some thousands of prisoners.

He called a council of war, and it was decided to despatch the prisoners. At 6 o'clock in the morning of March 13th, they were conducted to the sea-shore. There they were mown down by artillery and musket fire, and the bayonet finished all the bullets had spared. In less than an hour, 3,563 men were killed and thrown into the sea.

François—to whom nothing that Bonaparte did could seem wrong—finds some excuse for this wholesale butchery, he writes:

Far be it from me to wish to lessen the horror of this terrible measure, but considering the position we were in, without provisions, and fighting every day, how could we guard, with less than 1,100 men, thousands of prisoners, whose desperation might have had terrible consequences for us. Those who, like me, went through the expedition to Egypt and Syria, will never forget the hardships they suffered. Let us therefore take no notice of the recriminations of our enemies (the English) who are a thousand times more barbarous than we are. Can many of our generals, superior officers, soldiers and sailors forget the terrible time on the hulks, where they all suffered the horrors of a slow and calculated death?

Immediately after this massacre, Bonaparte moved his camp, and, on March 19th, was in position before St. Jean d'Acre. The Druses brought some provisions, and were very useful to the French all the time the siege lasted. They informed Bonaparte there were two men in the town who were worth the whole Mussulman army; the one was Sir Sidney Smith, the commander of the English naval division, and the other was a Frenchman, named Philippeaux, formerly an artillery officer, and very clever in that branch of military science. The *pacha* had entrusted the defence of the town to these two men.

To François and his comrades, the walls did not appear more formidable than those of Jaffa, and they expected the siege to be as short and end as fortunately; in spite of this clever and terrible Philippeaux, although they knew that he had constructed an inner line of fortifications, defended by the guns from the two English war-vessels.

But the help provided by the English would have been of no avail, if fortune had not also been against the French. The fleet, which was to have brought them siege guns and ammunition, was captured by the British, with the exception of one corvette. "This irreparable loss was announced to us in an order of the day, which also showed us how to remedy the evil."

Almost more serious was the want of provisions, for the convoys did not come from Egypt, the stores found at Jaffa and other places had long since been consumed, and, though the Druses were friendly, the French had to go a long way to get provisions, and pay heavily for bad bread, bad fruit, and bad wine.

Bonaparte was often implored by the soldiers to let them try an assault, and, a certain tower having been well battered by artillery, and a mine fired under it, the soldiers were sent to storm it. The grenadiers nearly took it, but they found a ditch, the existence of which they had not suspected, and the *pacha* having rallied his men, the French had to retreat with heavy loss. The ferocious *pacha* had the heads of the dead Frenchmen cut off and stuck along the walls on pikes. It was said that he presented them to Sidney Smith, who drew back in horror at the gruesome sight, but as Smith was an Englishman, François could not believe he would behave that way. The next day the garrison and the English sailors made a sortie, and, though they were driven back, they retired in good order, and inflicted considerable loss on the French.

To add to Bonaparte's other troubles, the Druses informed him that a large army was marching to the relief of St. Jean d'Acre. Ammunition, too, was running short, so Bonaparte issued an order of the day in which he offered to pay for the enemy's shot, according to the calibre—12 *sous* for a 24-lb. ball; 9 for an 18-lb.; 8 for a 12-lb, and smaller ones at the rate of a *sou* per pound. As soon as the order was read, the men picked up their weapons, took large sacks, and collected some thousands of cannon balls. This little business continued until the siege was raised. François and his comrades used to go out and tempt the enemy to shoot at them, and then pick up the balls, but a good many men were killed at this game, and when the garrison got wind of the arrangement they were more chary of their fire, in spite of provocations. François owns that, in collecting these cannon balls, the patriotic object of making a breach in the walls was secondary to the personal motive of being able to buy food from the Druses.

On his life he set small value. One day he stood on the earthwork of the trenches, fully exposed, and for an hour and a quarter fired at the enemy, with muskets two of his comrades handed to him. He received eight bullets, he says, but a bruise on his thigh was all the damage he sustained. He stuck to his dangerous post, "in spite of the observations of his officers and comrades," till he had used up seventeen packets of cartridges.

He was also in an assault which his regiment made upon the tower, but the 9th brigade fared no better than the grenadiers, and was obliged to retreat, leaving forty-two dead or wounded behind. For his conduct on these two occasions, François was promoted to sergeant-major.

Ammunition became so scarce that Bonaparte had to double the rewards he had been giving. After that the men used to go out and try to draw the fire of the batteries and the English vessels, and, after a volley, run after the cannon balls. Many fell victims to what they regarded as a game, but some of the men made from 20 to 30 *francs* a day. The Druses still continued to bring in a little food, but the other natives did not, for they had seen two assaults on the town fail, and they began to think the Turks would make reprisals when the siege was raised.

The brilliant victory which Bonaparte and Kléber won at Mount Tabor restored their confidence, and after that provisions were plentiful. The arrival of three French frigates with siege artillery and ammunition filled the besiegers with joy, but the besieged were by no means discouraged. They beat back every attack made on the ruins of the Square Tower (which the French called "the Infernal Tower") killed brave old General Caffarelli, and severely wounded General Vaubois. General Lannes whilst looking through a loop-hole, was hit by a musket ball, which passed through both cheeks, knocking out several of his teeth.

A night attack made by the French, failed, for the Turks had been taught by Philippeaux the inconveniences of the custom of not fighting after sunset, and the walls were made "as light as day" by lanterns and fire-pots. On the other hand, the sorties of the garrison were repulsed, on one occasion with the loss of 700 men to the besieged; but another time they succeeded, before they were driven back, in destroying a mine on which the French had been at work ever since the beginning of the siege.

This,—with the failure of the attacks and the fatigue and privations,—made the soldiers murmur, though they did not proceed to acts of insubordination. But, on the afternoon of April 27th, a fleet of thirty vessels was seen approaching. The rumour ran through the camp that these were French ships, bringing reinforcements and ammunition; and their hopes seemed to be confirmed when it was noticed that the two English war-ships hastily put to sea, evidently fearing to be captured.

But the joy of the French soldiers was short-lived. As the vessels approached, it could be seen they were flying the Turkish flag, and, in fact, were bringing troops, ammunition, and provisions for the garrison.

Bonaparte saw that his only chance was to storm the town before these fresh troops could disembark. He ordered another assault, which was delivered with all the impetuosity of the French; "who never before displayed such boldness and superhuman courage," says François, who was not a bad judge of those qualities. The "cursed tower" was carried, and the French took five flags (one was taken by François) and spiked nine guns. Cries of victory were already heard, when the French suddenly found themselves confronted by another obstacle. This was a wall, with a ditch 18 feet wide and as many deep, in front of it. They charged it gallantly, but, exposed to a hot fire from front and rear, they wavered and broke, and Lannes, who led the storming-party, was unable to rally them.

What rendered the defeat the more bitter to the French was that they had been within an ace of succeeding; for two hundred grenadiers and scouts, commanded by General Rambaud, had penetrated into the heart of the town, but, being left without support, were surrounded. They took refuge in a mosque, and, knowing what their fate would be if they were captured by the Turks, determined to fight to the last man. Most of them, indeed, including General Rambaud, were killed, but Sir Sidney Smith saved the remainder, by promising that if they surrendered to him their lives should be safe.

It needed a good deal to discourage men who had Bonaparte for their leader, and, though food was running short—for even the Druses had almost ceased to bring in any—the soldiers were not disposed to own themselves beaten. When Bonaparte appeared in the trenches, they would say to him, "General (or Bonaparte), we must try again." When some of the men were picked out to make an assault,. the others, who were passed over, would say to the officers, "Am not I as good a soldier, and as brave as so and so?"

To which the officers would reply, "Your turn will come."

There was plenty of fighting at close quarters, and François records that hand grenades were often thrown backwards and forwards several times before they burst. He had escaped serious damage, hitherto, he "does not know how." He recounts how, in one of the sorties, he was nearly taken prisoner.

Not fearing death, having escaped it so many times, and trusting to my good luck, without thinking of danger, I jumped right into the middle of the Turks. Several of them began to drag me away, some by my coat, others holding on to my sword, whilst one tried to get my gun. I was hardly able to defend myself in such a narrow space, and surrounded by the barbarians, who, fortunately, were somewhat scared, and not having recovered from the dangers they had run, contented themselves with trying to drag me into the town. But, at this moment, our men, following up their success, jumped into the trench where I was, and the Turks, getting frightened, left me and retired into the town. I was so dazed by the scuffle, which had lasted several minutes, that I did not even think of the risks I had undergone. Finding myself once more amidst my comrades, without any wound, and only having lost my hat, I laughed with them about the narrow squeak I had had. My tunic was torn from the waist up to the middle of the back, so I put on the coat of one of the dead men; there were few amongst us who had not changed their coats thus several times.

The adventure did not prevent this indefatigable fighting man from banging away all night, with a "short 32-pounder," at the enemy's works. At two in the morning, Bonaparte came into the battery, and watched the effect of one or two shots. Then he walked up to the gun, levelled it himself, and said, "Always shoot *there*"; which François did for several hours, Kléber's division arrived, and thus reinforced, Bonaparte ordered another assault. Captain Venoux, who led the storming-party, swore that he would either take the town or be killed, and he kept his word, for he and most of his grenadiers perished in the breach. The French lost 600 killed and twice as many wounded, in this attack.

The plague raged amongst both besiegers and besieged, but was worse for the former, on account of the number of dead who lay rotting in the trenches, François draws a grimly realistic picture of the horrors of the siege:

The fire from the town did not allow us to burn or bury the corpses. We were always in the trenches, so were compelled to pass the whole twenty-four hours amidst those rotting carcases, which served us as ramparts. The least rotten we used as seats! We were obliged to keep our handkerchiefs to our noses the whole time, and the horrible stench prevented us from eating or drinking the whole twenty-four hours we were on duty. Our commander-in-chief sent several times to Pacha Djezzar, to ask for an armistice to permit us to bury the dead. But the plague was too good an ally, and he would not accede to Bonaparte's request; he fired on our envoys, and the only one he did receive (who was a Turk) he kept prisoner. Perhaps he had his head cut off.

Bonaparte had no alternative but to raise the siege. On May 11th, some of the batteries were dismounted, and the guns sent to Kantarah. Many of the sick and wounded were also sent to the same place. But the siege was not quite over,—it would have been all the better for François if it had been, for the good luck he had so long enjoyed deserted him at the last moment. The besieged made a sortie in force, on the morning of May 16th, and somehow it happened that, as François was running full speed towards the trenches, he found himself surrounded by Turks, he says:

I received five sabre cuts on the arms and head, one of which cut off the skin of my forehead, which dropped over my right eye. I fell, but they had no time to come and cut my head off, our fire being too hot. When I recovered myself a little (the sabre cut on my forehead was about three inches long) I tried to run back, but, just as I was getting up, a shell burst over my head, and a splinter broke my left arm. I lay stretched out on the ground. My comrades were not far off, and seeing my state and hearing my cries, came to my succour, in spite of the danger, and led me to the ambulance. There I was attended to by Chief-Surgeon Larrey, who set my arm and sewed up the skin of my forehead. There was no lint, and he had to use cotton. I was the more grieved about my wounds as there was some talk of raising the siege, and I was afraid I should be sent away, like the other wounded to Kantarah, and put on board ship. It was proposed to me, but I refused. Events showed that I was lucky, for the ship with the wounded was wrecked on the coast near the Isthmus of Suez, and all on board perished.

Another thing, which also greatly annoyed François, was that the Turks, in this sortie, left behind them copies of a proclamation by the *grand vizier*, drawn up in French, promising a safe conduct and protection to all Frenchmen, of whatever rank, who would desert the army. At the bottom of the document was a note, signed by Sir Sidney Smith, "certifying the authenticity of the proclamation and guaranteeing its execution." Such a paper was hardly calculated to suborn the soldiers of Bonaparte, and, as François' opinion of it no doubt faithfully represented that of his comrades as well as himself, it will be interesting to hear his remarks concerning this document.

How pitiful was this stale trick, and how indignant this proclamation—which we guessed to be of English composition—made us! Could this Commodore Smith hope to seduce us by such promises? This leopard forgot, no doubt, that for six years we had not ceased to fight with glory and devotedness to make our name illustrious. Philippeaux is a monster to so misunderstand the character of his countrymen, and dare to suspect us of such disgraceful cowardice. Oh, that he could have heard our curses against him and the English! Deputations were sent to Bonaparte, asking him to try one more assault to revenge this insult, and to prove to the Turks and their allies that the conquerors of Holland, Germany, Italy, and Egypt, preferred death to dishonour. But Bonaparte had made up his mind, and knowing better than we did that all efforts to take St. Jean d'Acre would be useless, replied that he had determined to raise the siege. The deputations returned and made known his reply. All the army swore that its vengeance should only be deferred.

Three days later, the army marched silently away in the night, leaving only the 9th half-brigade, with a few artillery men and engineers, before Acre. The garrison perhaps guessed, or knew, that the main body had gone, and next day made a most determined sortie. If the 9th had not "surpassed itself in bravery," it would have been cut to pieces; but the men knew they were there to cover the retreat, and that no assistance could be hoped for, and fought like demons. The Turks were eventually driven back into the town with heavy loss, but the French lost 98 killed and five wounded. The difference in proportion was due to the Turkish custom of cutting off the heads of the wounded.

François, being in hospital at the time, was not in this engagement, but, with his arm in a sling, his forehead sewn up, and his head enveloped in cotton, stood in the rear with the other wounded, to defend the flag. As the enemy had advanced nearly to the aqueduct, the wounded retired to a trench still further in the rear, but had hardly arrived there when a ball, from one of the small forts near the sea, took them in flank, killing three non-commissioned officers, and cutting off both legs of Sergeant-Major Noel, and a leg of a quartermaster. The brains of one of the unfortunate sergeants were thrown full in the face of François. Noel was carried to the ambulance, and the tough old warrior survived the amputation of both legs, and was living in Paris when François wrote out his journal, many years later.

About two in the morning, the brigade evacuated the camp, dragging the field guns by hand, and leaving the siege artillery. The greatest silence was observed, as their road lay along the seashore, and any noise might have drawn on them the fire of the two English war vessels. But the English did not know of their flight till daylight came, and then did not pursue them. Bonaparte made the greater part of the retreat on foot, having given up his chargers for the use of the sick and wounded, and the other generals all followed his example.

Thus ended the memorable siege of Acre; the French lost there at least 5,000 killed, and took away 1,500 wounded. François consoles himself for the defeat with the satisfaction that at all events they had left some unpleasant reflections for Pacha Djezzar and the English; for the town was in ruins, Djezzar's palace destroyed, and Philippeaux dead of the plague.

The army, "if it might be so called," was at Kantarah on May 21st. Forty guns, which had been captured at Jaffa, were put on board ship, and the others were thrown into the sea, and the carriages burned or broken. The soldiers attacked with the plague were transported to a small island, opposite the port, and left there; in the hope that the English would help them, but, as the latter knew why these poor wretches had been abandoned, they left them on the island; where they probably perished, when they had consumed the few biscuits and the little water given them.

> This barbarous but necessary measure was very painful to us, but we knew that its object was to avoid greater evils, for the terrible disease assumed a character capable of making us tremble, if we had still feared death.

The fertile country between Acre and Jaffa was ravaged, "till it looked like a desert." François thinks the Syrians "well deserved this vengeance, which prevented them from pursuing us and troubling our retreat;"—which would be excellent logic if it could be proved that the French had any right in Syria. All inhabitants found with arms in their hands were instantly shot, and, at Jaffa, the fortifications were blown up, the artillery thrown in the sea, the magazines of grain and warehouses destroyed, and all timber burned; in short, everything was done to complete the ruin of the country. Bonaparte's friends fared little better than his enemies. Some hundreds of Catholics from Nazareth and Ramleh came to claim his protection, and asked permission to follow his army. Unfortunately for them, the permission was granted, for they nearly all perished in the Isthmus of Suez from want of food and water.

Much ink has been shed over the vexed question as to whether the plague patients at Jaffa were poisoned by Bonaparte's order. Some historians have asserted that several hundreds were thus killed, and, on the other hand, Bonapartist writers still maintain that no such order was ever given, and that, if any of the sick were poisoned, it was done without Bonaparte's knowledge and consent. As François was on the spot, and is not a witness likely to paint Bonaparte's conduct in the worst colours, the following extract from his diary is not without historic value:—

> At Jaffa, where there was a hospital for plague patients, and to avoid still worse evils to the soldiers attacked with that disease, Bonaparte ordered a secret committee to decide on the fate of these poor wretches. His plan was to poison them, to prevent the terrible fate reserved for victims who fell alive into the hands of our ferocious enemies. Orders were given that the comptroller at Acre should ship them to Damietta; but thirty were poisoned with opium. Eighteen of these poor fellows were saved; a man named Gariot, the son of my lieutenant, was one of them.
>
> Thus only twelve died of poison, and not 400 as was rumoured, because the army did not know that the patients capable of bearing the voyage had been sent to Damietta. Several of these ships were wrecked near El Arish; those who escaped from them wandered into the desert and perished there, except three who succeeded in reaching a little port called Tyneh.
>
> I saw them afterwards at Ibrahim Bey's hospital, near Cairo, where they related to me their misfortunes. They told me that the English were about to capture the vessel on which they were, but, finding out that the plague was on board, these leopards left it alone. Several ships besides theirs were wrecked. They added, that it was by a kind of miracle that they reached Tyneh by land. They were reduced to eating one of their comrades, and this food gave them strength to get to Tyneh, where, after some days' rest, they were brought back to Cairo, and then sent to the hospital.
>
> As will be seen, then, it is not true that all the plague patients at Jaffa were poisoned; only thirty partook of the brew prepared by one named Boyer, chief druggist to the army.

At Gaza, only the forts were blown up; the town was spared out of gratitude for the kind reception the inhabitants had given the French when they first came there. The plague reappeared amongst the troops whilst at Gaza, and the men affected were lodged in deserted houses in the town, and orders given to the authorities that they were to be well treated. To ensure this, some of the principal inhabitants were taken away as hostages.

Crossing the desert was a worse ordeal than on the first occasion; many of the horses, camels, mules, and donkeys which bore the wounded, died, and the men they carried were left to perish. Many men who were not wounded, died of thirst and heat, and others wandered off into the desert. When a well of bad water was at last reached, a cannon had to be fired to recall stragglers, many of whom came into camp during the night. Noel, who had both legs taken off by a cannon ball at St. Jean d'Acre, came safely across the desert, but seven out of the twelve men appointed to carry his litter died. François' wounds healed rapidly, in spite of the fact that they were never dressed. Republican soldiers seem to have been hard to kill.

At last Cairo was reached, and, thanks to having a splendid black Arab charger presented to him just before he came to the city, Bonaparte was able to make an imposing entry. Thirty-three flags captured in the Syrian expedition—of which François had taken two—were sent to the Grand Mosque, and the men were made happy by the announcement that they were to receive the back pay for the year VI. and two months of year VII.

Two of François' wounds gave him some trouble, so he bought some bedding, hired a negro lad, and asked the divisional surgeon to attend him. His comrades and officers said he was sure to be gazetted sub-lieutenant, and he told his captain that, if he were not promoted, he should like to join the Dromedary Corps. His wish was gratified; and on July 9th he was appointed chief sergeant in this famous corps. He much preferred this to being an officer in a line regiment, as the "Dromedaries" were the picked men of the army, and their pay was much higher. The men were employed as orderlies and scouts, and were often sent long distances.

Three days after François entered the regiment, Bonaparte reviewed it. Some 300 of the men were mounted and in uniform, François amongst them, though he was still very weak; his arm was in a sling, and he wore a black bandage over his right eye. His uniform was, at least, picturesque, and consisted of a *dolman* with a hussar's belt ("in which many of us stuck pistols in addition to those in the holsters"), wide cotton trousers, yellow morocco boots, and a white turban with black ostrich plumes. This was the ordinary or undress uniform; on grand occasions they wore a sky-blue tunic with red sleeve-facings, epaulettes, tight breeches, also sky-blue, and red boots instead of yellow.

Towards the end of the month (July), Bonaparte moved to Alexandria. François was present when he reproved General Marmont for having abandoned Aboukir, where the Turks were strongly entrenched. Marmont excused himself, on the ground that he had only 1,200 men against more than 20,000. *"Eh, bien,"* replied Bonaparte, "with 1,200 men I would have gone to Constantinople."

On July 25th, Bonaparte attacked the Turks, and routed them with immense slaughter, several thousand being shot, sabred, or driven into the sea. François was "tired of killing;" his arm being still weak. The French lost nearly 1,000 in killed and wounded, amongst them several generals. A cannon ball took off General Fugière's arm. François heard that he said to Bonaparte, who saw him a few minutes after his arm had been amputated by Larrey, *"Mon géneral,* you will perhaps some day envy my fate, for I die on the field of honour." He did not die, however.

Three thousand of the Turks shut themselves in the fort of Aboukir, and defended themselves obstinately, but, as they had no food, were starved into surrender. When they came out they looked like spectres. They expected to be all killed, but the French, "forgetting all feeling of hate, gave them all the attention their deplorable condition required." The French knew, by experience, the danger of eating too heartily after a prolonged fast, but they could not impress that lesson on the Turks, three-fourths of whom died from over-eating.

After the battle, Bonaparte gave orders that a fort at Alexandria should be henceforth known as Fort Cretin; the battery at Cleopatra's Bath was to be called Fort Leturcq, and another battery, Fort Duvivier, after three superior officers who were killed at Aboukir. François says:

> Such were the noble rewards with which our commander repaid our courage and devotion,—rewards which the army would rather have had than the mines of Peru.

A couple of French transport ships arrived a few days later. They brought a small reinforcement—about 300 infantry—but they also brought news that made Bonaparte determine to go back to France as soon as he possibly could. He returned to Cairo almost immediately, but left it again a fortnight later, and started from Alexandria for France, on August 22nd. His departure was kept secret, and the garrison of Cairo refused to believe the news at first, until "the Dromedaries" assured them it was true. Some then said that their commander had treacherously deserted them, but François reproves these "evil tongues," and says that Bonaparte left by order of the government, and to obey the desire of the nation.

Kléber was left in command, and Bonaparte—it was rumoured amongst the soldiers—had done all in his power to render his successor's task the easier. He had written (it was asserted) to the Divan at Cairo, to announce that he had abjured the dogma of the Trinity, and professed that of Unity, the fundamental principle of Mahomet's religion, and he reproached the Turks for having made an alliance with Trinitarian Christians. He promised to build, at his own cost, a mosque which should rival in magnificence Saint Sophia, and he recommended Kléber to give the preference to Mussulmans rather than to Christians, as the latter were sure to be on their side whatever happened. In fact, "owing to the political methods of this great man," affairs were left in a flourishing condition, except that there was a matter of seven months' pay due—which, however, Kléber was soon able to pay.

In discussing the effects of Bonaparte's departure, François is sometimes optimistic and sometimes pessimistic. Two or three days later, when noting the official announcement that Bonaparte had left, and Kléber had assumed the command, he sees things in a far less rosy light, he says:

> We were accustomed to regard Bonaparte as the arbiter of our fate, and we expected nothing but death in this foreign land. The officers and soldiers were indignant, and each man was guided by personal motives. They said that Bonaparte ought to have deemed their preservation a paramount consideration. Our leaders told us he had been called away to save France. Finally, having exhausted every conjecture and every probability, after having regretted and cursed our general, we were suddenly seized with joy, hoping that Bonaparte, when he had vanquished the enemies of the Republic, would return to us to conquer those who remained to be subdued in Egypt.

General Kléber—though loved by his own division, who had fought under him in the Rhine campaign, and now formed part of the army of Egypt—was not equally popular with all the army. Many would have preferred to see the command given to General Desaix, who was surnamed "The Just" by the Turks, and whose military reputation was quite as good as that of Kléber. He was, moreover, quiet, affable, and unostentatious; whereas Kléber was proud, brusque in his manners, and too much given to display. When he rode through the streets of Cairo, he was preceded by running footmen, carrying sticks six feet long, who cried: "Here comes the Lord Commander-in-Chief! Bow down before him!" This may have pleased the Turks, but was very distasteful to his soldiers, for they remembered that Bonaparte often went about the city on foot, accompanied only by an orderly, and his faithful Mameluke, Roustan.

In October, François and the other Dromedaries helped General Desaix to disperse a small body of the enemy; and, in the following month, General Verdier defeated a body of 7,000 *janissaries*, who had been landed by Sir Sidney Smith's vessels, at the mouth of the Nile. But, in spite of these small successes, the French were far from being in a comfortable position. A regiment mutinied because it could not get its back pay (the men had not been paid for ten months). General Kléber was jealous of the rising importance of Bonaparte, and his temper was not improved by the intimation he received from Sir Sidney Smith that the negotiations for peace, which he had begun, would not be considered by the Sublime Porte without the consent of England and Russia. To make matters still worse, a letter which Kléber wrote to the Directory denouncing Bonaparte and imploring assistance, fell into the hands of the British Government, the vessel which conveyed it having been captured by an English corvette.

# CHAPTER 6

# 1800

Early in January, 1800, the Grand Vizier of Turkey arrived at Gaza, accompanied by Sir Sidney Smith, to confer with General Desaix and Citizen Poussielque on the terms of peace. François was sent there with a detachment of "Dromedaries," with a letter from General Kléber, empowering the French envoys to "accept any terms that did not compromise the honour of France and the army," and would ensure the return to France of all the forces, numbering about 18,000 men. He was also inclined to insist on a rupture of the alliance between Turkey, England, and Russia, but, as it was pointed out that the alliance was purely defensive, he had to withdraw his objection.

The Dromedaries were well treated all the time negotiations were going on, and were fed on roast mutton, game, very black bread, date cider, *sorbets*, and coffee. Before their departure, they were reviewed by the *grand vizier*, who gave each man five gold pieces (about 40 *francs*), but, in spite of the hospitality he had received, François was ill-satisfied with the peace that had been made. He and his comrades said:

If Bonaparte had been here, he would not have signed the treaty, and, if he had judged it necessary to evacuate Egypt, he would first have forced the Turks, by a fresh victory, to grant more honourable terms, and made the English ratify them.

Their wrath was increased by the fact that some twenty French soldiers, part of the post at El Arish, had been surprised by the Arabs and cut to pieces; which disaster was, of course, attributed to "the criminal intervention of English policy."

Preparations were rapidly made by Kléber to leave Egypt; the wounded were put on an English ship, the *Bison*, to be conveyed to France, but, at the last minute, orders were received from Sir Sidney

Smith that no vessel was to leave Alexandria, and Admiral Keith, commanding the English Mediterranean squadron, also informed General Kléber that no terms would be made with the French unless they laid down their arms, and that all troops found on board ship would be sent back to Alexandria, even if provided with Turkish passports, and if not provided with passports would be regarded as prisoners of war.

"This strange and abominable letter," as François calls it, caused Kléber to give orders to re-arm the forts, and unload the ammunition from the boats that were going to take it down the Nile to Alexandria;—orders which the soldiers obeyed with alacrity, for they all thirsted for vengeance.

The French saw that the Turks, prompted by the English, wanted to force them to fight, in the hope that their small army would be annihilated. General Kléber called a council of war, read the letter he had received from Admiral Keith, and then said:

Generals, you know the contents of this letter. It shows you your duty and mine. This is our situation: The English refuse us an egress, although their plenipotentiaries agreed to it; and the Turks, to whom we have given back the country, want us to evacuate it, according to treaty. We must conquer these latter, the only ones we can get at. I count on your zeal, your coolness, and the confidence with which you inspire your men. Here is my plan of battle.

The army marched out that night, formed in hollow squares, and next day attacked the Turks at Heliopolis. Kléber's address to the men, before the battle, was short and pithy:

Soldiers! you know the justice of our cause; the enemy must learn your valour; prepare for combat. And you, drummers, if the enemy enters your squares, knock out their eyes with your drum-sticks.

Although the Turks were nearly twelve to one, they were routed with great slaughter. Their camp and effects fell into the hands of the French, who had plenty of loot. Two days later, the fort at Belbeis was compelled to surrender. The garrison had to lay down its arms, and François, who was present, reports that one man, a fanatic, would not be disarmed, and said that he preferred to die. He fired his musket, at close quarters, at Colonel Latour-Maubourg, Kléber's *aide-de-camp*, but the bullet only grazed that officer's shoulder.

The next moment all the other Turkish soldiers threw themselves at our feet and said they all deserved death. They wished us to revenge on them the act of their comrade, but the commander-in-chief pardoned them all, except the author of the attempt, who was executed on the spot.

Kléber energetically followed up his advantage, and on one occasion went almost too fast. Hearing, by the sound of the guns, that his advance-guard was engaged with the enemy, he pressed on with only his guides and cavalry. The Turks, seeing only such a small body, bore down on him. He was wounded in the left shoulder by a spear, and his escort, of which François was one, would have been cut to pieces, if the 14th Dragoons had not luckily come up in time. In the course of this quick march across the desert, some of the soldiers died of the hot wind, and others had their eyes burned by the glare of the sand.

The Turks were expected to rally at Salhieh, but, when Kléber arrived there, he was surprised to find that they had fled, and the Arabs were busy pillaging the camp. The French fell on these marauders, killed "some hundreds" of them, and put the rest to flight. François, with ten other Dromedaries, pushed on to the mosque, where they expected to find a large stock of provisions. In addition to the stores, they found there two French artillerymen, naked, and loaded with chains, which François made the peasants break.

The camp contained plenty of loot. There were boxes of rich clothes and perfumes, saddles, 40,000 horseshoes, a dozen richly carved and gilded litters, and many horses and camels. The Turks were in full retreat to Syria, but, as they had abandoned all their stores, and their army was pursued and harassed by the Arabs, who killed all the stragglers, François reasonably doubted whether many of them would get there in safety. At least 50,000, he thinks, must have been killed in the various battles, without counting those who fell by the hands of the Arabs. The total French loss, killed and wounded, was only 300.

When Kléber returned to Cairo, which he did almost immediately, he found both the city and the important suburb of Boulac had revolted against the French. Having only a limited number of men, and very little artillery ammunition, it cost him some trouble to take Boulac, though his losses were trivial. Some English officers and French deserters were found amongst the rebels, and orders were given that all Europeans taken prisoner were to be immediately shot without trial. François says:

For my own part amongst several prisoners I made, I recognised an Englishman by his language. To be better assured on this point, I spoke Arabic to him, but he could not reply, so I asked him, 'Are you English?' He replied to me in German mixed with English; so, being sure that he was really English, I blew out his brains. I thus proved my hatred for that nation, which had caused all our misfortunes. I took the other prisoners to General Friant, who, having ascertained that they were not soldiers, sent them away. The loss to the enemy must have been considerable, for we killed men, women, and children.

Besides the throat-cutting, every French soldier carried a lighted torch, to set the houses on fire!

A similar scene was enacted when Cairo was besieged. In one attack, 500 houses were burned, and more than 2,000 of the enemy were killed; François calmly points out:

But that does not include the number of insurgents, of both sexes and all ages, who were burned in their houses.

The city surrendered, after two or three days of such carnage, and François was employed as orderly to carry Kléber's conditions to the Turkish and English leaders. The duty was rather dangerous, for he ran a risk of being killed by the infuriated populace, but was not without its compensations, for Nassif Pacha gave him a handful of gold.

On April 27th, the French made a solemn entry into the city, amidst the booming of the big guns, and in the presence of more than 200,000 people, witnesses of this triumph, who, with folded arms and bowed heads, seemed to await their fate in fear and trembling. In this march in, Kléber not only showed his liking for theatrical display, but condescended to a trick not unknown to stage-managers, which François describes:

All the shops were shut, and the greatest silence reigned during the passage of the troops, who passed several times through the same quarters and down the same streets, to impress the inhabitants with the idea of a numerous army. The trick succeeded admirably, but caused us a lot of work, because we had, so to speak, to multiply ourselves to keep up the illusion.

General Kléber imposed a fine of twelve million *francs*—half in cash and half in stores—on the city; which the Turks,—who had expected to be all killed, and their city sacked, and who had richly deserved that fate, François thinks,—regarded as being very generous terms.

François has little of importance to record during the next month. It is interesting, however, to note that General Kléber, being very short of men, bought slaves from the caravans and enrolled them in the French Army, and that these "idolatrous negroes" soon became good soldiers. The system had been begun by Bonaparte, who wrote to the Beys of Tripoli and Algiers, offering to buy all the male slaves from sixteen to nineteen that could be procured. The proceeding does not appear to be altogether in keeping with Republican principles.

On June 14th, General Kléber lunched with General Dumas, and afterwards went with his architect, Citizen Protain, to the Staff office, to consult with him about some repairs to his palace, which had been damaged in the siege. Whilst traversing a long, vine-covered terrace, a native approached and stooped as though to kiss the general's hand, and stabbed him in the side with a large dagger. Kléber staggered against the low wall of the terrace, and cried, "Help, Guides, I am murdered!" to some soldiers who were walking in the square below. The architect Protain, who had only a light cane in his hand, rushed at the murderer, who stood motionless, looking at his victim. There was a short struggle, and then the architect also received a stab which stretched him senseless by the side of the general. The assassin turned to the general, gave him three more stabs, and then fled and hid himself in the garden. The Guides arrived soon afterwards, and Kléber was carried into the house of General Dumas, where he died nearly two hours later.

The news of the assassination quickly spread through the city. The French soldiers snatched up their arms, and ran through the streets crying: "To arms! Vengeance! our commander is murdered!"

The startled inhabitants fled in every direction, and had good reason for their flight, for the French sabred or bayoneted all they met. The officers had the greatest difficulty in preventing the men from setting fire to the city, and destroying this "nest of brigands."

François confesses that, on the way to the quarters, he and his comrades sabred all the men and children they came across. Patrols scoured the streets, and the Sheik El-Sadhut was arrested, he; being suspected because he had been punished for having protested against the fine of twelve millions levied on the city; but he easily proved that he was guiltless of all knowledge of the murder.

Protain, who had recovered consciousness, stated that the murderer was a poorly-dressed Mussulman. The gardens were searched, and two of the Guides brought to General Dumas a young man they had discovered hidden in a thicket. The architect identified him, and several of Kléber's servants stated they had often seen him hanging about the general's residence. When interrogated, he said that his name was Suliman El-Halebi, of Aleppo, aged twenty-four, and a writer by profession. He denied all knowledge of the murder, and said he had never seen the commander-in-chief, but, after being bastinadoed, confessed everything. A further proof of his guilt was the discovery of a blood-stained dagger close to the spot where he was hidden. François, who saw and handled the weapon, says it was a kind of cutlass, with a curved blade fifteen or sixteen inches long.

General Ménou, who as the oldest lieutenant-general took temporary command, ordered all the priests of the great Mosque to be arrested. One of them had fled, but three others were brought to head-quarters, and confronted with Suliman. They denied all knowledge of him, but Suliman called them cowards and heartless wretches, so they ended by confessing their complicity, but said they had tried to dissuade Suliman from carrying out his murderous design. After this confession, they were sentenced to be beheaded. Suliman was to have his hand burned off, to be impaled, and his body exposed until it was devoured by birds of prey.

The account of the execution is too ghastly to be reproduced, and loses nothing of its grim horror in the artless telling of the bloodthirsty, revengeful soldier. It seems almost incredible that, barely a century ago, such a barbarous and savage sentence should have been passed by a tribunal of civilized men. Curiously enough, as a further satire on civilization, the executioner, who gloated over the victim's sufferings, and even added to the tortures he was empowered to inflict, was a renegade Italian—Bartolomeo Serra, the leader of a newly-formed corps of Mamelukes. Suliman displayed all the stoical contempt of pain of an Eastern fanatic; he told his cowardly accomplices that:

> His greatest regret was to have been associated with wretches so weak in faith, and so little worthy of the honour the Prophet had granted them, in being associated with him in an act so glorious to Islam.

The day of the execution, an English officer arrived with a signed copy of the agreement for the evacuation of Egypt; but General Ménou refused to see him, and ordered François and twenty-five other Dromedaries to escort him to Katieh. On the road, the English officer, who spoke French, told François that 100,000 Turks, 50,000 Russians, to say nothing of Albanians and *émigrés* were coming to drive out the French. François contented himself with replying, that they would await all these bands and make them suffer the same fate as they had at Heliopolis.

General Ménou was not at all popular with the soldiers "on account of his marriage and his change of religion," François says, but when the men were informed by their officers that the general had returned to his original religion, "confidence was restored amongst us." This deep concern about their commander's religious belief seems almost touching. Perhaps the facts that the pay was no longer in arrears, and the bread much better, may have contributed much to renew confidence. Moral and theological objections disappeared when the commander-in-chief visited and presented every soldier and non-commissioned officer with a *franc*. The Turks, too, had some of his bounty, for, when the dam of the Kornieh Canal was cut, he threw into the water 100 purses, each containing 1,000 *carats* (about 28s.). In spite of the strong current, many Turks jumped in after this money, and several of them were drowned, whilst others were carried by the current as far as the centre of the city, holding a purse in their teeth.

In a very short time, however. General Ménou had, by his incapacity, estranged the affections of. officers and men, and though his appointment had been confirmed by Bonaparte—who probably was not sorry to have somebody on whom the evacuation of Egypt could be saddled—many of the officers proposed to arrest General Ménou, and send him back to France. Nor were the Egyptians better pleased with him. He had issued a decree abolishing the payment of blood-money by an assassin or his family to the relatives of the murdered man; and the consequence was that, as the natives thought they could henceforth murder on the cheap, assassinations were rife throughout the country.

Though liberal to the soldiers, whose good opinion he wished to purchase, Ménou was parsimonious in other respects, and refused to provide enough funds to enable the scientific men Bonaparte had brought with him to fully explore Egypt. They did, indeed, make a short tour up the Nile, and to the borders of Abyssinia, and François, who dearly loved to see strange countries and extraordinary things, was glad that he was one of the escort, but returned somewhat disappointed because the *savants* had not confided to him the nature of their discoveries.

On his return, he seems to have become quite domestic; his description of his household, and the young Oriental beauty he proposed to make his wife, are best given in his own language.

We were often ordered by the commander-in-chief, in the time of Generals Bonaparte and Kléber, to make night attacks on wandering tribes of Bedouins. We brought away nothing but their camels, horses, goats, and sheep, and never took any prisoners. Men, women, and children were put to the edge of the sword. On one occasion, however, I took to serve me a young Bedouin, whose tribe we had destroyed near Mount Sinai. He was fourteen or fifteen years old, and I found him very honest and faithful. He died of the plague in March, 1801.

The bazaars at Cairo are open every day, from ten in the morning till three in the afternoon—the hour of prayer of the Turks—for the sale of slaves. The other bazaars are open from sunrise to sunset, for the sale of merchandise.

All the soldiers, from the generals to the drummer-boys, used to go to the bazaar where the slaves are sold, to see the sales, and even to buy the unfortunate wretches. I went there many times, and I ended by buying two negresses, one aged fifteen, and one seventeen. The one cost me fifty-five Spanish *piastres*, and the other seventy. I presented them to a little demi-princess, the daughter of a Georgian mother, whom I had kept for several months past.

This young woman belonged to a *bey's* family. She was young, and as lovely as a Cupid. I only won her by force of money. I gave her a *piastre* a day; a Turk and the two negresses were her servants. My costume pleased her greatly, and, as I had some money, she thought me a great *sultan*. Consequently, this young woman loved me very much, and sometimes, at critical moments, ran a risk of falling a victim to her friendship for me. Her name was Anif, and she was the daughter of one of Effi Bey's concubines. Her father's palace, on the Esbehieh Square, was the headquarters of the army.

When she was fifteen or sixteen, she was the prettiest woman I have ever seen to this day. Her dress was in keeping with her birth and beauty. She was clad in the richest stuffs, her turban was a cashmere of divers colours, and on her head was a plate of gold, enriched with different stones more or less precious. She wore necklaces and bracelets of solid gold, as thick as my finger, and anklets of the same metal.

I was proud of possessing this young person, who introduced me to her mother, with whom I arranged to take her daughter to France and make her my wife; but events, and the misfortune to which I succumbed, as I shall relate, deprived me of a woman I loved, and by whom I was beloved.

He could not have had frequent opportunities of enjoying the company of his beloved, for General Ménou employed the Dromedaries constantly for carrying despatches, slaughtering Bedouin families, and escorting caravans. It was on a duty of the last sort that François, with twenty-four other Dromedaries, ten Mamelukes, and twenty-five Arabs, quitted Cairo, on December 25th, 1800, being ordered to escort a caravan returning by Suez to Mount Sinai.

# CHAPTER 7

# 1801

By January 21st, 1801, François and his comrades had returned to Cairo, and, three or four days later, made a second excursion to the Pyramids. A couple of French frigates arrived at Alexandria, early in February, bringing a small reinforcement of 600 men, some guns, ammunition, and, of course, letters and news from France. The most serious item of the news was, that an alliance had been made between England and Turkey to drive the French out of Egypt. Mourad Bey, and the other Turks who had espoused the French cause, warned General Ménou of the dangers he was likely to incur, but Ménou replied that he had the most thorough contempt for English, Turks—and Mamelukes. The addition of the last-named showed a want of tact on the French commander's part, for Osman Bey, who had given him notice of his danger, was the leader of a band of Mamelukes, and had shown himself a good friend to the French. He had taken a special liking to François, and offered to enrol him in his Mamelukes, where he would be safe if the French should chance to be annihilated, but François declined the offer.

Ménou evidently did not put any faith in these rumours, but, on March 4th, he was aroused from his lethargy by the arrival of a "Dromedary"—who had ridden from Alexandria to Cairo in twenty-seven hours—bearing a despatch from General Friant, announcing the appearance of a hostile fleet off that port. As the enemy had appeared on the north-west, General Ménou immediately sent off a force of cavalry to the south-east; by which route he feared the *grand vizier* and his forces would arrive. The other generals protested against this useless measure, and recommended that the whole force should be brought to bear against the British, but Ménou haughtily replied that he was not in the habit of asking advice from his subordinates, and all they had to do was obey.

A week later, news arrived that the English had landed at Aboukir Bay, inflicted a check on General Friant's forces, and compelled him to surrender the fort. General Ménou, after a good deal of hesitation, consulted Generals Lanusse and Reynier, and, by their advice, marched to attack the English, and save Alexandria from falling into their hands. François says:

> The march was very slow, but the common danger made us forget his conduct. The soldiers wished to show that he might count upon their zeal and bravery, if, on his part, he would show some firmness and military talents.

The battle, which was fought on March 21st, is one of the glorious feats of British arms. It has been described, from the British point of view, in dozens of military or general histories, and it will therefore no doubt be interesting to many military critics to give somewhat fully the account of what François saw or heard of the fight. He had not the facilities for observation of a modern war correspondent, and his comrades, in what they told him, may have exaggerated their deeds—as they certainly did in the instance of Sir Ralph Abercromby's wound,—but, on the whole, his description is graphic, impartial, and intended to be correct.

> *21st March* (30 *Ventose*).—The army was under arms at three in the morning, and drawn up in front of the camp, which was beyond the Rosetta Gate, one of the gates of Alexandria. General Reynier waited till the action was fully begun. Then he marched to the left of the English, to prevent them from moving on Alexandria. The cavalry remained in the rear of the infantry, until General Lanusse had driven back the English right, and General Bon, who commanded the cavalry, could seize the right moment to decide the victory by a home charge.
>
> We, of the Dromedary Corps, commanded by our brave leader and bold rider, and all mounted, attacked, a little before daybreak, a redoubt raised near the Alexandria Canal; we climbed the sandhills on our dromedaries, many of which fell; others were wounded, as well as seven men. We captured the redoubt, and took twenty prisoners, but three of them were killed by our wounded, who expected they would all suffer the same fate.
>
> "As soon as the redoubt was taken, we dismounted, and at once turning our two guns, we fired several rounds of grape-shot at

the men who were running away from the redoubt, and then balls at the nearest entrenchments, to attract the attention of the enemy, to whom we did a lot of damage.

At that moment, General Lanusse and the columns of the centre and right, began to advance. A company of carabineers had also captured a redoubt on the enemy's right, in spite of the fire of their first line, and that of the gunboats. General Gilly charged the large redoubt, and made an English detachment lay down its arms. Just then. General Lanusse saw that General Valentin had left the seashore, and was within the re-entering angle of the redoubt and the Roman camp, where the cross fire of the enemy held him back.

General Lanusse marched to this spot, encouraged the men, and made them advance. The worthy general was hit in the thigh by a ball from a gun-boat; four grenadiers tried to carry him off, but a second ball killed two of these brave fellows. This event caused some confusion amongst General Thevenin's brigade, which, having suffered severely from the fire of the gun-boats, scattered amongst the sand-hills. At this juncture, the 4th Light Infantry, of General Gilly's brigade, met, at the angle of the great redoubt, the 32nd regiment, who, in the darkness, had strayed too much to the left. These two corps charged each other by mistake. This accident caused a confusion, which damped the ardour of the soldiers, and caused a loss of valuable time.

General Rampon rallied the 32nd, and charged, at the double, on the first English line, but was driven back by their fire. The general's uniform was riddled with bullets, and two horses were killed under him. Many of the men were hit. Adjutant-General Sornet, at the head of three companies of carabineers of the 2nd Light Infantry, was mortally wounded. General Destaing, who had followed the Aboukir road, was met by a heavy musketry fire from the English, and fell seriously wounded. The officer commanding the 21st Light Infantry had his leg carried off by a cannon ball, and his half brigade was left, without a leader, amidst the enemy's army, and one battalion, outflanked by the enemy, was captured. Thirty men, who guarded the colours, let themselves be killed rather than give up the flag. General Eppler brought up the grenadiers of the 25th Line Regiment to support the 21st Light Infantry, but he was dangerously wounded, and his grenadiers driven back with loss.

During this attack, we Dromedaries, who had taken the redoubt and were firing on the enemy with the guns we had found there, saw the commander-in-chief, Ménou, walking about quietly, with his head bowed, in the rear of the army. He often stretched out his arms frantically, like a sailor who is shipwrecked in port and appealing for help. He seemed to trust to the bravery of the generals and soldiers, and gave no orders.

The right wing, commanded by General Reynier, had not yet engaged, and that general, seeing that the commander-in-chief was demoralised, and issued no orders, took it upon himself to try an attack on the English right wing, and left General Dumas with the 13th of the Line, between the two lakes, to occupy the left and drive the skirmishers towards the Alexandria Canal.

General Reynier ordered General Friant to march towards the enemy's left, and the light artillery to advance to silence the enemy's redoubts. Whilst this movement was going on. General Reynier climbed one of the sand-hills, to see where he might attack with most advantage. The English general, commanding at least 6,000 men, did not dare to attack General Dumas, who had only 800 men of the 13th Regiment, 350 cavalry, and 100 dromedaries.

Just as General Reynier was preparing to attack. General Ménou, who had not hitherto taken any part in the action, as I have previously said, went to the reserve cavalry, which was commanded by the brave General Roize, and ordered him to charge, Roize ventured to make some remark, but Ménou would not listen to him, so there was nothing to do but obey. Turning to his brave men, General Roize said, "Friends, they are sending us to glory and death! March!" The charge was terrible. The first line, commanded by General Broussard, charged the English lines in the rear of the big redoubt. The enemy's infantry was overthrown, and obliged to retreat, under the protection of the fire of the second line. But the guns of the redoubt took our cavalry in the rear, and the not less murderous fire of the second line brought down a great many officers and dragoons. General Broussard ordered a retreat, and at the same moment he was hit by two bullets.

Brave General Roize, seeing his first line driven back, advanced with the second, made a desperate charge, and penetrated to the camp of the second English line, sabring and overthrowing all in his road. The terrified English threw themselves on their faces on the ground; others fled to their tents; but this obstacle stopped the terrible rush of our cavalry and caused our ruin. The English had dug wolf-pits in their camp, and strewn caltrops about, plentifully. The horses fell into these pits, or were entangled amongst the cords and tent pegs. The brave and unfortunate General Roize, finding there was no chance of escaping from such a position, dismounted, fought like a lion, and was killed, as were also his men. In this terrible *mêlée*, an officer of the 16th Dragoons, after having killed all the English who surrounded him, penetrated to the tent of General Abercromby, whom he found there, and in a hand-to-hand struggle, gave him such terrible wounds that he died a few days later.[1]

The destruction of this reserve left us no alternative but retreat, to avoid the destruction of the entire army. We Dromedaries kept the position we had occupied, and remained there till the evening, after having defended ourselves desperately, and been often attacked and besieged. We finally retired, having spiked the guns and left our wounded Dromedaries in the redoubt, and passing through the English sharpshooters, reached the Rosetta Gate. We lost eleven men killed, and seven wounded. I had nothing but a bruise on the left shoulder, caused by falling off my mount, which was hit in the thigh and brought down by a round shot. This battle cost us 800 killed, amongst whom were seven Generals and eleven superior officers, 2,000 wounded at least, and 400 missing—an enormous loss for an army which numbered only 9,000 combatants.

Alexandria was full of wounded French the next day, all "cursing the commander-in-chief, and telling their unwounded comrades that a similar fate awaited them." There was no medical aid, and more than a third of the poor fellows died for want of assistance.

François was one of a detachment sent to Cairo with the news of this defeat. All agreed, when they heard the tidings, that their days were numbered, and, like true French soldiers, resolved to enjoy what was left them of life. So they all sent for their lady-loves, and François sent his faithful Turk to fetch Anif, and consulted with her and her

---

1. This is not correct. General Abercromby was not in his tent, but on horseback at the head of his troops, and was wounded in the thigh by a musket-ball; but he did not even reveal the fact that he had been wounded till the battle was won and the French in full retreat.

mother about the best means of getting that charming young lady to France. He was the more anxious because he was aware that if the fact that she had an *infidel* lover became known, he would be the involuntary cause of her being "put into a leather sack, sewn at both ends, and thrown into the Nile."

Being of a practical, as well as an amorous disposition, he calculated his resources, and found that he was well able to support a wife. In fact, he had not done badly in the way of prize-money, and had a small but weighty portmanteau deposited with the paymaster of the Dromedary Corps. It contained six pounds and three quarters of gold, in bracelets, necklets, rings, etc.; forty-three diamonds of different sizes; 3,000 *francs* in gold and silver, and six of the finest cashmere shawls. He thought the lot was worth something over 60,000 *francs*—which if any of the diamonds were of fair size and good colour seems a very moderate estimate. Anif also had 11,000 or 12,000 *francs* in dresses and jewellery, and no doubt they would have been able to marry and live comfortably ever afterwards, if the fates had not decreed otherwise.

The incapacity of General Ménou had caused much dissatisfaction amongst the soldiers, who openly said that he ought to be deprived of the command. General Reynier was regarded as the only man who could get them out of their difficulties. Of course, General Ménou heard these rumours, and the fear of seeing himself removed made him take a very extraordinary measure; which was to get rid of all the Generals who had been intimate friends of Kléber. He accordingly sent 300 infantry, 50 cavalry, some sappers, and artillery with one gun, to arrest Generals Reynier and Dumas, and a civilian official named Daure, put them on board ship, and conveyed them to France.

The generals were naturally much surprised, and the men sent to arrest them so disgusted that they offered to mutiny, and even arrest Ménou instead, if Reynier would give them the order, but he wisely declined.

This arbitrary removal of two of the bravest and wisest officers did not render the position of the French more easy. The only man left, who was capable of any energetic movement, was General Belliard, who was at Cairo with some 4,000 men; and a Turkish army, supported by 12,000 British, was moving on that city. It was moving very slowly, for the English generals had recommended the Turks to be circumspect; and this circumspection,—François thinks with some reason,—was the highest homage that could be rendered to the French, considering the enormous difference between the two armies, for it showed that the English thought that the Turks would meet with another Heliopolis if they should encounter the French.

General Belliard refused to surrender Cairo, but, with two powerful hostile armies against him, a disaffected city, the plague as well, and 269 desertions in one day, his position was hopeless. He called a Council of War, on June 20th, to discuss what was to be done. General Donzelot advised that they should retire to Upper Egypt and carry on a guerilla warfare till reinforcements arrived, but General Belliard pointed out that no reinforcements could ever hope to reach Upper Egypt, even if they dodged the English fleets and succeeded in crossing the Mediterranean.

Brigadier Dupas was of opinion that there were only two alternatives before them, surrender or death, and of the two the latter was to be chosen. His speech was worthy of one of the old war-dogs who helped to make France feared and famous.

> What a subject of pride for our country and of admiration for Europe, when both shall learn that 5,000 Frenchmen have preferred the imperishable glory of being buried under the ruins of their conquest, to the shame of ceding it to the enemy!

Several of the members of the Council of War highly approved of these sentiments, but the majority thought the price to be paid for the admiration of Europe was too high. General Donzelot pointed out, that though Kléber had defeated a large Turkish army with 10,000 men, it was hardly probable that 4,000 men could repeat the same feat, especially when the Turks were helped by 25,000 British. There was no shame, he said, in an honourable capitulation, when nothing better could be done. The French force now, though small, was strong enough to get good terms; but if they fought and lost they would have to put up with any terms they could get. A capitulation was agreed to eventually. There was a crowd of soldiers waiting to hear the result, and when they were informed that the Council had decided to ask for an armistice, in order to negotiate terms for the evacuation of Egypt, many of the soldiers wept.

The following morning, General Belliard ordered twenty-five of the Dromedaries to prepare to start next day, to escort Captain Millet, of his Staff, to the headquarters of the English commander. Lord Hutchinson. François informed Anif that he was to form part of the escort, and, when he returned, he would take her to France, where they would be safe from all their enemies, and supremely happy.

The little princess was very uneasy in her mind. She warned François not to go on this expedition, for she had a presentiment that a misfortune would happen to him and she would never see him again. He laughed at her fears, but his heart was sad, and he could not help thinking of her words when he said farewell to her the next morning.

The party started at 8 o'clock in the morning, and had got but a little way from the city when it was assailed by a body of Turkish horsemen. The trumpeter waved his white flag, and the interpreter yelled, "Envoy!" but the trumpeter was killed, François says:

And in less than six minutes we were all thrown from our dromedaries, trodden under foot by the horses of these barbarians, and half the detachment killed or wounded. The captain was amongst the number. The firing brought up other bands of these brigands; a detachment of English arrived, and saw the flag of truce which one of the brigands was carrying off. The officer who commanded the detachment had the greatest difficulty in stopping the carnage, though he was assisted by some of the Turkish officers. The skirmish ceased. The Turks, seeing their error, made off, carrying several heads of our men with them, and dragging me along, with two other men of my detachment.

I received a lot of bruises, one of which, on the left shoulder, was due to a fall from my dromedary. I had also a few slight wounds from lances, and a couple of sabre-cuts on the head, which cut through several folds of my turban, also a few knocks from the horses' feet. One of my comrades had received a dagger-stab in the arm, and some bruises. The other was seriously wounded with several sabre-cuts, and a pistol ball in the side.

I was so dazed that at first I felt nothing of my bruises, and we arrived at El-Kanka before I thought about them. There we were surrounded by hundreds of barbarians, several of whom took the heads of seven of our dead comrades, and presented them to us, and insulted us. One of my comrades wept, but I had not the strength to do even that. The other lay on his face on the ground; he was dying.

Two hours after our arrival at El-Kanka, my comrade and I were led to the tent of one of the chief officers of the *grand vizier's* army. The other man could not move. The Ottoman of-

88

ficer put some questions to us through an interpreter. I had been less mauled than my comrade, and having recovered my senses, I told the officer about our mission and the officer we escorted. He did not appear to believe it, but, however, he told the men to take care of us, and give us some food, and we were lodged near his tent. In the evening, they gave us each a black biscuit, some rice, and water; and we passed the night amidst the guard, who asked us so many questions that I could get no rest, and the night appeared endless. I was deep in thought, could not believe the reality of what had happened, and wondered what would be the upshot of it all. My second comrade was not brought before the officer, for he had not the strength to move. I believe he died, for I never heard of him again.

The next day, François asked to be brought before the *grand vizier*, or one of his chief officers, but the soldiers laughed at him, and said their officers did not talk to dogs. He and his comrade were sent to Gaza. One of the escort had the heads of two of the French soldiers suspended at his saddle-bow, by a rope passed through the mouth and a hole cut in the cheek. He ordered François to carry these ghastly trophies. The other Dromedary was also ordered to carry a couple of heads, but he was so weak that the officer spared him this horrible burden. François, however, being practically unhurt, had to carry these unpleasant trophies, in spite of his protests. The rope was put over his head, and with the heads of two of his dead comrades dangling on his shoulders, he made the journey to Salhieh.

There he was relieved of this uncomfortable burden, and was kept three days in a mosque, which served as both hospital and prison. This rest did François a good deal of good, and encouraged him to ask an officer for his liberty; but he doubts whether he was sufficiently respectful in his demand, for the officer called him a dog, and told him to be silent. Poor François owns that he often said to himself during these dark days:

You say you like extraordinary adventures, my friend; but you have more than you bargained for this time.

On July 2nd, they set out for Gaza. François and his comrade were separated from each other.

My unfortunate brother-in-arms often looked at me: he appeared sadder than I was. I assumed a confident air, but perhaps my heart suffered more than his.' I thought of the last farewell of my little Georgian; of my prize-money deposited with the quartermaster of my regiment, and my notes on all the wars I had been in, which I had left with Huet, the quartermaster of my old regiment—the 9th Infantry.

Fortunately Huet kept them, or we should, perhaps, have been deprived of this interesting book.

As we were not very well guarded, I constantly thought of making my escape. At night especially, the temptation was very strong, for our guard bivouacked and slept in little groups without sentinels, but I could not inform my comrade of my plan, and besides, I was without money and my arms had been taken from me, to my great regret, principally on account of my Damascus sword and my pistols, which were a present from Mourad Bey. Otherwise, I knew the country well enough to hope to be able to rejoin our army, either at Cairo or Alexandria. But I dared not put my plan in execution, for fear my comrade should fall a victim; besides, I hoped that, when I arrived in Syria, the army having capitulated, I should be sent back to France. So, on reflection, I gave up the dangerous attempt.

After four days' march, they arrived at Gaza, and François, despite his protests, was put in the gaol with the common criminals, many of whom had lost their nose and ears. He saw nothing of his fellow-soldier, and came to the conclusion that he must be dead. The society being uncongenial, François did not speak to any of the "brigands" who shared his prison; and after twenty-three days left Gaza, and was taken to Damascus. Four days later, he was brought before the governor, who asked him, through an interpreter, who he was, and how he came there. François related the circumstances of his capture. The *pacha* shook his head, and said that the army of *infidels*, the usurpers of Egypt, had embarked, to return to a place they never ought to have left. He spoke of Bonaparte and Kléber. François praised them both "to the skies," and asked for liberty to join the first-named, but the *pacha* again shook his head, said he could hold out no hopes of that, and sent François back to the prison. He was on better terms with the prisoners there, some of whom were janissaries, and, taking him to be an Egyptian, treated him as a comrade. At the end of a month, he was told he would be sent to Aleppo, and thence to Alexandretta, to be shipped to France,—news which made his heart beat with joy.

He was again doomed to disappointment,—but he had better tell his own story.

*September 15th.* I arrived at Aleppo, and was handed over to the Governor of that city. After eight days of solitary confinement, I was brought before Pacha Achmet Ali Mustapha, Governor of Aleppo, with whom was another *pacha*, who appeared to me to be more important than the governor, who paid him every mark of respect. I was questioned through an Arab interpreter. I related what I had already said several times before; and I added that the Pacha of Damascus had sent me to Aleppo, to be conducted to Alexandretta or elsewhere, and thence to France. The two *pachas* declared they could not give me my liberty until they had obtained further information about me. The difficulty arose from the fact that I spoke Arabic, and that I was dressed almost like a Turk when I was captured. After an audience of an hour, the *pacha* with the green turban asked me if I would enter his service whilst the information was being obtained, and he would place me in his military household. Without knowing who this personage might be, I replied that I would accept. Then he informed me that his residence was at Adrianople, not far from Constantinople.

On September 27th, François accordingly became one of the armed retainers of the Emir Esseid Katif-el-Bekir, Governor and Viceroy of Adrianople. He lodged and messed with the officers of the "*spahis*," most of whom spoke Arabic, and who told him that he ought to be happy in the service of such a powerful prince. He replied that he had already been in the service of a more powerful man; and then they asked who this Bonaparte was. François replied that he was the first general, and supreme magistrate, of France. These ignorant people reported the conversation to the prince, who, however, being better educated, took no notice of it.

The prince, in fact, knew a good deal about France and liked the French, for he had visited Paris, his father having been Turkish Ambassador at the Court of Louis XVI. in 1787. François, who rarely has a good word for anybody who is not French, had "nothing but praise for this prince during the twenty-one months that I lived with him." Indeed, after the hardships and privations of the campaign, life in the service of this Turkish *emir* must have seemed a pleasant holiday. François was well-fed, richly clothed, had plenty of money and nothing to do but accompany the prince, on foot or horseback, when he went to pay a visit.

The *emir* seems to have been on a tour of inspection, and François accompanied him through the Holy Land, which he says, "hardly keeps up its reputation, for it is infested with Arabs and Bedouins, and you cannot travel there unless you are well escorted." His remarks about Palestine are not very interesting or original, so there is no need to reproduce them here. He saw the Holy Sepulchre, and the prior wanted him to become a monk there, but he diplomatically replied that he had no calling that way. Jerusalem did not impress him, for that city, so much vaunted in history, is one of the most wretched places in Palestine and has most beggars. The inhabitants are generally thieves,—superstitious and lazy.

François would have greatly liked to visit Saint Jean d'Acre, but he did not dare to tell the prince so, and the *emir*, though he went there, did not take all his bodyguard. François was left at Jaffa, and saw the hospital. He wisely refrained from telling any of the inhabitants he was a Frenchman.

On November 21st, 1802, the prince embarked at Jaffa, and after calling at Rhodes, reached Smyrna before the end of the year.

CHAPTER 8

# 1803—1804

The *pacha* had several more places to inspect, and left François for a month at Athens, whilst he visited other parts of Greece. Finally, he returned to Smyrna, and the whole party embarked there for Constantinople, on February 12th, 1803, and arrived at that city three days later.

The duties of the bodyguard were far from onerous, and François, finding time heavy on his hands, went about the city, Scutari, Galata, and Pera. He naturally fraternised with the French merchants he found there, and was especially friendly with a commercial traveller who represented a Lyons house, and, having but recently quitted France, could give him the latest information regarding his native country. From him, François learned that an army would soon assemble at Boulogne, with the object of making a descent on England. He hated the English—to whom he attributed most of his misfortunes—and he longed for more fighting under his beloved Bonaparte. From that moment he determined to make his escape, and return to France.

He was not able, however, to put the plan into execution for some time, for his master returned to Adrianople. Being very much trusted, and a great favourite with the *pacha*, he was often sent with messages to the prince's wife, and on some of these occasions was allowed to penetrate into the harem, and as he was a great admirer of *le beau sexe*, he frankly owns that he would "have willingly turned Turk, if they would have left me in that paradise." The young women gave him many little presents, and he had "quite a complete Turkish wardrobe," but he wisely refrained from any love affairs with the *odalisques*.

After a few weeks at Adrianople, the *pacha* returned to Constantinople, and François, meeting again with the French merchants, the feeling of home sickness once more assumed its sway. On the morning of August 10th, he put on his best clothes, armed himself with his Damascus blade, dagger, and pistols, and having found that his master had no orders for him, made his way almost mechanically—for he was so troubled in mind that he did not know where he was going—to Pera.

He passed the door of the French Embassy several times before he could summon up courage to go in; but at last he asked to see General Sebastiani, the ambassador. He told the ambassador the story of his adventures, and General Sebastiani promised to send him back to France; and, until the arrangements could be completed, offered him hospitality at the Embassy.

François wished to travel to France by land, and the ambassador granted that request, and gave him 400 *francs* for expenses, as well as some European clothes,—for he had hitherto been dressed in the Turkish fashion. His pistols and dagger he sold to one of the attaches for fifty *francs*.

Towards the end of the month, François started, with a small caravan consisting of forty-one persons,—Turks, Montenegrins, Italians, Swiss and two Frenchmen. François and four others were the only ones who were not mounted.

"At leaving even the most unpleasant people and places, one keeps looking at the steeple," and though François was not much given to sentiment, he was sad and dreamy for some days, and could not help thinking of the pleasant time he had passed in the *pacha's* service, and the adventures which had preceded it. The conversation of the two Frenchmen—who were cheerful, as bagmen usually are—drove away these melancholy thoughts. The caravan dwindled down, as one member after another turned aside towards his destination; and when Trieste was reached, François had only one companion left—a young Italian who was going to Padua.

On the road thither, they passed through the town of Udine, where there was a French garrison. By a very extraordinary chance, it turned out to be the 9th regiment of the line, to which François had previously belonged. His comrades had naturally concluded he was dead, and were much astonished to see him. He was led in triumph to the colonel, who invited him to mess, and made him relate all the adventures that had befallen him. The colonel was very anxious he should rejoin the regiment; made flattering offers, found comfortable lodgings for him, and wrote to Beauharnais, the Viceroy of Italy, to request that François might be made a sub-lieutenant. The viceroy replied that he had written to Paris, and François would be appointed as soon as the papers came back signed by the First Consul. He had also asked six months' furlough for François. Pending the return of the courier, François was to be the guest of the regiment.

His life was one "continual holiday." He visited all the towns where detachments of the regiment were placed, and found that all his old comrades were delighted to see him, and all made certain that he would rejoin the regiment. François also desired it, for he had never been ambitious of promotion, and was so glad to see the old regiment again that he would willingly have returned as a private soldier; though he was not ignorant that, as a sergeant of the Dromedary Corps, he was entitled to a lieutenancy in a line regiment.

Nine days after François had rejoined the colours—October 11th—there was a change of garrison, and the 9th received orders to proceed to Strasburg and Landau. François, who was still awaiting his brevet, accompanied the regiment, and lodged at Landau with a M. Weber, a baker, who had a pretty sister, aged 20 or 21, who was very anxious to hear the wanderer's story, some details of which had been told her by some of the soldiers. Perhaps "she loved him for the dangers he had passed, and he loved her that she did pity them." All that he says in his diary is that "I told her my story, and many other things, etc.,"—but the "etc." may stand for a good deal.

If he gave information, he also received it, and learned, from some of the officers, particulars of the evacuation of Egypt. The Dromedary Corps, he was told, had been disbanded, and some of the men had been drafted into the *gendarmerie*, others into the Consular Guard. As senior sergeant, which entitled him to rank as lieutenant in the cavalry or line, he could have entered the Consular Guard, but preferred the sympathy of his old officers and comrades, and elected to stay with the regiment he had joined when a beardless boy.

November 12th was a red-letter day. Colonel Pépin sent for François, embraced him, and told him that he had received his papers. Not only was François created sub-lieutenant, but he was granted six months' leave of absence, the pay that was due to him at the time he was made prisoner, and half-pay during the whole period of his detention. He thanked the colonel, lunched with the mess, was congratulated by the other officers, and "wept with joy to see himself again united to such worthy friends." There was an inspection that afternoon. One of his comrades lent him a uniform, that he might appear at the review, and, in the evening, François dined with the inspector, the colonel, and other officers, and the regimental band played, "Where can a man be better than in the bosom of his family?"

Not having heard from any of his relatives—his father had been dead some years—François did not use his leave of absence. Towards the close of the year, he went, with part of the regiment, to Belfort; which he found "a small town with plenty of society and not bad-looking women." His landlord had four daughters, "all tolerably pretty;" and he made many agreeable acquaintances.

On January 28th, 1804, he mentions that the "order of the day" stated that a person named Georges Cadoudal, coming from England, had disembarked in France with thirty-four of his accomplices, and they had gone, separately, to Paris; where Cadoudal had plotted, with General Pichegru and others, to seize the First Consul and carry him alive to England. Of course, the conspirators were aided by English gold, and abetted by English statesmen. The conspiracy, as we know, failed, and on February 24th all the corps of the division were ordered to assist at a Mass; when a *Te Deum* was sung to thank God for the discovery of the plot contrived by England for the assassination (!) of the First Consul.

Bonaparte choose to believe that the Duc d'Enghien was concerned in this plot. François, who had returned from Belfort and rejoined the regiment at Strasburg, learned that two *aides-de-camp* of the First Consul (Savary and Colimourt) had come to Strasburg to ask General Leval to appoint a superior officer, or an intelligent subaltern, to take some important papers to an English spy, who had been instructed by his government to get up a plot to kill Bonaparte. Colonel Pépin was asked to undertake this delicate mission; but he pleaded ill-health, and General Leval appointed Captain-Adjutant-Major Rosey. He went and saw two English spies, named (according to François) Kack and Smitz; and, thanks to false papers with which the *aides-de-camp* had supplied him, completely deceived those two emissaries and learned all particulars of the supposed plot. As François played a small part in the great historical drama which followed, it is preferable to give his account *in extensor.*

> Captain-Adjutant-Major Rosey, having obtained full knowledge of the plot, and the residences of the agents and the Duc d'Enghien, returned to Strasburg, and gave an account to General Leval, and the *aides-de-camp* Savary and Colimourt; who had orders from the First Consul to arrest the Duc d'Enghien.

On March 17th, 300 men of the 9th Regiment, of whom I made part, 200 and odd *gendarmes*, and two 4-pounders, in all about 600 men, commanded by *chef-de-bataillon* Grandjean of the 9th Regiment, and *aide-de-camp* Colimourt, assembled silently about 10 o'clock at night, and marched to the Kiel bridge, where an officer was sent to inform the Prince of Baden of our entry into his States. The little column continued its march. Having arrived near the *château* of Ettenheim, we surrounded it, knowing that the Duc d'Enghien and the Princesse de Rohan were there.

The troops preserved the strictest silence: and the captain of the *gendarmerie*, with Adjutant-Major Rioust of the 9th Regiment entered the *château*. The captain of the *gendarmerie* presented himself before the prince, who had not yet gone to bed, and was in a shooting jacket. Captain Rioust of the *gendarmes* (four *gendarmes* were at the door) informed the prince that he had been ordered to arrest him. The prince made a movement, and said to the captain: "I could blow out your brains, but you are too fine a fellow for that. I will go with you." On the table, in front of the prince, were two pairs of pistols and a shot-gun. He was brought back to Strasburg, as were also seventeen peasants, and guarded in the citadel by a battalion.

The officers on duty dined with the prince; he did not seem much affected, and talked little, but never about his position. He remained eight days in the citadel, and left with two officers of the *gendarmerie*, who took him to the *château* of Vincennes; where a special court assembled, composed of generals, who condemned him to death, and he was executed by the Invalides on leaving the court, in the ditch at Vincennes. He was about thirty-two years of age, and a fine handsome man.

Nothing else of importance occurred during the remainder of the year. A detachment of the regiment was sent to Paris to be present at the Coronation of Napoleon, and François was lucky enough to form one of this detachment. He was the more pleased about this as he had never used his leave of absence, and he found at Paris a brother and a married sister. He saw all the rejoicings, and was present at the distribution of eagles in the Champ de Mars; but "fortune was always against him," and he did not get the Legion of Honour, though crosses were given away wholesale on that occasion.

But he had compensating advantages. As recruiting officer, he was entitled to extra pay, he boarded with a married sister, lived six months in Paris with little to do, and was happy—as he deserved to be after the trials through which he had gone. He paid twenty-four *francs* a month for fencing lessons from the best masters, but, when he took part in assaults at arms, he found he was no longer "the best swordsman in the army," as he had been called when he was in Egypt.

CHAPTER 9

# 1805—1806

Except that he made a trip to Stolzermann, in Westphalia, with a draft of eighty-nine recruits, François did nothing during the first six months of 1805, but, towards the end of June, he was informed that he would be attached to the "elite company" of the regiment—the sub-lieutenant of that company having been promoted—and must join his brigade, then stationed at Arras.

The brigade consisted of the elite companies of several regiments. In August, it was ordered to Boulogne-sur-Mer, where "the finest army that Europe had seen for centuries shared the wishes of the emperor, and incessantly demanded to embark and make a descent on England"; but the preparations were not yet completed, and the time was spent in drilling, and also in decorating the camp, which had assumed an almost semi-permanent appearance. The stagnant puddles at the foot of the arid sand-hills had been drained; and the men camped there lived in neat wooden huts, thatched with straw, arranged in streets, and ornamented with turrets, gardens, lawns, etc. The streets bore the names of soldiers dead on the field of honour, or of recent battles. The greatest harmony existed amongst the soldiers; and, when the duties of the day were over, there were balls, fencing matches, and performances of military pieces, by actors who came expressly from Paris.

The emperor's *fête* was celebrated on August 15th, with more pomp and ceremony than had ever before been displayed, but, five days later. Napoleon left for Mayence, to rejoin Josephine; and, within a fortnight, the troops were informed there was to be no descent on England, but they were to hold themselves in readiness to march to Germany; for there was a third coalition against France, and Austria had begun hostilities by invading Bavaria.

The "united" brigade, to which François belonged, made the journey to Strasburg in carts or wagons, with ten to twenty men in each vehicle. Hostilities began early in October, with a few cavalry skirmishes, in one of which a dragoon and an officer captured a standard and took a hundred prisoners, single-handed. The dragoon was deservedly decorated. Murat and his cavalry defeated the troops of Prince Ferdinand, and very nearly captured the prince himself, just as he was going to sit down to dinner. The dinner, prepared for the Austrians, was eaten by the French General Klein and his *aides-de-camp*. The garrison of Ulm offered to capitulate, if they were allowed to return to Austria.

"I might," replied Napoleon, "grant that to the officers; but, as to the soldiers, what guarantee have I that they will not serve again?" After reflecting for a minute, he added, "Well, I will trust Prince Ferdinand's word. I wish to give him a proof of my esteem; and I will grant what you ask, in the hope that the Court of Vienna will not repudiate a promise made by one of its princes."

Prince Lichtenstein owned that Prince Ferdinand was not at Ulm. "In that case," answered Napoleon, "I do not see who is to give me the guarantee I require."

The Austrians, to the number of 30,000, did surrender, and as many more capitulated a few days later. The French soldiers said—and François remarks that soldiers often reason justly, and many of them know how to appreciate the talents of a general—

Our emperor has discovered a new way of making war; he uses our legs more than our bayonets.

The French were far from being comfortable, in spite of their extraordinary success. François says:

Although the campaign had only lasted two months, we were barefooted, and were paid in paper money, on which we lost ten *per cent*. We were wretchedly poor, and could not procure any comforts, and, moreover, were worn out with fatigue, wet through with rain and snow, nipped with cold, and camped in the mud; but, in spite of our misery, the presence of our emperor, and our successes, made us bear it all. The emperor knew of our wants and our fatigue, which he shared. He was aware, too, that the soldiers grumbled, especially those of the Guard, and he said, "They are right; but it is to spare their blood that I make them undergo these hardships." When we heard that, he could have made us do what no one else could. An Austrian colonel, who had been made prisoner, was astonished to see Napoleon covered with mud, and his uniform soaked with rain. He made some remark about this, which the emperor overheard. "Colonel!" said Napoleon, "your master has tried to make me remember that I was a soldier; I hope he will acknowledge that the throne and the imperial purple have not made me forget my original profession.

On November 2nd, there was a smart brush with the Russians, who opposed an obstinate resistance, but they could not stand a bayonet charge, and lost 500 men and 300 prisoners; whilst the French had barely a hundred killed or wounded. The Russians were pursued in their retreat by the 9th and 10th Hussars, who killed "as many as they liked," and captured 1,500 more prisoners.

The Emperor of Austria, seeing himself beaten and pursued, retired on Vienna, and proposed an armistice, but Napoleon replied that "It was not for an army of 200,000 men to make an armistice with a flying foe." A few days later, Napoleon entered Vienna, and established his headquarters there in a very quiet and unostentatious manner, without pomp or ceremony; "which modesty gave the inhabitants a high opinion of him."

Napoleon knew well the value of time, and General Lannes' division (to which François belonged) had orders to closely follow up the Russians. An *aide-de-camp* of the *czar* came to Murat, to propose a surrender, and ask for an armistice of four hours whilst the terms were being arranged. Napoleon did not approve of the articles of surrender, and came to the conclusion that the truce was a trick to gain time and receive reinforcements, which were advancing from Upper Moravia. As soon as the four hours had expired, the French made an attack, although it was late in the evening and dark. The darkness, and the smoke from the burning village, prevented the men from distinguishing friends from foes. General Vandamme's division came across a body of troops, the officer commanding which called out, "Don't shoot: we are French!"

But the next moment the French received a murderous volley. Vandamme was so indignant at the trick which had been played him, that he fell on the Russians and slaughtered every one. The battle ended at 11 p.m., when the field was covered with Russian slain. They lost, in addition, 1,800 prisoners, twelve guns, and more than a hundred waggons. Their losses would have been heavier still if Murat, acting on express orders from Napoleon, had not slackened his pursuit to give time to the Emperor Alexander to rejoin the bulk of his army. Thanks to that the Russians got safely into Breslau, which the King of Prussia—"a big beast with a long tail," François calls him—opened to them.

The last days of November were passed in manoeuvres, in the vicinity of Austerlitz. On the morning of December 1st. Napoleon surveyed the camp of the allied armies from the top of a hill, and then turning to General Berthier, who was with him, said, "Before tomorrow evening all that army will be mine." Later in the day he told several of his generals that:

> If it were his intention to stop the enemy, he should await them where he was, but that would only lead to an ordinary battle; whereas if he strengthened his right, and withdrew it towards Brünn, and this false retreat induced the Russians to quit the hills they occupied, they are caught in a trap and hopelessly lost, even if they were 300,000 strong.

The same evening, he issued his famous proclamation, in which he said that:

> If his soldiers behaved with their usual bravery he should keep in the rear, but that if the victory were for a moment doubtful, they would see their emperor in the front rank.

During the night, he visited the bivouacs of the soldiers, to learn the effect of his proclamation; but he was everywhere recognised and received with cheers, the soldiers lighting wisps of straw, and placing them on the points of their bayonets. One of the grenadiers said:

> Sire, you will have no need to expose yourself, I promise you in the name of my comrades. You will only have to fight with your eyes, and tomorrow we will bring you the flags and artillery of the Russian army to celebrate the anniversary of your coronation.

The emperor was much touched by this little speech—it was even said that he had tears in his eyes, and when he returned to the little hut he occupied, he cried:

> This is the happiest day of my life! But I am sorry to think that tomorrow I shall lose so many of these brave fellows.

The corps to which François belonged was under the command of Marshal Lannes, on the left wing, which was centred round Santon—a strong position, defended by eighteen guns. More than a week before the battle, Napoleon had visited the spot, and said to his *aide-de-camp*, "Note this place well, for it will play a great part before long."

The Battle of Austerlitz has been so often described that there is no need to give François' account of the fight, which is short and naturally imperfect, though he saw more of it than he wished, for he was in the reserve intended to support the divisions of Saint Hilaire and Vandamme, if required; but that necessity never arose. He and his comrades were tired of continually changing their position and doing no fighting; and when the emperor passed near, some of the men implored permission to share the glory of the day. "Be glad," replied Napoleon, "that you have nothing to do. I keep you in reserve, and it is all the better that I have no need of you today."

A great deal of ink has been spilled over the vexed question as to whether the French artillery broke the ice of the lake on which the Russians were massed, and so caused the needless death of several thousand men. Bonapartist writers maintain that the breaking of the ice was caused by the weight of the men, not by the fire of the French guns, and this view is borne out by the evidence of François, who says:—

Some battalions passed over the frozen lake; but the ice gave way under the weight of the men, and several thousand officers and men were drowned. Those who escaped, to the number of 6,000, were surrounded in the plain of Sokolnitz and made prisoners; so we saw these poor Russians in the greatest disorder.

The ice on another lake broke under the weight of a park of artillery which was passing over it, and men, horses and guns were engulfed, together with four battalions of infantry, but in neither case does François intimate that the catastrophe was caused or hastened by the fire of the French guns, though, had such been the case he would have been almost sure to boast about it.

The allies lost 40,000 men and 120 guns, the mortality on the French side being 2,000 killed and 5,000 wounded. So many feats of bravery were accomplished that Napoleon said, "It would need a power greater than mine to worthily reward all these brave men."

Two days later, there was a meeting between Napoleon and the

Emperor of Austria, near a windmill, by the side of the high road, some little distance from the village of Saruschitz. A fire was lighted in the open air. Napoleon said, "I receive you in the only palace I have lived in for the last two months."

"It suits you so well that you ought to be pleased with it," replied Francis II., with a smile.

An armistice, and the general conditions of peace, were soon agreed to, and the Emperor of Austria also asked for a truce for the remnants of the Russian Army. Napoleon replied that their army was entirely surrounded at that moment, but he added that:

> To oblige my brother, the Emperor Alexander, I will agree to stop the march of my columns and let his troops pass; but your Majesty must promise me that this army will return to Russia, and evacuate Germany, and Austrian and Prussian Poland.

"That is the Emperor Alexander's intention, I can assure you," said Francis II., "But you can satisfy yourself on that point by sending one of your officers to him."

"I am committing a mistake," said Napoleon; "for I could follow up my victory and capture all the Russian and Austrian Army, but, at any rate, there will be some tears the less shed."

Alexander gladly acceded to the terms demanded, and Napoleon sent back all the Russian nobles who had been taken prisoners. François was one of the escort of these "braggarts" and remarks that they were far less "cocky" than they had been a week ago.

Although peace was proclaimed, the French army was not withdrawn, but encamped in Germany, awaiting orders to return to France. Six months passed, and these orders did not arrive; on the contrary rumours began to arise that there would soon be another war with Prussia and Russia. These rumours were confirmed a little later, when it was known that the King of Prussia had sent an ultimatum to Napoleon, ordering him to recross the Rhine, evacuate German territory, and renounce the thrones of Italy, Naples, and Holland. Napoleon, it was said, did not even finish reading this insolent document, but remarked that he was sorry for the King of Prussia, who did not understand French, and had certainly never seen the rodomontade that was sent in his name.

On October 7th, Napoleon rejoined the army, and an advance was immediately ordered. The next day there was an engagement between the advanced guards of the two armies. In the course of this skirmish,

Prince Louis of Prussia was killed by a sergeant of the 10th Hussars, named Guindé, who was rewarded, and entered the Imperial Guard. A few days later, the emperor arrived at Jena, and made preparations for the forthcoming battle. On the night of October 13th, he was sitting over his camp fire, when one of the sentinels, who was shivering with cold, approached to warm himself. Napoleon looked up, and said, "Young man, do you know music?"

"No, Sire."

"Tomorrow you will hear a full orchestra."

At daybreak next morning, a cannon was fired as a signal for the troops to fall in, and skirmishers at once pushed forward, for there was a dense fog which prevented the armies from seeing each other. About nine, the fog cleared away, and the battle soon ended in a complete defeat of the Prussians. François was in the thick of the fighting, but, with his usual good luck, escaped unhurt, except for the usual bruise on the thigh, though he had a bullet through his hat and two through his coat. He records that, in several instances, when a regiment received the order to fire, the men replied, "Oh, there is plenty of time. Wait until we are within fifteen paces." In another case, a cadet gave the order to charge to a regiment Napoleon wished held in reserve, just as the emperor was passing. "What?" he cried sharply, "Does some beardless boy dare to forestall my orders? Let him wait till he has fought thirty pitched battles before he pretends to teach *me*."

The Prussians were vigorously pursued, and the queen was very nearly captured the next day, at Weimar. On October 25th, Napoleon was at Potsdam, where he found the sword of Frederick the Great, the belt he wore in the Seven Years' War,[1] and the ribbons of his Orders ("I saw them all," says François). The emperor told his officers that he would rather have those trophies than twenty millions of money, and would send them to the Governor of the Invalides as a proof of the victories of the Grand Army. Napoleon also visited the tomb of Frederick, which is in black marble without any inscription, and took off his hat when he entered the vault.

François thinks Napoleon was quite justified in laying hands on the sword of Frederick, for no one was so worthy to wear it. Besides, Frederick had said, "If I had the honour to be King of France, not a cannon should be fired in Europe without my permission," and Napoleon successfully filled the part which the Prussian hero had

---

1. *Frederick the Great & the Seven Years' War* by F.W. Longman is also published by Leonaur.

envied.

The day the emperor visited the tomb, there was a heavy shower of rain, and though he little feared rain or tempest, he dismounted and entered the house of the chief huntsman to the King of Saxony. Napoleon was plainly dressed, and wore his usual grey overcoat. He was therefore surprised to find himself recognised by a young woman who was there. She was an Egyptian, the widow of a French officer, and after many adventures had reached Prussia, where she had been sheltered by the official in whose house she was. Napoleon granted her a pension of 1,200 *francs* a year, and promised to see that her son was educated in a French school. "It is the first time," said the emperor, "that I ever dismounted to avoid a storm; I had a presentiment that I was called to do a good action."

François learned of this incident from an officer of the escort. The Russians had also renewed the war, and Napoleon entered Warsaw before the end of the year, but there was not much fighting, except at Golymin on December 26th, when Lannes' division, backed by those of Benningsen, Murat and Davoust, inflicted a check on the Russians. A sudden thaw prevented the French from following up their victory.

CHAPTER 10

# 1807

The army encamped in Poland, and, on February 8th, was attacked by the Russians, when the famous Battle of Eylau was fought, which resulted in a crushing defeat for Alexander. The French also suffered severely, but François came off with only a bullet through his hat, and the usual slight bruise on the thigh. The troops remained nine days on the field of battle, after having driven away the Russians; but the men complained bitterly of want of food.

A month later (March 7th) the Russians were again defeated at Ostrolenska and lost 3,000 men, two standards, and seven guns. Then followed the blockade of Dantzic,[1] and a lot of skirmishing in various places. Both sides were short of provisions, and the men used to agree amongst themselves on a kind of informal truce for the purpose of foraging, and robbing the poor Polish peasants. The description of these foraging parties, as given by François, is not without interest.

The scarcity of provisions obliged us to agree with the Russians in order to procure food, and we made a kind of truce by means of signs,—a truce which was faithfully kept by the outposts of both armies, and persons who knew nothing of war would have found it hard to believe that soldiers who seemed so peaceable in each other's presence, were ready to cut one another's throats at the first signal. Our necessity was so great, that we fraternized with these villainous and dirty irregular Cossacks, of whom we had no fear, especially those of us who, like me, had not feared the Arabs. The much-boasted wild and

---

1. *The Long Siege, Danzig,* 1813, a double edition *The Siege of Dantzic, in* 1813 by Louis Antoine François de Marchangy & *Dantzig and Poland:The Background & History of the Siege of Dantzig,* 1813 (Extract) by Simon Askenazy is also published by Leonaur.

savage aspect of these islanders (*sic*) little intimidated us; and it often happened that we shared provisions with them, as we did with other nations as soon as we understood their language. I give an instance of this, which the soldiers who made this campaign can confirm.

The *chasseurs* on the banks of the Omuler River crossed over to an island in the river, to carry off the potatoes, which the unfortunate Polish peasants had buried there. They met some Cossacks who had come for the same purpose, and the two parties, though they could not converse owing to difference of language, agreed by signs that they would leave their arms in the boats which had brought them, and that they would search together and divide the spoil equally, all of which was faithfully observed. The *chasseurs*, being quicker and cleverer than the Cossacks, soon found potatoes, and religiously observed the clauses of this tacit agreement.

They divided the potatoes with the Cossacks, and each party returned to its own side of the river like good friends, and after shaking hands. Similar instances often happened, even to the *voltigeurs* of my company.

Early in June the Russians were defeated at Spanden by Bernadotte—who was wounded in the breast in this engagement—and at Gutstadt by Murat's cavalry; but at Heilsberg (June 10th) they defended themselves obstinately, and the French obtained no good advantage, in spite of their intrepidity. The loss was very heavy on both sides. Marshal Lannes had two horses shot under him, and many officers were killed or wounded, François escaped with three bullets through his clothes, and without the ordinary bruise. The 5th Cuirassiers, commanded by Colonel Davenay, made several brilliant charges. At the end of the battle this officer said to Prince Murat, at the same time showing his sabre dripping with blood, "Prince, you may go all through my regiment and not find a *cuirassier* whose sabre is not like mine."

One officer of this regiment was wounded in fifty-two places, and did not leave the field till he was too weak to sit on horseback.

A few days later, the bloody Battle of Friedland was fought, where the Russians lost at least 15,000 men, and twenty-five Generals were killed, wounded, or captured. Napoleon was seen in the most exposed positions, and François and his comrades trembled for him when they saw shells passing near him, and men falling almost at his feet. The Russians retreated, and, as has always been their custom, destroyed most of their supplies, but some fell into the hands of the French, who badly wanted them, for, says François:

We needed provisions of all sorts, and I do not know how we endured so much fatigue and so many battles on empty bellies, for we rarely got any brandy and never any bread, so the unfortunate Poles had to pay dearly for our invasion of the country.

A treaty of peace between the two emperors was signed at Tilsitt on June 21st, much to the satisfaction of the French soldiers who were glad to get some rest after their trials and privations. François and his division were encamped on the banks of the Niemen, and on the other side of the river were some "monstrous savages" called Kalmucks.

These Tartars have no offensive weapons but arrows, which they shoot whilst riding, like the ancient Parthians, and which are often poisoned. The way in which these soldiers fight often made us laugh, although many of our men were wounded by these arrows, which we feared but little.

The Russian and French officers told the soldiers to have no dealings with these Kalmucks during the armistice, as "they were treacherous barbarians," but with the other Russian nations, François says, "we made ourselves understood by signs, and often had a glass together."

On the morning of June 25th, the troops were under arms, and lined the streets of Tilsitt. Napoleon was at his pavilion on the Niemen, where the Emperor of Russia and the King of Prussia called on him, and all three monarchs returned to the headquarters at Tilsitt, where they dined together. As they passed down the principal street, the French soldiers cried "*Vive Alexandre!*" and "*Vive Napoleon!*" but not a single cheer was raised for the King of Prussia.

That the French soldiers should have showed a contempt for Frederick William III. was but natural, considering the way Napoleon treated him, but it does not say much for their gallantry that they should have deliberately tried to annoy his beautiful queen (Louisa of Mecklenburg Strelitz). The king and queen lodged in a mill, which was used by the soldiers to grind their corn, and the men vied with each other to see who could make the most noise, although they knew that the queen was ill. The king, however, bore all these annoyances patiently.

The Russian and Prussian monarchs, and Prince Constantine several times reviewed the French troops. The prince once put François' company through an exercise in squad firing, and was so pleased with their regularity that he gave François twenty gold pieces to divide between the men. At these reviews, the King of Prussia ("a great gawky with a long tail") was always behind the two emperors and seemed ashamed to be in their company. Napoleon had continually to say to him, "Your Majesty is requested to advance." François could not imagine that "a king could be such a simpleton." Nor was this unfortunate ruler more popular with the Russians. The French and Russian Imperial Guards dined together, and the repast passed off merrily in spite of lingual difficulties. After the dinner, the men changed coats with each other, marched up the street, and passed before the lodgings of the two emperors, crying "*Vive Napoleon!*" "*Vive Alexandre!*" The Russian soldiers said that the French and themselves were *obrai* (good) but the Prussian soldiers were *nient obrai* (no good)—a verdict which time has reversed, if it were ever true.

As the French were to occupy Tilsitt for some time to come, they made themselves wooden huts, which were arranged in streets, named after great battles, or soldiers who had fallen on the field of honour. The huts were made of wood, whitened outside, with thatched roofs, and doors and windows. François says:

> The camp had ruined the villages for five or six leagues round. Our soldiers had carried off furniture, doors, and windows from the habitations of the unfortunate Poles, who belonged to Prussia. The camps were very pretty, but they were expensive to humanity and us. Food was badly wanted; the country, for twenty leagues and more round, had been ruined, and we died of hunger in our palaces.

This was doubtless an exaggeration, but at any rate it did not for long affect François personally, for, in July, he was named Lieutenant in the 5th Legion of the Reserve, and ordered to rejoin his regiment, which was then in Italy[2] and then proceed, with two of his fellow-officers who were also promoted, to Grenoble, the headquarters of the legion to which they were appointed.

He passed rapidly through Italy, but had time to see some of his old friends—notably a certain *marquise* with whom he had been on

---

2. It will be remembered that, in this campaign, François was attached to the "United" Brigade, composed of drafts of picked men from several regiments.

more than friendly terms, and by whom he was well received, though he seems a trifle annoyed to find he had a successor in the lady's affections—"but such is the custom of the fair and gallant Italian women," he philosophically remarks. He was not long without another lady-love, however, for in a fortnight later he was in Grenoble, and, before he had been there four days, he had made the acquaintance of a young and rather nice woman, married to an Italian employed in the *octroi*. It was rather against his principles to have a love affair with a married woman, but he explains that:

> When I first knew her I thought she was a *demoiselle*, and I did not learn till afterwards that the goddess was married; but, as the first step had been taken, I stuck to her, chiefly because she was pretty, very *coquettish*, and extremely fast.

The new legion was drilled six hours a day, and two months later (October 20th) was ordered to Spain. His new "princess" was inclined to be what the French call "*une femme collante*," and wished to go with him, and when he raised an objection to that, she grew desperate and threatened to come and join him. The legion marched south, passing through various towns, including Béziers; which is such a fine city, and has such a splendid climate that the inhabitants say that "if the *Bon Dieu* came to live on earth he would choose Béziers." When the legion neared the frontier, François was sent on into Spain to prepare food and lodgings for the forces. He was selected for this duty because he spoke Italian—"a language which has some affinity with Spanish."

He did not think much of the Spanish inns, for he says that:

> When a traveller arrives, he must find out where the butcher, the baker, and the wine merchant live, and when he has procured all his provisions it is doubtful whether he can get them cooked at the inn; and unless he has brought his own bedding with him, he will find nothing but a bare room, the floor covered with dirty matting, on which he can lie if he likes. In addition, he will be charged for the noise he makes, and even the air he breathes. The people are proud, haughty, and ragged. As for the Castilians, the dirtier they are the more noble they think themselves. They imagine they confer an honour on a stranger by drinking with him, and if he is worthy of that mark of distinction they offer him the cigarette from their own dirty mouth

A favour which François invariably declined.

# CHAPTER 11

# 1808

The year 1808 was fated to be an unlucky one for François. To begin with, a post-chaise arrived at ten o'clock in the evening of January 3rd at his lodgings, and from it stepped two women, one of whom was the sweetheart he had left at Grenoble, and the other the mistress of his comrade, Ferdinand. François scolded the unfortunate girl for committing this *sottise*, and sent her back to Bayonne next morning.

At Valladolid, where his regiment was in January, François noticed that the people did not appear to like the French, though they treated them civilly. At Zamora, on the other hand, the civil and military authorities and the clergy came to meet the troops with cries of "Long live the French and the Emperor Napoleon," and the officers were invited to a collation. The French were not behindhand in hospitality, and the carnival passed off merrily, but soon afterwards François noticed that all the cadets at the School of Artillery, and many of the leading citizens, were leaving the town. He had formed a sort of platonic attachment to the daughter of a colonel of cavalry. She was of noble birth, and very fond of balls and dinners, and as General Poinsot was the cavalier of her elder sister (they were aged 45 and 38 respectively), François was able to give her plenty of amusement at no great cost to himself, his share being to arrange the entertainments.

François asked this lady the meaning of the exodus, and, after some hesitation, she replied, that the men were bound for Andalusia, to take up arms against the French, who would never return to France. François laughed, but she said, "You will see, and I recommend you to stay with me, or you will die along with the others." He told this to his comrades, who said, "We quite believe it; for the people are not the same as they were."

A detachment was sent, under François, to Segovia, where his coming aroused some curiosity, as he was the first Frenchman to enter the town. The division joined him here, and they learned, a few days later, that General Muller had been killed in a street riot at Valladolid, by one of his own men, who had incautiously fired off his ramrod, which hit the general in the forehead. The corporal who fired the fatal shot had a month's imprisonment!

François was attacked in the street, on the evening of March 28th, by two Spanish soldiers, one of whom aimed a blow at him with his sword, which cut off one of the corners of his hat and part of his epaulette. François drew, and being a skilful swordsman, wounded one of the men; whereupon the other fled. The wounded man was found in the hospital the next day, having received a thrust which had gone nearly through his thigh, but no information could be got out of him, and as the division left a few days later, François never heard of him again.

The division went to the Escurial, where they received a visit from the King and Queen of Spain. The king, François describes, as looking like a respectable workman. He was dressed in grey cloth, with white silk stockings fastened with garters above the knee, shoes with very large silver buckles and purple velvet bows. The queen wore a plain white dress, cut so low that it showed half her back, a pair of skinny, yellow shoulders, and a yellow neck without any bust below it. She had a little nose, a large mouth, and rather pretty black eyes, with yellow and black rings round them. She was very short, and both spoke French. On leaving, the poor king asked General Verdier where he was to go, but the general could give him no information.

On April 12th, the division encamped a league from Madrid. François and some of his comrades visited the city, dined at a good restaurant, where they had a dinner well served but dear, admired the *cocottes*, who were young, pretty, and nicely dressed, and gazed at the public buildings. On their way back, they crossed a bridge over the Manzanares, and were "potted at" by some of the natives from the banks. Having only their swords, they could not reply to this fire, which accompanied them nearly all the way to the camp. None of them were hit, and they said nothing about the incident, as there were strict orders that they were not to leave the camp, or even to go out at night.

These orders were very necessary, for assassinations were rife. A captain of *voltigeurs*, who was ill, was lodged in the house of the cure at Caramancelli, and for a fortnight was very well treated. One morning the *curé* came with a gun, rapped at the captain's door, and told him his chocolate was ready. The officer threw open the door, and the priest immediately shot him dead. The rumour spread amongst the troops that it was François who had been killed. Many of the soldiers called at his lodgings to know if the report were true, and when they found him alive and well they shed tears of joy.

He had a narrow escape a few days later, for he was sent into Madrid, accompanied only by an orderly, to make purchases of clothes, musical instruments, and cooking utensils. He lodged with a banker, who warned him to go out as little as possible. He did, however, go out, but took his sword and a pair of pistols. He was occasionally called a *bandido*, or *demonio*, but took no notice of these compliments. The departure of the Royal Family caused riots to break out, and Lagrange, Murat's *aide-de-camp*, who brought the order for the departure, was nearly murdered. François says:

> I was present at this scene, as I wished to see the queen leave for Bayonne, but when I heard the officer of the guard give the order to fire on the people, I returned home, and my host made me stay. However, when I heard the shooting, saw the people running towards the palace, and a soldier killed under my window, I could stand it no longer. I handed over my effects and money to my host, and he gave me two receipts, one for me and the other for my orderly, whom I left at the house, making my hosts responsible for him and also my money and goods, and made my way to the St. Nicholas quarter, where the troops were under arms.

He joined one of the French battalions, and a sortie was made. The French were assaulted with stones, tiles, bricks, tables, and chairs, thrown out of the houses, and shots were fired from windows and cellar gratings. The fire of the infantry, the charges of the Mamelukes, and the grape-shot of the artillery, dispersed the mob, and the troops from outside entered at the double and completed their discomfiture. Napoleon and his officers took no half measures in affairs of this sort. No prisoners were taken, and even after the disturbance had been quelled, the streets were patrolled, and any Spaniard found with a weapon, even a knife, was arrested and taken to the Retiro, where 337 were shot that same night. A patrol of Mamelukes found two of their own men dead in front of a respectable-looking house. Some friendly Spaniards said they had been killed by shots fired from that house, so the Mamelukes entered it, cut off the heads of all the men and women they found therein, and threw them out of the window; after which they remounted and continued their round.

The abdication of Carlos IV., and the accession of Joseph Bonaparte, caused insurrections to break out all over Spain. Small detachments of French were set upon and murdered with horrible tortures. General Rene, his wife, and child were sawn in two. François saw, at Val-de-Penas, a large house, used as the hospital, where 400 French had been cut to pieces and fifty-three buried alive. A convoy he was escorting was attacked, and two of his men killed by stones, but François, leaving twenty men to guard the carts, turned back with the other eighty, stormed the village, burned down the *alcade's* house, and took eight of the principal inhabitants as hostages,—a feat for which he was greatly complimented by General Poinsot, his commander.

The next few pages of the diary are filled with similar ghastly details of men who had their ears and nose cut off, and suffered worse, and nameless, mutilation. In one place they found a man who was raving mad; he was the sole survivor of twelve hundred and odd invalids who had been hacked to pieces. His life had been saved by one of the inhabitants; but he had lost both his ears as well as his reason.

When the division arrived at Val-de-Penas—the scene of some of the worst atrocities—the inhabitants, fearing the vengeance of the French, had decamped in a body, and the town was entirely deserted. But the cellars were still full of good wine, and the soldiers carried off such quantities that, in less than an hour, all the men and many of the officers were drunk; even the men left in the camp had liquor brought them. Several died of intoxication and others were drowned in the wine, which was two or three feet deep in some of the cellars. To prevent farther mischief. General Vedel was obliged to move his camp a league away from the town.

The division was moving to the relief of the First Legion, which was surrounded by insurgents, and reduced to living on green corn and radishes. The road lay through the Sierra Morena, and the passes were defended, but the untrained Spanish peasants could not stand against Napoleon's veterans. François, who commanded 100 men of the advance guard, took two of these batteries without any aid from the main body. In the first affair, he lost three men, and his musket was cut in two by a round shot. The second was more serious, there were six guns, mounted on tree trunks. Sending his lieutenant, with forty men, to make a circuit and attack from the rear, he advanced with fifty-four men, and, in spite of a volley at close quarters from four of the guns, carried the battery, killing seventeen of the gunners and capturing thirteen prisoners. He had a knock on the head from the butt end of a musket, but he thought little of trifles of that sort. When the division arrived, the generals asked him to dinner, and promised to recommend him for "the Cross."

He managed these little businesses so well that, on July 4th, he was sent, with three companies of sharpshooters, to the town of Linares, where it was reported there was a powder mill and lead works.

I arrived, without any obstacles, at the town (he says), presented myself, with a captain of artillery, before the *alcade*, and showed my order. He gave us every assistance, led us to the powder mill, and we took half a ton of powder and 1500 lbs. of balls, which we put in the carts. My mission being accomplished, I caused bread, meat, rice, and a bottle of wine a piece to be given to the soldiers, and they prepared their meal on a plateau overlooking the town. Very soon, more than 600 peasants surrounded my bivouac and called us *amigos*. Knowing this expression, I distrusted these *amigos*, and told them to leave. Many of them did so, and my soldiers had their lunch, and slept quietly two or three hours. I left at nine p.m. and had hardly started before there came a shot which wounded one of the sharpshooters, so I formed sections with the carts between and continued my march, but was hardly more than half a league from the town when I was attacked on all sides. I formed square, with the waggons inside, and continued my march, blazing away in all directions.

These brave *amigos* accompanied us with gunshots until five o'clock in the morning, when I entered a wood, where, very fortunately, I found a company of sharpshooters of the First Legion, which the general had sent to meet me. On leaving the wood, I met a second company of the same legion. The *amigos*, seeing us in force, retired. I had a man killed, and five wounded. I do not know what damage my *voltigeurs* did to these *amigos*, two of whom were taken with arms in their hands and sent to General Vedel, who had them shot the same day.

A day or two later, a peasant was arrested on a charge of trying to suborn the soldiers. Luckily for him, he was tried by court-martial, and it turned out that he was a poor devil with six starving children, and was asking the soldiers for bread, but, as they did not understand Spanish, they put a wrong construction on his words.

The want of Napoleon's presence was keenly felt; the generals did not work in unison, and made terrible blunders, especially General Vedel, who evacuated Baylen, a position he ought to have held at all costs. General Dupont then tried to take possession of the place, and engaged the Spaniards. Vedel's men, who were only four leagues away, heard the firing and begged to be led to the relief of Dupont. Vedel complied, but when halfway, as the men were hot and thirsty, he called a halt for three or four hours, thus losing valuable time. The men cursed and swore at the delay, but a large drove of pigs came along the road, and the men, having been on short commons and reduced to two ounces of boiled cheese a day, set to work to kill the pigs, to the great amusement of General Vedel. When the advance was at last ordered, the men had to throw away the pork. They did at last engage the enemy, but it is not very easy to make out from François' description exactly what did happen, but there is every excuse for him, as he met with a serious calamity, which led to one of the most dramatic episodes in his adventurous career, and the account of which is best given in his own words.

The First Legion, of which I was part, took two guns, three caissons, and 800 prisoners of the Irish regiment. At that moment I was ordered to attack a chapel where the Jaen regiment was posted. I had sixty-five men, thirty being employed in guarding the equipages of General Poinsot and his w—. I sounded the charge, and my young soldiers received the Spanish fire, crying out "*Vive l'Empereur!*" At the moment when a Spanish officer waved a white handkerchief as a sign of surrender, I was hit by a bullet in the right hip, which knocked me over amongst the brushwood.

I lost in this affair nineteen men and thirty-three wounded, myself included. Eleven of the wounded rejoined the battalion, and reported that they believed me to be killed, as they saw me fall twenty or thirty paces from the chapel, and as it was dusk, the men sent to pick up the wounded did not find me, as I had crawled into the brushwood, and was unconscious through loss of blood. In the night, I came to, and found myself alone, surrounded by my dead *voltigeurs*, and expecting the same fate. Not having the strength to move, nor to cry out, I did not know what had happened.

The next morning, the Spanish soldiers and peasants came to the field of battle, to pick up the weapons and search the dead. Two peasants found me, and seeing I was alive, insulted me, pulled me out of the brushwood, searched me, and took my watch and my belt, which contained eighty-three *napoleons* and five *piastres*, tore out my earrings, and left me, despite my prayers that they would either kill me, or take me to the ambulance at Baylen. They replied that I was a brigand, and had lived long enough, and went away insulting me. A few minutes later, some other peasants came, and I persuaded them to take me to the ambulance at Baylen. I cannot describe the suffering I went through to get there; I was weak from loss of blood, had passed a whole night on the battlefield, and felt hopeless.

His wound was dressed, and in a few days he was able to rejoin his division, but, owing to the blunders and want of mutual confidence of his commanders, both Dupont and Vedel had been forced to capitulate, and though the French were supposed to have surrendered with "all the honours of war," and with full liberty to return to Madrid, they soon found that they were prisoners of war. The description of his captivity, given by François, is so interesting that it is here given almost as he wrote it, only details of no importance being omitted.

Being, as I have already said, wounded, I was taken, at my own request, to join my comrades of the Fifth Legion of the Reserve, who hastened to help me, and obtained leave from General Vedel to place me in his waggon, in which I journeyed to our cantonments in Andalusia, where we were regarded as prisoners of war, the articles of capitulation having been violated in the most flagrant manner. The Junta of Seville pretended that it was obliged to wait for passports from the King of England, ensuring the safety of our sea voyage to France, but the mask was soon lifted. The English Admiralty, by agreement with the insurgent government, refused the passports, and the infamous English policy was the cause of this unfortunate *corps d'armée*—which had already been robbed, ill-treated, and partly murdered— being thrown into fortresses and jails.

The legion, like some other *corps*, was imprisoned in deserted houses and stables in the villages of Andalusia, the officers being in *posadas* guarded by *alguazils* and peasants. Afterwards, as

I shall relate, some of them were put on hulks in the harbour and port of Cadiz (I was of the number). The greater part of these unfortunate victims of English and Spanish perfidy died of hunger and misery. Those who survived were afterwards removed to the island of Cabreira, some leagues to the south of Majorca, where they were in want of the necessities of life, and where they found themselves again given over to the persecutions and ill-treatment of a half-savage population, who had been taught to believe they were heretics and wretches deserving the worst fate.

Finally, as a crowning instance of the atrocious English policy which had directed the Spaniards in this monstrous violation of the laws of war and humanity, the poor remnant of General Dupont's army was, as I have said, treated as prisoners of war, and some of them taken to England to share, in the hulks, the fate of the other Frenchmen whom the luck of war had caused to fall,—more legitimately at least,—into the hands of our most implacable enemies. Such was the deplorable result of General Dupont's expedition to Andalusia—the most unfortunate recorded in history.

(*August 23rd.*) To get to our cantonments we were escorted by infantry of the Alcantara regiment. We had nothing but praise for the way they behaved. At my arrival at my cantonment, at Aralur in Andalusia, our escort left us, after handing us over to the Junta of the town, by whom we were examined. The non-commissioned officers were deprived of their swords, and the men were divided into companies, and conducted to their lodgings by a guard of peasants. They were lodged in stables and yards, and given straw to lie on; the poor wretches wept when they left us, and so did we. The officers were put up at inns. I and four others occupied one room and slept on mats. Being convalescent, and walking with difficulty, I had made the journey from Morron on a donkey. When I arrived at the cantonment I was leaning on the arms of two of my comrades. The inhabitants, seeing that I was wounded and my trousers all covered with blood, insulted me in the most outrageous manner; many of them threw stones and mud at me. I cannot describe how much I cursed my fate.

On September 1st there arrived 200 men of the Alcantara regiment, who were supposed to guard us. As a preliminary, they sabred three of our soldiers, who had asked permission to fetch water. One of the three belonged to my company, and I obtained permission from the *alcade* to have him with me. He had a sabre cut on the head, and, in a few days, though it was hardly healed, was very useful to me. I also obtained leave for a surgeon to visit me. He said there was some foreign matter—linen or cloth—in my wound, and wanted to reopen it, but I would not let him, and the pain never returned.

(*September 3rd.*) Today, we officers were confined to our lodgings, and guarded by armed peasants. About eight in the morning, a crowd of peasants assembled before our lodgings, threw stones at the windows, and insulted us. They cried, "By noon you will have ceased to live—your heads will be cut off;" and displayed their knives. Our guards did not interfere with the mob, but laughed, and seemed pleased to see us insulted. We did not know what to think of these proceedings, and seized our weapons, resolved to sell our lives dearly if we were attacked. Towards 11 o'clock, five members of the *junta* came to our lodgings, escorted by 100 dragoons of the Alcantara regiment, to examine our valises.

As I could not walk, I was sitting on mine, and they did not examine it. Having finished this operation, the escort went off, with my four companions in misfortune, to the stables, where our soldiers were. On the road they were insulted and stones thrown at them, in spite of the dragoons who accompanied them. Our soldiers were ordered to bring out their haversacks, which were minutely examined to see that they did not contain any Spanish goods. Luckily for the poor wretches, they found nothing. Then the *junta* took away the men's cartridge-boxes, broke the point of their knives, and went away, telling the people they had found no Spanish property. The officers were led back to their lodging; the inhabitants crying as they passed, *A la manana a matar* (Tomorrow you die).

My comrades were very anxious about the soldiers, and we resolved to go and live with them, which we did that evening. We lodged in the loft over the stables, and had our sabres with us. This was a great relief to the soldiers and to us too, and we all decided to defend ourselves if we were attacked by peasants or others.

(*September 6th.*) The same *junta* came again to search the soldiers and make an inventory of our money and effects. I had in my portmanteau a pair of Spanish pistols I had bought in Madrid. Unfortunately, one of them was still loaded. A Franciscan monk, a member of the *junta*, asked me a lot of questions, and, seeing that I was wounded, called me brigand, scoundrel, said I was not fit to live, and, cocking the pistol, placed it against my breast. Luckily, another man snatched the weapon from him. That evening I was put in a cell, and remained there thirty-six hours, tortured by anxiety. I was at last taken back to the inn, where I found my comrades, who showed joy at seeing me once more amongst them, and told me how anxious they had been on my account.

After that we were not disturbed. We went to Mass at noon on Sunday, and the people, being used to seeing us, no longer insulted us. Our soldiers worked as labourers, and many of them earned twenty to twenty-five *sous* a day.

(*September 11th.*) The people are getting a bit used to us; many of us have made acquaintances amongst them. I had hardly begun to walk, but supported by my comrades, I accompanied them in their walks in the town. I thus made the acquaintance of Don Alonzo, the vicar of the parish, who took a liking to me. He came to see me, and often took me to his house. I never much cared for people of that sort, but he was a good, honest man, and did us some services.

Some foreign officers in the Spanish service tried to seduce the French soldiers from their allegiance. They had no success with the real French, but a good many of the Swiss, Italians, German and Dutch were compelled by force to join the Spanish Army. Nothing is recorded as having taken place in October, but, in the beginning of November, François and the other prisoners were escorted to Marchena, where, after waiting two hours in the public square, amidst the gibes of the populace, they were ordered back to their old quarters. But, at the end of the same month they were again sent off, and this time for good, to Moron. There François hired a room "furnished in the Spanish style"—that is to say, four bare walls—for ten *sols* a day and five *sols* for a straw mattress. On December 6th they were removed to the town of Arcos, where the peasants assailed them with stones, and several of them were badly hurt. They passed through the town of Bruno, where the officers and soldiers of the 4th Legion were confined. The soldiers were lodged in an old castle in the public square, and if one of the unfortunate fellows dared to show his head at a loophole, it was saluted with a bullet, or a stone thrown from a sling.

The next day, François and his comrades were at Xérès, where they arrived at 2 p.m., and halted to await the orders of the Spanish officer. He did not come till 4 o'clock, which gave the crowd time to prepare their plans; and when the prisoners did at last start they had to be taken down bye-lanes to avoid the mob, and, as it was, were followed for half a league by harridans, who threw stones at them all the way. They arrived at Santa Maria at nightfall, and were conducted to a prison where they found a number of French soldiers and sailors, who were glad to have an officer to command them, for matters became more critical every day, as was quickly proved *by* the events of the next twenty-four hours, which François describes.

(*December 8th.*) This was a *fête* day, and on those days the fury of the populace was always worse. This particular date had been fixed for our assassination. We were informed of this by one of the authorities, who came to warn the major of the 5th Legion. Our soldiers were told about it, and determined to sell their lives dearly. A proposal was made to one of the members of the *junta* that we should be furnished with 200 muskets and cartridges that we might disperse this vile mob, the numbers of which increased, and drew together many of the inhabitants, who would not have come of themselves, but were attracted by the hope of seeing us murdered.

We promised this official that we would return to the prison at the first summons. He gave us several good reasons why it was impossible to comply with our request. He assured us that the clergy, and civil and military authorities would use means to make the mob withdraw;—in which, as a matter of fact, they succeeded, patrolling the streets continually and showing the Holy Sacrament before the prison, and the priests passing through the crowd brandishing their crucifix.

Our soldiers—for the most part men of the marine artillery, of seven or eight years' service,—were determined to sell their lives dearly. They were armed with stones, balusters, iron bars, knives, and razor-blades fastened to sticks, and there was no doubt about their determination. The people knew we intended to defend ourselves vigorously.

(*December 9th.*) There were the same gatherings, which, in the afternoon, dispersed little by little. They satisfied themselves with insulting us, and making signs with their knives that they would cut our throats. The women made the same sign with their fans.

Our portmanteaux, which we had left in a room by order of the commanding officer, were examined by several officers and a member of the *junta*, but were restored to us. The major of the 5th Legion was the only person who paid for this search, for they took more than 3,000 *francs* belonging to him.

(*December 10th.*) Today we learned from the officer on guard that a revolution had broken out in several places where the French were confined, and that at Sebrya the people had killed twelve officers out of fifteen, and sixty-five dragoons, commanded by Major Baron, who was the first victim. Only Brigadier-General Privé, his *aide-de-camp*, a medical officer, and two officers of the 14th Dragoons had escaped. One of them saved his life by climbing into an olive tree. The general and the officers were hidden in a cell, and the mob were made to believe they were dead.

(*December 11th.*) General Privé and the officers who had escaped the massacre at Sebrya, arrived at our prison. Nearly all these poor wretches were covered with the blood of their comrades, and wounded by daggers and sticks. They told us they owed their lives to the Holy Sacrament being brought to their quarters. The barbarians left their victims, and prostrated themselves. A sermon was preached to them, telling them to pardon their enemies; they promised they would and solaced the last moments of the dying.

(*December 13th.*) General Privé and his *aide-de-camp* left for Fort Saint Sebastian at Cadiz. The unfortunate general died there; his mind was deranged and he talked of nothing but murders and massacres.

At Santa Maria, a little town two leagues by sea and seven by land from Cadiz, we were pretty well off, though not allowed to go out. We slept on the tiled floor, for the Spaniards never provided any accommodation, not even straw to lie on.

(*December 25th.*) A corporal of the Marine Artillery had obtained the post of master-at-arms on board one of the ships. Either through natural depravity, or by poverty caused by gambling, to which he had lately become addicted, he robbed one of his comrades and sold what he had stolen. Complaint was made to the Spanish officer, and the offender was arrested and put in a cell. There, being left to himself and repenting of his act, he hanged himself. A doctor was fetched to him, and said, "Oh, what a fine sight! I should like to see them all like that, along with their *Napolochon!*"

He declared that the man could not have hanged himself, and that his eyes turned up to heaven, demanded vengeance, and that the best way to find the guilty parties would be to decimate all the prisoners, as the people wished.

The authorities did not comply with the advice of this singularly blood-thirsty medical man, but they locked up all the roommates of the deceased, and the non-commissioned officers charged with the police arrangements of the prison. François was sent away about a month later, and so never heard what was done to these poor fellows.

CHAPTER 12

# 1809

During the whole of this year, and good portion of the next, François was a prisoner on the Spanish hulks. His plain unvarnished story of the horrors of that period is best given, as far as possible, in his own words. It casts a lurid side-light on the glories of war,—creates a feeling of wonder that any of the unfortunate French prisoners were able to live through such a long period, exposed as they were to dirt, disease, and starvation,—and is a proof of what splendid material the veterans and conscripts of Napoleon were made.

François, and the other officers of the 5th Legion, were, on January 26th, 1809, removed from prison and taken to a hulk with the not in-appropriate name of the "Terrible Castilian." They were kept for a day without food, and, on making complaint, were transferred to another hulk, named the "Old Castille," where they found General Dufour and about 700 officers of all grades. There were eight of these vessels in the harbour or roads of Cadiz, and all of them were filled with French prisoners, one of them being reserved for civilians—who were chiefly merchants established at Cadiz and other ports. François was not long in discovering the nature of the floating hell he had entered.

(*January 28th.*) What was my surprise, the morning after my arrival in going over the vessel, to find half the soldiers ill, and learn of the death of several officers; amongst others of one of the 5th Legion, of which I was part, who, covered with vermin, had thrown himself into the sea in despair.

This terrible disease broke out when the French were first tak-en to the hulks; it was looked upon as an epidemic. I was struck by the want of order, and the dirtiness of the ship. Ten French sailors, also prisoners, were, however, paid by the Spanish Navy to clean the ship, but the poor wretches were as ill as the others. All the prisoners were devoid of everything; no food, no water. Several of the wives of the officers were not exempt from the scourge. The air we breathed was pestilential. Yet the major of the 3rd Legion wrote daily to the Spanish officer . charged with the care of the prisoners; but the only reply he received was that there were no military hospitals, and the sick could not be admitted to the civil hospitals. At any rate the Spaniards were glad to see us perish.

The disease began with a violent headache, a weakness in all the limbs, followed by a fever and delirium which was little short of madness.

(*January 30th*) A Spanish commissioner came on board. He kept his handkerchief to his nose, and, as may be imagined, did not stay to listen to our complaints.

(*February 2nd.*) An officer of the 3rd Swiss regiment, in a moment of delirium, threw himself into the sea. When he was in the water, he recovered his senses, and had the courage to take off his clothes. He struggled amid the waves, and called for help, but when he was taken out it was too late.

(*February 24th.*) An officer, who had been ill for a long time, felt better, and came on deck, but suddenly dropped dead. The day on which this sad spectacle was presented to us, was the last day of carnival. What a contrast! At four o'clock in the afternoon, a momentary sorrow; at five o'clock, follies of all sorts. Many of us, to create a diversion, gave ourselves up to joy. We took advantage of the talents of some of the officers on board, dressed ourselves up in absurd disguises, and danced, sang, and drank. The ship looked like a booth at a fair. Such is the French character, which can in an instant convert a horrible prison into a place of pleasure.

(*March 10th.*) For several days we had been short of provisions. We saw a vessel which appeared to be that of our caterer. Our joy was in proportion to our wants, but what was our surprise, and what horror we felt, on finding that the boat was loaded with some fifty naked, gaunt corpses. It was a boat that came, for the first time, to take the dead from the hulks. It visited the neighbouring vessel, and the boatman, a modern Charon, asked if we could increase his load. Every day this boat made its round, and never took away less than 20 to 40 bodies, most of them with a cord round the neck and towed behind the boat. That was the spectacle that was offered us every morning.

A hospital was opened in March, and the patients there were looked after by French doctors, but admission to this establishment was not easy. Patients were robbed, left for hours on the shore exposed to the broiling sun, insulted and assaulted. Once a week, and sometimes oftener, crowds of the townspeople used to go and demand that the patients should be given to them to be put to death. They died fast enough without that—3,000 in three months at the hospital, and as many more on the hulks. Those who had received extreme unction were buried in the hospital cemetery; the bodies of the others were put in a hole dug in the sand at low water, and were washed out by the next tide. The corpses were dragged down to the beach, and the Spanish soldiers prodded them with their bayonets as they passed, but the chaplain of a Swiss regiment complained, and the practice was stopped. After that, the soldiers contented themselves with spitting on the corpses.

Three hundred officers and 200 men were taken from the "Old Castille" to be transported. They were selected by lot from all regiments represented on board, and, luckily for François, the 5th Legion drew No. 61, so the draft was made up before his regiment was reached. After the departure of this draft, provisions and water were scarcer then ever, but, in April, a new caterer was appointed who was "deaf to the insults of the Spaniards," and so provisions came more regularly, and the number of invalids decreased. On April 21st, François learned, from some fresh prisoners who had been brought on board, that the Portuguese had also revolted, and were even more barbarous than the Spaniards, and that Napoleon was in command of the army, and had completely beaten the English in Estramadura, Galicia, and on the Portuguese frontier; but that there was much talk of a war with the Emperor of Germany and that an army corps destined for Spain had been recalled and sent to Germany.

In June, several officers tried to escape from Cadiz by swimming, with the intention of getting across to Tangier, but some of them were recaptured, put in irons for a week, deprived of their pay, and treated like private soldiers. Although the prisoners received no correspondence, they heard of Napoleon's entrance into Vienna on May 12th, and of some successes in the Peninsula. "The silence of the Spaniards told us more than their gazettes."

On August 25th, more officers tried to escape, were caught, and treated as already described, but François and the others on board voluntarily gave up a portion of their pay. Three days later, more prisoners were brought in; they had been captured at Talavera, where the Spaniards and the English were beaten, but the French also suffered heavily.

(*September 6th.*) Some boats came, and all the sub-lieutenants were ordered into them, and were taken on board a hulk called the *Polonia*, a merchant vessel belonging to the India Company. On arriving there, they found on board a colonel, an *aide-de-camp* of General Mondragon (who had charge of the prisoners) a commissary, and a guard of 50 men. The French were drawn up in line, and the colonel, who spoke French, pulled out of his pocket a placard that he said was an order from his government, in reply to a report from General Mondragon concerning the attempted escapes of many of the officers.

This order said, that to remove the means of flight and attempts at bribery, they were going to take away all the money and jewels the officers possessed, with the exception of 25 *francs* for each man. The prisoners were then stripped and searched in the most rigorous and indecent manner. The lieutenants were then fetched and searched in the same way. They took from François twelve *napoleons* which he had managed to save by the most rigid economy, by living only on his pay. The same operation was performed on the captains.

(*September 7th.*) The same Spanish officers came on board the "Old Castille" to examine the superior officers. A *chef de bataillon* asked the Spanish colonel the meaning of this search, and, on being informed, he pulled out his watch, crushed it under his heel, and then threw it into the sea;—an example which was followed by all the other brave fellows. After threatening to report their conduct to General Mondragon, the search began, but was conducted with more delicacy and decency. Perhaps, they were satisfied with the booty taken from the subaltern officers, who had lost not only their money, but also part of their effects, which the Spanish soldiers stole as well as our provisions.

(*September 13th.*) Four officers of the 4th Legion tried to escape, with the help of a Spanish peasant, to whom they had promised a sum of money. But the peasant did not come to the place appointed, and they were obliged to write to the captain of a Spanish frigate, who sent and fetched them and put them in a cell, heavily ironed.

(*September 15th.*) A captain, having first well primed himself with wine—less by custom than to give himself the courage to execute his design—threw himself into the sea, but, as he was on the point of drowning, he was saved, and taken to the hospital. Two days previously, a sub-lieutenant of *chasseurs* tried the same means, and was sent to the hospital, but, five days later, was taken to the hulk where the private soldiers were confined, and deprived of his pay.

(*November 11th.*) The English Ambassador, Wellesley, left for England. He was dissatisfied because the Spaniards had refused to make over to him Cadiz, Ferrol, Ceuta in Africa, and Porto Rico and Havanna in America. We heard that the English Army, under the command of 'my lord Moor,' (*sic*) had retreated into Portugal.

(*November 20th.*) Several officers escaped. An adjutant-major of the 5th Legion was arrested at Cadiz, locked up for nine days, put in irons for ten days, and then taken to the hulk for the private soldiers.

(*November 21st.*) The *Gazette* of the 17th says that the English took the island of Walcheren on September 15th, but that, out of 15,000 men, 10,000 are sick, and the island is not of sufficient importance to justify such a sacrifice. The same *Gazette* says also that Brigadier-General Monet, who commanded Flushing, having surrendered after a few days' siege, the emperor has had him arrested, and he will be tried by court-martial, on the ground that he must be either a coward or a traitor to his country.

# CHAPTER 13

# 1810

(*February*). The frequent desertions of prisoners from the hulks caused active measures to be taken to put a stop to these attempts. Putting the men in irons, and cutting off their rations were no good. The offence, our enemies declared, deserved death, but, out of kindness, this exemplary nation had hitherto contented itself with trying mild measures, under the impression that they would suffice to put an end to this longing for liberty. But now, orders were given to fire on prisoners, no matter of what grade, the moment they jumped into the sea, and any soldier or sailor who was captured trying to escape should receive six strokes with a birch rod, and subsequent attempts would receive more severe punishment, and even death.

An officer who deserted would be put in irons for six months, and receive a private soldier's rations; but a repetition of the offence would entail the penalties above-mentioned. The officer commanding the guard was instructed to enforce the regulations, which were to be posted up on all the hulks.

This did not put a stop to the escapes, for the prisoners learned that these severe measures were caused by the near approach of the French Army. This was further confirmed by the fact that English sailors towed all the hulks into the roads, where they were surrounded by English vessels. The English also blew up Fort St. Catherine, which defended the entrance to the roads, presumably to prevent its falling into the hands of the French, but François does not explain. The caterer announced that in future he would come round every two days, and could not give any more credit, as there was a fortnight already due to him. The fact was that the officers had not received their allowance all that time, and as they had no money they could not procure food. They wrote to the Spanish authorities to complain, but received no answer.

Several more forts were blown up by the English, Cadiz was in consternation and confusion, and the French soldiers "had nothing to eat for two days."

Under the date of February 2nd, François reports:

The poor wretches on board the *Rouffine*, which was moored near us, were dying of hunger; they obtained some help from us by means of a rope passed from one ship to another, but the little aid we could give was quite insufficient for 600 men.

At 4 o'clock in the afternoon, an English officer, who was passing in a boat near our ship, was hailed, and consented to take a letter to Vice-Admiral Lord Gervas (Jervis). The letter concerned our condition and that of the soldiers.

At six in the evening some water was brought, and the master of the boat told us that seven or eight thousand men of the Spanish troops, commanded by the Duke of Albuquerque, had entered the town, and the bread intended for the prisoners had been distributed to the soldiers. This makes three days that we have received no food.

(*February 3rd.*) This morning three dogs that we had on board were killed and eaten.

About 9 o'clock, a sailor jumped into the sea and swam towards the English admiral's vessel. Everybody watched him. A boat put off from a Spanish gunboat and rowed after him, but the English sailors also jumped into a boat, picked up the poor fellow right under the noses of the Spaniards and took him on board their ship, and we could see them give him food and clothes. They made him drink, and he handed them letters to the admiral. The deck was full of Englishmen, who offered him provisions. He left on board the Spanish boat, and divided amongst his comrades the biscuits the English had given him.

At seven o'clock in the evening, a sailor swam to our vessel, and stated that forty of his comrades, driven by hunger, had started to swim to the English admiral's vessel. The sailor also said they had eight negroes on board their ship, and the next day they were going to kill and eat them!

(*February 4th.*) When the sergeant came round to receive the

131

daily reports, the sailors on board our ship seized his boat, and went on board the English admiral's vessel. Major Degromaty explained our situation, and stated that we had been without food for five days, and were on the point of eating each other. The admiral showed the letters to Venegas, the Governor of Cadiz, who said it was not true the prisoners were without food.

At four p.m. the boat that brought round the provisions visited all the hulks, but we only received one day's provisions.

Provisions also came the next day, the Spaniards perhaps being rather frightened, for the French were already at Xérès, only a few miles inland, and outposts had pushed forward to Santa Maria. Very soon the bivouac fires could be seen at night, and the cannon of the English war vessels began to speak. On February 11th, François saw several dead bodies, which he presumed were those of French sailors who had tried to swim ashore. These attempted escapes became more frequent now the French were in sight, and the Spaniards announced that any officer caught escaping would have six months' imprisonment, and a private soldier the same, with the addition of six strokes with a gun-strap. In spite of this, 20 officers, 5 surgeons, 2 sergeants, and 8 soldiers or sailors, seized the boat that brought fresh water, and made their escape in it on February 22nd. The others had to pay for it, however, and were informed they would be kept on half-rations till the value of the stolen boat had been made up, and for a month the prisoners were fed on bread and potatoes.

François hated the English so cordially that he rarely has a good word for "those leopards," but he is more than once obliged to bear testimony to their courage, and their kindness to the prisoners, as the following extracts will show:—

(*March 5th.*) A strong south-west wind, with heavy rain, made this a terrible day. At half-past one, our bowsprit broke, and at two o'clock the main mast also went, giving a violent shock to the vessel, but no one was injured. The English sent an officer on board to see if anyone was hurt. We were pleased to see what a difference there was between our two enemies. The storm continued for several days, and several ships, including an English brig, were wrecked, but the crew saved.

(*March 8th.*) Last night was as bad as the preceding one. At nine in the morning we saw lots of our men on the beach, by the Trocadero and Fort Réal. About ten o'clock, the English brought on board three casks of water, and four hundredweight of biscuits with a cask of wine; also cocoa and raw sugar for the sick. They took the same to the other hulks, as well as to the one which served as the hospital. It said that the Spanish admiral has left the work of looking after us to the English. During the tempest, we saw the English brave every danger to help the shipwrecked. Those cowards of Spaniards stayed on their vessels, and never tried to help their allies.

(*March 10th.*) Yesterday our new caterer brought us provisions. That was the seventh day we had been without any, except what the English gave us on the 8th. Several officers returned on board from the hospital ship. They say that the sick are well cared for during the last few days, thanks to the English.

(*March 11th.*) The Spanish Government has capped all the repeated vexations it has made us suffer for nearly two years, by an order which says, that if a prisoner escapes, two others, chosen by lot from those remaining, shall be hanged. Instead of trembling at seeing themselves surrounded on all sides by our troops, they are more insolent than they have ever been. The English tell us that when they brought us food on the 8th, they found more than twenty men had died of hunger, and that on the *Terrible*, where there are about 1,200 men, 400 are ill from the same cause, and from want of water.

The French officers drew up a reply to the astounding order just mentioned. They said they had been obliged to read it several times before they could persuade themselves that it was possible that a nation calling itself civilized should use such barbarous threats. Such a measure as that threatened was never practised, even by savage nations. The conclusion of this temperately-worded reproof—which is too long to give *in extenso*—is not devoid of dignity.

You little understand the character of our nation. You have not foreseen that such degrading measures, so far from diminishing in us the longing to escape from you, must, on the contrary, add to the desire we have to rejoin our brothers-in-arms a still more powerful incentive to get away from a country where such unheard of cruelties are practised. You wish to reduce us to despair, but we all swear that whatever fate may be in store for us, we will bear it with the dignity worthy of the great nation to which we have the honour to belong. We prefer death to ignominy, and can submit to it, when the time comes, in a manner to leave behind us an example of courage and coolness, whilst you will leave one of injustice and cruelty.

What the Spaniards thought of this snub is not stated, but matters appear to have gone on much the same as previously. François heard from an English officer, on April 9th, that twenty men had that day made their escape from the hospital-ship; but, two days later, he was informed that only eight had tried to escape—four officers, two privates, and two civilians—and had been recaptured and the six soldiers shot. A little war news is mixed with the old story of privations and escapes. On April 21st the French took the fort of Montagoido, although it was gallantly defended by an English garrison. After the French took possession, there was an artillery duel between the fort and the ships, and as the Spanish gunboats took up a position behind the hulks, some of the prisoners were wounded by the French fire. Another hardship was that, as the coast was in the possession of the French, the prisoners received no fresh water and had to cook their provisions in sea-water.

With their countrymen within gunshot of them, it is not a matter for surprise that many plots to. break prison were organised amongst the captives, but they were all discovered; information being given by "false brethren,"—amongst others Major Morla of the 4th Legion, who had his wife with him, and 30,000 *francs* he wished to save. François says bitterly:

It is to him that we owe ten months more captivity.

François does not seem to have been in any of these plots, or at least he makes no mention of any share in them. Though brave as a lion, he was eminently practical, and it may be that all the plans seemed to him too quixotic to succeed. But when a plan which promised some hope of success was mooted, he went into it heart and soul. His account of the escape and his subsequent adventures, is one of the most dramatic episodes in his career.

(*May 13th.*) Naval Lieutenant Mosseau proposed that we should try to make our escape. There were seventeen of us in the plot. For that purpose we met in a cabin in the keel, and I brought down some bottles of wine. Lieutenant Mosseau told us to be prepared on the first sign from him, and to be always armed with our daggers, because he hoped that the weather would soon prove favourable to our plans, and the wind that he knew was coming would serve us.

As I was steward on board, I had been able to obtain from our caterer, a saw, an axe, and two files. With these tools, four of our sailors had built, in the keel, a little skiff, and made two oars for it: with the files, we made fifteen daggers out of iron hoops. These weapons were to serve us to attack our guards at night, disarm them, and make them go below.

Two non-commissioned officers—one of the 9th Cuirassiers, and the other of the Paris Guard—were entrusted with the axe and the saw, and they were to cut and saw the cables, under the direction of an officer. The duty of the others was to prevent the guards doing any harm, to take their weapons, and to fire on any soldiers or sailors who tried to approach the vessel. One of the four Spanish sergeants, who commanded the guard, was in the plot. The guard consisted of fifty men and four sergeants.

(*May 15th.*) The 14th we had no provisions and no water.

On the 15th, we met together at a sign from our old sea-wolf, the brave Lieutenant Mousseau. As usual, we went down into the keel, where we found already assembled the four sailors and *chef d'escadron*, Fressard, of the 14th Dragoons, who were, as soon as the cables were cut, to get into the skiff and try to reach land; in order to inform Marshal Victor and General Leval, whose division was at the Trocadero, of our escape, and ask them for assistance and support. Lieutenant Mousseau and Fressard gave each man his instructions and appointed him his proper post, and the Lieutenant, who was sixty-three years old, and well acquainted with the sea and winds, said, 'If this wind continues, be all ready for nightfall.' We had ropes all ready to work the rudder, and some sacks and blankets sewn together to serve as a sail. The rest of the day we passed in drinking and singing. I gave wine and brandy to all who wanted either, the day being that on which we were to try to recover our liberty, or perish.

All Europe knows that through the shameful violation of the terms of surrender of General Dupont's division, thousands of men died of want at Cabrera and on the hulks in England, or those which were moored in the roadstead of Cadiz. Prisoners who had languished for seventeen months in the most horrible captivity, recovered their liberty through a bold and difficult enterprise, as I am about to tell you.

Today, about eight o'clock in the evening, the wind being propitious and keeping in the south-east, was the moment when seventeen brave fellows saved their comrades.

Nine officers—I was of the number—each with a dagger hidden under his rags, went into the guardroom on the bridge, and said to the Spanish soldiers, 'If you make the least resistance, or utter a single word, you are dead men!' The poor devils, who were still sleepy, threw themselves at our feet. They were disarmed, and sent below, with two officers to guard them. Meantime, the cables were being cut. But the strokes of the axe woke up the officers who were sleeping near by, and who, not being in the secret, cried: 'We are lost!' They all got up, and wanted to know who were the originators of the plot.

The two non-commissioned officers who were cutting the. cables, dropped the saw and axe, and slipped away amongst the groups of prisoners. Taking advantage of the confusion, the officer who had been appointed to command them, seized the tools, and finished cutting the cables, whilst, from the bridge, we fired upon all the boats which tried to approach the vessel. Then, seeing that the deed was done, some of the others who were not in the plot, set to work to defend the vessel.

The vessel rolled from right to left, and almost bumped against the twenty-six gun galleon which guarded the hulks. The Spanish sergeant, who was in the plot, asked the captain of the galleon for help, saying: 'Sir, our cables have parted, send assistance on board.' Thereupon, boats left the galleon and other vessels, but, when they were close to us, we fired on them, and they pulled back and informed their officers that we had revolted. Several broadsides of grape were fired at us, which killed several officers, amongst others, brave Lieutenant Mousseau, whose body we threw into the sea along with the others, in order that the timid ones should not know of their death.

During the tumult, Fressard and his four sailors made the greatest possible efforts to bring their frail skiff to land, and, in spite of the state of the sea, reached the shore, and informed the generals of our escape. They immediately sent to our assistance, and some of Marshal Victor's forces, and Leval's division, snatched up their arms, and marched to the shore.

Meanwhile, armed with ten muskets, we fired at all the vessels that came near us, and many of the superior officers—amongst others Colonel Buquet, and Major Beaufranchet of the artillery, rigged up chains and fetched cannon balls, which they placed near the bulwarks to defend ourselves in case we were boarded by the English or Spanish. Many of the prisoners wept, uttered curses, and tried to find the man who had started the undertaking to sacrifice him to their vengeance, but could not succeed owing to the confusion which reigned on board. To give themselves courage, several of them went down to the steward's room, which I had left, got drunk, and lost their lives in consequence.

Towards one o'clock in the morning our ammunition was exhausted, so we went between decks, and persuaded our comrades, who had remained neutral until now, to defend themselves. They were to throw cannon balls from the bulwarks on the heads of any who might try to prevent us reaching the shore, to which the rising tide and the wind were driving us. At that moment, a galley with about sixty armed Englishmen on board, approached the vessel's side. The defenders stationed on the bulwarks were frightened. Then I and several comrades seized cannon balls and threw them on the heads of the English soldiers and sailors. Others did the same, and in an instant many were killed and others wounded. The officer who commanded them said he would withdraw and leave us alone.

During this time, the hulk continued to drift with the rising tide, but sometimes in the contrary direction, when the wind dropped, and knocked right and left all the vessels that came in the road. At last, about three in the morning, the hulk touched ground in some nineteen feet of water. Then those who knew how to swim, jumped into the sea. Those who did not know, but to whom wine had given courage, followed their example; many were drowned. However, 300 were saved.

(*May 16th.*) Our vessel having grounded in about nineteen feet of water at high tide, three English bomb-ketches came and placed themselves between us and the land, and cannonaded us, with the help of the Pontules Fort. It was not till about eight in the morning that the light artillery of Leval's division forced these bomb-ketches to make off; and, when the tide was low, those swimmers who had remained on board, jumped into the sea and reached land, which was about three hundred fathoms away.

Besides Fort Pontules and the other forts, more than twenty armed vessels were behind our hulk, and engaged in blazing at us. I counted as many as eleven shells in the air at the same time, all directed on our prison, and this fire continued from seven in the morning till half-past four in the afternoon. Some of the officers were killed or wounded.

About nine o'clock at night, the vessel had been lightened of nearly 500 soldiers of all ranks. I heard that six of the officers who were in the plot had been killed, and two wounded.

Towards ten o'clock, we saw gallop up two boats, brought in waggons from the Trocadero; they were launched, and rowed by sailors of the guard, who, in spite of the rolling fire of the enemy, reached our vessel. Then, hope and joy appeared on every face. We made arrangements to embark. First, we put in the boats the women and children, the wounded, and the elder men. Then the rest disembarked, under the active direction of Generals Leval and Daboville, and this continued until 4.30 a.m., under the fire of more than 150 guns. Some eleven hundred soldiers of all ranks were more than eight hours in the water, under the enemy's fire. At last, about half-past four, everybody was rescued.

I, with twelve of my comrades, jumped into the sea at that hour, but we did not reach land till 5.30, after fighting against the waves of a rough sea. Two *carabineers* of the 16th Light Infantry, named Mirebeau and Berger, saved me by swimming out to meet me and led me, half-dead, to Fort Napoleon, where the surgeons restored me to life.

We twelve jumped into the sea, without waiting our turn, to escape the fire, which, for the third time, had broken out on board, and we could not succeed in putting it out. I had tied my clothes, and some papers, on my head, but they were all soon wet through. I was very hot, and very weak. Just as I was reaching land, a wave threw me back thirty paces, and—as I said above—it was to the two brave carabineers who faced death— perhaps for the hundredth time that day— that I owe my life.

When I was out of danger, one of the carabineers lent me his cloak, and I went to the town of Ponti-Real, where I was received by the bandmaster of the 16th Light Infantry, who gave me a shabby great coat; an officer of the same regiment gave me a pair of cotton trousers and a pair of shoes, and one of the soldiers contributed a grey cloth cap. I lodged with the bandmaster, who had with him all the bandsmen, and they all showed me every attention.

I glory in being one of the chief actors in this escape. The certificate, which I have, proves it. It was given me at Seville by the superior officers who came, safe and sound, out of this perilous enterprise.

On the whole, more than 900 officers, and about 280 non-commissioned officers and soldiers were saved from the hulk; 127 prisoners were killed.

The sergeant and the Spanish soldiers, to whom we partly owed our escape, received from Marshal Victor passports enabling them to return home.

I forgot to mention that, at the moment when I jumped into the sea, a bomb fell on deck, killed a major and three other officers, set fire to rags, sacks, and blankets, and the fire spread to the vessel which was burned down to the water's edge.

This evening we received orders to leave the following day for Santa Maria, in order to go from there to Seville, where Marshal Soult was to hold a review.

(*May 17th.*) After having lunched with the bandmaster and several other officers, my host gave me six *francs*, a musket, and a packet of cartridges. I thanked him, and hoped to have the pleasure of meeting him again. Along with several other officers, who were nearly as elegant as I was myself, I went to Santa Maria, where we were to be quartered. The inhabitants stood at their doors and watched us, but said nothing.

My quarters were at the house of a rich proprietor, in a little street to the right, at the entrance to the main street opposite the port.

It might have been about eight o'clock in the evening when I arrived within fifty paces of my appointed lodgings. I asked a citizen to inform me where it was. He pointed out the house to me, and my host, who was standing at the door. I asked him,

'Are you Señor? ———?'

'No,' he replied, 'it's lower down.'

I went to the house he showed me, and they told me there I was wrong, and the house I wanted was the one I had just left. I went back and knocked, but there was no reply. I banged loudly with the butt-end of my gun; I was sure there were people in the house, for, in passing, I had seen my host and a young woman at the window.

An hour passed without any success. I went to the *corregidor*, who sent an *alguazil*, with whom I returned to the house. My conductor knocked, said who he was, and the door was opened. The master of the house said to the *alguazil*, 'What! have you brought back that brigand?'

'Yes,' replied the other, 'by order of the *corregidor*,' and with that he went away.

My host left me nearly an hour without a light, and would take no notice of my complaints. My position was getting intolerable. My musket was loaded, so I fixed my bayonet, and then knocked at the two doors, which, by groping round, I found were in the room. I was dying of hunger and uneasiness. After a good deal of noise on my part, I heard in the darkness the voice of the man threatening me. I replied to his threats. Soon afterwards he opened a door, and appeared holding a light in one hand and a mallet in the other. He continued his threats, promising to knock me on the head if I would not keep quiet. I asked for a light, and something to eat and drink. He replied that he had nothing to give to a brigand, and tried to leave. I prevented him, threatening him with my weapon, and as he raised his stick I plunged my bayonet into his side. He fell without a word, and dropped his candlestick and mallet. Luckily, the candle was not extinguished.

At this moment the man's daughter and a servant girl came. The first-named was at least thirty years old. The two women were astounded at first, but then tried to run away. I stopped them, threatening them in my bad Spanish. The daughter threw herself on her father, weeping. I succeeded in compelling the servant to give me the key I had demanded.

I left the daughter and the servant to look after the old scoundrel, and, provided with another light, I searched every corner of the house, and being sure that no one could leave without

140

my knowledge, I insisted on having something to eat and drink. I let the two women weep, and refreshed myself; then, about one o'clock in the morning, I left the house, with the consolation, at least, that my host would never threaten another Frenchman.

My situation was far from being pleasant. I carried away the key of this inhospitable house, and when I reached the port I threw it into the sea.

About three o'clock I rejoined some of the officers, with whom I journeyed to San Lucar, thinking that my liberty had begun sadly, but glad to have revenged myself.

I did not relate my adventure to my comrades till I got to Madrid, and they were surprised at the patience I had shown under the circumstances. The 20th I was at Seville.

The late prisoners were reviewed by Marshal Soult, who gave them each some clothes and 200 *francs*. François, as one of the principal surviving actors in the drama, was recommended for promotion and reward, and Soult also recommended the Spanish sergeant, Manuel, who had taken no small part in the plot, to King Joseph (Bonaparte) for promotion and a decoration.

François and the other ex-prisoners were formed into a company of scouts. They had no uniform, and looked like very ragged civilians, he says.:

> The Spaniards thought us worse brigands than themselves, and when they knew that we had broken out of a Spanish prison, they did not dare to attack us. In fact, we had only one brush with the enemy all the way from Seville to Madrid.

When "he had the honour to kill a Spaniard, who wore a thick red cloth cloak," which François found very useful on the journey.

At Madrid, they were reviewed by King Joseph, who wished to know if any of them would enter his bodyguard. Only seven accepted the offer, and one of these was the Spanish sergeant before mentioned, who was made lieutenant. The king gave all the ex-prisoners 100 *francs* a-piece—which was all he could afford—and the leaders of the plot (including François) 300 *francs* each in addition.

Most of the officers wished to rejoin their old regiments, and their request was granted. The headquarters of the 5th Legion were at Vendôme at that time, so François had an opportunity to revisit France. He got to Bayonne on July 26th, but there he was taken ill with a fever, the result of his cold bath on the occasion of the escape. Here he also learned that the recommendation for promotion to a captaincy had not been confirmed by the authorities in Paris, and he must remain a lieutenant for the present; whereupon he remarks—for the third or fourth time—"I consoled myself, never having had an ambition to become a Marshal of the Empire."

Recovering from the chill, François moved to Bordeaux, where he had a sharp attack of congestion of the lungs. His hostess, Mme. Latapie, had a pretty daughter, and the two ladies nursed him through his illness, which lasted nearly a fortnight. When he was getting well, his bedroom was often full of visitors, some of whom wished to hear the story of the escape from the Spanish hulks, whilst others came to gaze on the beautiful Mlle. Latapie.

On September 3rd, he was well enough to leave. Neither his hostess nor the doctor would accept any payment; both saying they were happy to have been of service to a brave man. François wept, and gave forty francs to the servants. When he rejoined his regiment, he was immediately given a furlough, on full pay, to go and see his relatives in Paris. He had twenty-two months' half-pay, four months' whole pay, which, with 400 *francs* he had received from King Joseph, made 1,600 *francs* in his pocket when he entered Paris.

He was ordered to Hamburg on October 12th, but obtained from the Minister of War a prolongation of his leave of absence, and did not start till November 25th.

CHAPTER 14

# 1811—1812

The year 1811 was the only uneventful year in François' career. The first nine months he was in garrison at Lubeck, and the last three at Hamburg. His stay at the latter place was very agreeable, in spite of six or eight hours' drilling a day, for, he says, "the inhabitants like us very much, especially the women, who are most amiable, generally pretty, and not at all 'cruel,' no matter what may be their rank or condition."

In January, 1812, there were rumours of war with Russia. The regiment left Hamburg February 28th, and, on March 17th, François received the long-expected promotion, being made a captain "by "Imperial decree."

During the next two months the regiment marched about and visited various towns and villages, but no incident of interest is recorded. In May, François and his company camped at the village of Swarasin—which appears to be somewhere near the left bank of the Vistula. There he lodged:

> ... at the *château* of Baron Werguikosky, proprietor of seventeen villages, having two sons, a daughter, and a niece, all speaking French. I had plenty of amusement in this house in the way of society, hunting parties, love affairs, etc.
> The girls—the daughter of the house and her cousin—were both named Justine; one of them who was twenty years old and rather pretty, afterwards grew quite sociable and I became her little *malosky*[1] that is to say her little—in short I was happy, etc.

The baron kept a good table, which, perhaps, was the reason why

---

1. Presumably the Hungarian word *malacozni* = *cochonner*.

General Bonamy, commanding the regiment, came to lodge there—but François was "the firstcomer, and always stood well with all the family." One day the regiment assembled to receive a new standard which the emperor had sent, and the ceremony was followed by a review and evolutions. "Our host and his sons and the Justines brought provisions, by which many of my comrades profited. My Justine had not forgotten her *malosky*."

Four days later he had to tear himself away from these comfortable quarters. The baron gave him a week's provisions, and offered to accompany him as far as Dirschau. "My" Justine was of the party, and when she left she gave him a ring containing her hair, and a locket with her portrait in ivory, painted by herself.

The army advanced towards Russia, and François notes, with some pride, that he was the first man across the Niemen. A few days later the Russians evacuated Wilna, after having set fire to immense stores of provisions, provender, and clothes. There was very little fighting. A Russian division was supposed to be advancing from Turkey, and forces were sent to oppose it, under the King of Westphalia (Jerome Bonaparte), but "he was not very clever and made nothing but blunders, so he was recalled by the Emperor and sent back to his kingdom." The French soldiers often came across proclamations written in French, and signed by the Emperor of Russia and General "Barklay" (*i.e.* Barclay de Tolly) promising to any French soldier who would desert, a sum of money and a safe refuge—"in Siberia probably," François sarcastically remarks. There were also other proclamations addressed to the Russians, requesting the nobles and priests to persuade the serfs that their religion was threatened, and the Emperor of the French intended to make them worship idols. François says:

> These crude absurdities of the sovereign produced on his half-savage people the same effect as the sacred name of Liberty would upon us.

It was not till nearly the end of July that any serious fighting took place. At Vitebsk, two companies of the 9th crossed the Dwina, and for more than an hour sustained an unequal combat against large bodies of Russian cavalry. The battle was watched from the other side of the river by nearly the whole French Army, who were powerless to render assistance. Napoleon asked what regiment it was.

"The 9th," was the reply, "and more than three-quarters of them are Paris lads."

"Tell them," said the emperor, "that they are brave fellows, and all deserve to be decorated."

Everything seemed to presage a pitched battle, as soon as the main body of the French should cross the river, but the Russians withdrew in the night. The French started in pursuit, but were recalled to Vitebsk, where Napoleon encamped, and where they remained ten days. The hardships the troops had hitherto undergone were only those usual to other campaigns, but worse treats were in store, as François proceeds to relate.

(*August 7th.*) Today the army received orders to hold itself in readiness to march, and to procure provisions for fifteen days, an extremely difficult matter, as I shall show. In the first place, the bulk of the army was stationed and encamped in the environs of Vitebsk, where the Guards were with the First Corps in the front of the town; the bulk of the army, I say, was in a state of penury, which was ill-calculated to restore the soldiers after the fatigue and privations of all sorts, endured during a march of thirty-eight days, and a distance of eighty leagues from the banks of the Niemen. It occupied a district devastated by the Russians, who, faithful to their system, had burned villages and stores, and destroyed the crops. Nearly every corps was compelled to live by its own means, by making excursions which were contrary to discipline, and completed the ruin of the inhabitants. For the last week we had been in the same situation, having received no rations and having nothing to live on but the proceeds of the marauding expeditions of the soldiers, who strayed a long distance from the flanks of the army; and many of whom were captured by the Cossacks or murdered by the inhabitants.

For my part I never wanted for anything. My soldiers used the rights which had been granted them, and I often had from five to nine waggons of provisions following me, until we reached the environs of Maloski, fourteen or fifteen leagues from Moscow.

In spite of the emperor's efforts to procure us provisions, his orders were only executed on paper. He was deceived by the accounts which the military purveyors gave him. Those brigands made him believe that the army had received food and was provisioned for fifteen days. It was on the strength of their

145

reports that he ordered the march on Smolensk.

At this time the army was much diminished, not only by marches and battles, but by dysentery, by which many of the soldiers were attacked.

This disease was caused by the scarcity of bread, which obliged the soldiers to live chiefly on meat, which they could get easily enough. The stagnant marsh water we drank also contributed to spread the disease. Few of the men, or even the generals, were exempt from it. The hospitals were full of sick, who had but little medical aid, for the ambulances and the medicines remained in the rear.

The Russians continued to retreat, and so prevented the French from offering Napoleon a victory as a birthday present, but two days later (August 17), they made a determined stand at Smolensk. Their artillery fire was very hot, and in less than half-an-hour two standard-bearers were killed in François' division, one having his head knocked clean off by a cannon ball. A good deal of mischief was also done by a kind of shell with three holes, and filled with an "inflammable combustible." François relates a plucky action he performed with one of these shells.

> About two o'clock in the afternoon, one of these shells fell in front of a squad, near Col. Buquet, Major Hervé, and Commandant Pléche. I sprang forward and seized this shell, which was vomiting flames out of all three orifices; my hands and hair were burned, but I was fortunately able to throw it into a well which was a little distance behind my company. My commanding officers, and the men, who witnessed this bold act, cried: 'Bravo!' and 'Live Captain François!'
>
> Had it not been for my presence of mind, two ammunition chests which were to my left, in the space between the battalions, might have blown up, and caused a lot of damage to the left of the first battalion and the right of the second. Col. Buquet, who liked me, made a report, very much in my favour, to the emperor; but, as usual, I was forgotten, and had no reward except my own satisfaction, and the esteem of my commanding officers and my comrades.

The Russians, finding that the town was on the point of being taken, set fire to it and retreated. It was said that Barclay de Tolly had orders to defend Smolensk at all cost, because a Russian proverb said,

"*When Smolensk is taken the czar will be dethrone*d." Another heavy defeat was inflicted on the Russians at Valatina, which caused Napoleon to say, "With such troops one could go to the end of the world." François was not so hopeful, as we see from the entry in his diary under date of August 22nd.

In his retreat the enemy destroyed the bridges, the villages, and the magazines. We were wholly without resources, the country we passed through being nothing but a vast desert covered with wood, lakes, and sand. Not a single inhabitant remained in his hut, and the dearth of provisions was felt more and more. The Russians did not leave a single vehicle behind them. We did not see even a trace of their bivouacs.

Another obstinate stand was made at Chewarino, and after a series of hard fights, the Russians retreated in disorder, losing seven guns, but the French had more than a thousand killed and wounded. François records that, at two in the morning, the Emperor visited the outposts, reviewed several regiments, and asked the colonel of the 61st what had become of one of his battalions. "Sire," replied the colonel, "it is in the redoubt of Chewarino!" The emperor said nothing, but passed on.

There was a sharp interchange of musketry fire the whole of the next day, and François was wounded. He writes:

During the day the regiment lost 300 men, of whom 67 were killed. I was amongst the number of the wounded, a ball having hit me in the left leg. I received this wound about eight o'clock in the evening, and in spite of the pain and loss of blood, I remained at my post, firing with "my company, and did not return to the regiment till eleven, when the battalion was relieved. I had the roll called, and had twenty-three men missing, of whom sixteen were killed. Then I went to have my wound dressed by the surgeon-major, who put a probe in the hole the bullet had made and extracted the projectile. I limped back to my comrades, with whom I passed the rest of the night.

Fortune had other and worse calamities, but he had better tell his own interesting story and relate, in his own way, the gruesome episodes of that terrible retreat.

(*September 6th.*) This afternoon, whilst out with the skirmishers, I saw there was a good deal of excitement in the Russian lines. I learned afterwards that a proclamation had been read to the soldiers, and the image of St, Sergius had been carried by the priests through their lines. The saint, who was thus carried in the front of the army, is held in great veneration in Russia. Every soldier wears him round his neck. As for us, our only amulet was our emperor, in whom we had every confidence.

(*September 7th.*) Towards three o'clock in the morning the army was under arms. Although wounded, I was at my post, on the right of my company, the regiment being in order of battle. My colonel, and several of my comrades, said to me, 'Retire, go to the ambulance, or guard the colours.' I replied, 'My wound is nothing; I want to share your glory.' At half-past three, we began to move, to pass the ravine. On our march, we learned from the orders of the day that the Emperor was at the post he had occupied the previous evening, and that he had said to the marshals who had come to receive their orders, 'This cloudless sun is the sun of Austerlitz; the army accepts the omen.'

About half-past five, we of the 30th halted halfway up the ravine, and the following order of the day was read to us:—

Soldiers,
At last has come the battle you so much desired. Now victory depends upon you. It is needful for us; it will give you abundance, good winter quarters, and a speedy return to your country. Conduct yourselves as at Austerlitz, Friedland, Vitebsk, and Smolensk, that the most remote posterity may cite with pride your conduct this day, and that it may be said of you, "He was at that great battle under the walls of Moscow."

The army, accustomed to this energetic language, replied to this order by the cry of '*Vive l'Empereur!*' which was always uttered at the moment of combat as well as after the victory. . . .

General Morand, after having received orders from the viceroy to march on the great battery, transmitted this order to General Bonamy, who commanded the regiment. General Morand went down the line exhorting the soldiers to conquer. When he came to me, seeing I was wounded, he said, 'Captain, you cannot follow, retire, and guard the Eagle.' I said to him, 'General, the day has too many attractions for me to make me hesitate to share the glory that the regiment is about to gain.'

'I recognise you in that,' replied the general. He shook hands with me, and went down the line, whilst hundreds of balls and shells were passing over our heads.

The redoubt was captured, but the regiment lost nearly half its strength, and brave General Bonamy, wounded in fifteen places, remained a prisoner in the hands of the enemy. The attack on the large fort was still more bloody. François and some of his men got into the fort, and sabred the gunners; but overwhelmed by numbers, and getting no support he was obliged to retreat.

He writes:

I have seldom been in such a tussle against soldiers so bold and obstinate as the Russians. I was badly damaged; my shako and coat tails were shot away, and I was bruised all over. A ball which passed through my left leg, in addition to the one I had received the previous day, left me so feeble from want of blood that I could neither breathe nor move. When I recovered a little from my weakness, the soldiers led me to the ambulance, where, at that moment. General Morand, who had been hit on the chin, was having his wound dressed.

The general shook hands with me, and, when he had been attended to, made a sign to the surgeon to look after me. The doctor came to me, put his little finger in the bullet-hole, and with his *bistoury* made the customary cross-cut at each hole, put in a probe which passed through my leg between the two bones, and said, 'A lucky wound,' then he put on the first dressing, and told me to go to the army ambulance at Kologha, where there were thousands of wounded. The ambulance was at a convent. I was placed in a room where there were twenty-seven officers of my regiment, five of whom had undergone amputation; all lying on straw, and absolutely in want of everything. There were more than 10,000 wounded in this hospital. Eight or ten days after this battle, three-fourths of these poor fellows were dead from want of medical assistance and food.

The soldier who served as my orderly, and who had escaped the carnage, after having searched for me on the field of battle, learned that I was at the hospital. He came and joined me, and brought my horses. It was to him, as well as to several of my comrades in misfortune, that I owe my life, for he was very active in procuring provisions. I paid as much as 3 or 4 *francs* for an egg; 5 to 6 *francs* for a pound of meat; and 10 to 15 *francs* for three pounds of bread. The commanding officers, who had escaped unhurt, sent us the money.

In the evening some soldiers of my regiment, who had been only slightly wounded, came through the ward. One of my company said when he saw me, 'Oh, Captain, they said you were killed. I am glad to see you again; but why were you not satisfied with your first wound?' This soldier was a great help to me, as well as to my comrades. He told me that my lieutenant was killed, that my sub-lieutenant had the underpart of his left arm and a part of the thigh carried away by a cannon ball. My sergeant-major, three sergeants, six corporals, fifty-seven soldiers, and a drummer were killed; that there remained only five men in my company, and, in the regiment, about 300, and eleven officers, out of 4,100 who had been alive that morning. In the night, seven officers in my ward died!

By the 28th I had sufficiently recovered from my wounds, and although I could not walk without the aid of a crutch, I asked to leave, as a detachment was to start the next day for Moscow, under the command of Prince Poniatowski. It was composed of 700 men of all ranks.

I said farewell to my brothers-in-arms; my soldier had my horses ready, and, as I had lost my portmanteau, my preparations did not take long.

(*September 29th.*) I quitted my companions in misfortune, and left them the few provisions my soldier had procured, either by his own efforts or with my money. We passed Mojuisk and saw hundreds of wounded horses. I saw Russian soldiers, who had lost an arm or a leg, who had lived on what they found in the haversacks left on the field of battle. One man had his leg shattered, and hanging only by a few shreds. Half his body was in the belly of a dead horse, of which he was eating the inside, like a dog. He came out when we approached, and we gave him some food and water.

(*September 30th.*) We had to pass through a wood in which, we were assured, parties of Cossacks were hidden. The mounted men of our party, and some officers, formed the advance guard. I was of the number. Arrived at the entrance of the wood, a brigadier and four hussars who were in front, along with a captain, *aide-de-camp* to Prince Poniatowski, were attacked; three hussars

150

and the *aide-de-camp* were captured, and a hussar wounded. We, who were fifty or sixty paces in the rear, charged, but hundreds of Cossacks came out of the wood, fell upon us, and drove us back to the head of the column, which opened fire. The Cossacks came out so suddenly that they cut us off, and sabred a good many of us. Thanks to my horse, I passed through them, and reached the column without getting any harm, but my first wound re-opened, and I lost a lot of blood, and could neither walk nor sit on horseback. I was put in a waggon. We reached Moscow about eight in the evening.

Each soldier returned to his respective regiment. As for me, supported by two comrades, I went to the palace of the Prince of Galicia, where my regiment was. I was well received by my chiefs and comrades, and by the seven men who remained of my company. These latter showed their affection, and each of them made me a present, besides the provisions which they procured for me in abundance, as well as wine, sugar, and coffee. The presents consisted of twelve silver forks and spoons, a soup ladle, a sauce ladle, a cloak lined with ermine, and a roll of roubles, which was worth about 46,000 *francs*, and a good bed. As I shall relate hereafter, I lost everything in the retreat, as well as the horse which carried my fortune.

A troop of French comedians came, and gave us three performances per week.

(*October 1st to 5th.*) Our duties were done regularly, but the officers, like the soldiers, murmured at the long stay in Moscow. Provisions began to fail. To procure any it was necessary to have recourse to the soldiers of the Imperial Guard. They searched everywhere, and took away from the soldiers they met whatever they might have found. They had established at their quarters, and in the street opposite the gate of the Kremlin, a sort of fair, where could be found wine, spirits, coffee, and furs. Everything was sold very dear. Such conduct towards their brothers-in-arms might have led to serious results afterwards, if the greater number of the Guards had not fattened the Russian soil.

(*October 7th, 8th and 9th.*) My wounds were much better, and I began to go out without crutches. I had no pain at all.

(*October 10th.*) The First Army Corps received orders to prepare to be reviewed by the emperor. Today, I put one of my crutches

151

in the fire, in order to be able to go to this review. I was, for the sixth time, proposed for decoration and another reward. The next day Colonel Buquet reviewed the regiment. I was there.

Napoleon reviewed the troops the following day, promoted some twenty officers, gave some forty odd crosses, 'and a dotation to the worst *chef-de-bataillon* in the regiment, procured by force of importunity. He did not profit much by it, for he left his bones in the retreat.' Colonel Buquet was promoted to be general.

The emperor, passing in review those proposed for advancement or decoration, asked Colonel Buquet where I met my wound. He replied: 'At Chewarino, and he is one of our old Dromedaries of Egypt.' The emperor approached me, and said: ' What do you ask? ' My colonel did not give me time to reply, but cried, 'The Cross!' 'Granted!' replied the emperor.

Having made so many campaigns, I was going to ask for a dotation, which would have been granted me, but my colonel, although he wished me well, did me a wrong under the circumstances. To crown my misfortunes, when the list of names of those decorated was sent back to the regiment, my name was omitted.

The letter announcing my nomination had been sent to the 13th Light Infantry, and I had a good deal of trouble to get it. A captain of that regiment was also named François; but he had not been recommended for a reward, and the letter was sent back to me. It will be seen that the fortune of war was not very favourable to me.

Snow began to fall heavily in the middle of October, and "this change of temperature was the cause of our misfortunes." The emperor believed the statements made to him, as to the rigour of the climate, to be exaggerated. The Russians regarded this sudden change as a sign of the protection of heaven.

François, though recovered of his wounds, "was not very agile "and obliged to walk with a crutch, being unable to mount a horse. The retreat began on October 19th, and the terrible difficulties of that calamitous march commenced almost the same day. The rearguard could not go a mile without having to face round and drive off the Cossacks; who "came within a hundred paces of us, and deafened us with their cries." At Maloszki—which the French had taken on September

7th—the houses were full of rotting corpses, both French and Russian. The wounded had been left to die of starvation. François saw the body of a French captain who had eaten his own arm to the bone!—and this was not a solitary instance.

(*November 1st*). Our situation seemed desperate. I will say little about myself, for many of my brothers-in-arms were equally miserable. Since my departure from Moscow, in spite of two bullets in the left leg, and various contusions not yet healed, I had still marched, with a boot on the right foot, and an old shoe on the left. I foresaw so many future evils that I felt no present pain. I never had my wounds dressed, I walked mechanically. My horses still carried some resources for me; they had to content themselves with the rotten leaves that they found under the snow, which began to cover the ground. Such was our situation at about thirty leagues from Moscow.

We began to want food, and those who had any hoarded it carefully. The soldier who formerly would have shared a bit of bread with his comrades, had become an egoist, and took pains to hide the little he possessed.

The horses, which were so useful to us for drawing the field-pieces, perished by thousands. It sometimes needed fifteen to drag a single gun. Every day we blew up ammunition chests, burned waggons, and broke guns. We of the rearguard were charged with these operations. Thus the army material disappeared in a fearful manner. As for us of the rearguard, our resources were exhausted.

We were passing through a country that we had ourselves ruined, and where we had fought by the light of burning houses. And hosts of Cossacks and armed peasants always followed us, passing through our ranks, and carrying off horses and chests, which, they thought, contained great riches. The soldiers had no means of preventing these disorders; for many of them were without arms, or not in a condition to use them.

Our foragers, that is to say those who had the strength to stray from the route to procure provisions, were often murdered by the inhabitants. Many went with the intention of getting killed, or rather of being taken prisoner; but the Cossacks would not have them, and the poor wretches retired into the woods, where they perished, not having the strength to rejoin the army.

The soldiers no longer sought to keep the gold and jewels which they had found in the smoking ruins of Moscow. When the weather became excessively cold, they tried to get furs, at no matter what price. As to provisions, they could not be procured.

Today, November 1st, after a march of about six leagues, the army halted after a slow and painful march, and bivouacked on a soil covered with snow, without straw, and unable to light a fire because the wind blew it out again.

The soldiers were impatient to see the sun rise, that they might start off again, without having taken the least nourishment to renew their strength. They were demoralized. They marched without looking before them either to the right or left, and knocked against generals or comrades without distinction. And these dull, apathetic men were those who, six months previously, had made all Europe tremble.

With a boot and an old shoe on my feet, a crutch in my hand, and dressed in a pink cloak lined with ermine and a hood over my head, I marched along with my faithful soldier and my two horses, which strayed at will without ever losing sight of us.

We ate the horses which died every day, and, as I was in the rearguard, we never found anything but the remnants of those; happy was he who could even get that.

Thus did I live till we reached Vilna, except for a pound of oat-bread, that a grenadier of the Guard sold me for a *napoleon*.

I ate horseflesh half-cooked, and was sprinkled with grease and blood from the chin to the knees. My face was begrimed, my beard long, and I looked like a Mayence ham, and, in spite of my condition, I often laughed at my own costume and those of my comrades. We marched with long icicles on every hair of our beards; the skins which half covered us, singed at the few bivouac fires we were able to light.

Dead horses were not sufficient for three-fourths of a starving army, and it was only the more courageous who could get that. Those who had neither knife, sabre, nor axe, and whose hands were frozen, could not eat. I have seen soldiers on their knees, and others seated near these carcases, and biting the flesh like hungry wolves. Thanks to my soldier, I was never short of horse-flesh, and every day I ate two to three pounds of this meat, without salt or bread.

For drink we had snow, melted in a saucepan, which my soldier carefully guarded, both for us and for the horses.

In spite of their demoralisation, the soldiers of all ranks had still the humanity to respect the horses of the wounded, although their owners could not use them; for in that region and at that season, a man on horseback, in spite of the warmest garments, would have been frozen in a few hours.

Such was the condition of the army in the early days of this month, and I leave to the imagination the situation of the unfortunate wounded, sick, and amputated, huddled pell-mell in carts, of which the horses died of fatigue and hunger. These poor wretches were abandoned at the bivouacs, and on the road, and died insane. Those who had the strength killed themselves. The companions and friends of these sad victims could give them no help, but turned away their eyes in order not to see them.

Though half the men were without weapons, they beat back a determined attack made by a strong Russian force, thanks chiefly to Marshal Ney. Colder weather came, and the temperature went down in a few days to—16° C. (= 3° F.), but the indomitable courage of François never deserted him.

He writes, under date of November 5th:

I, though never eating anything but half-cooked or thawed horse-flesh, felt nothing more of my wounds. My stomach was good, and I marched well, following the remnant of the regiment, which I never quitted. I shared with my comrades pieces of horse. I would not be discouraged, and used to say to my comrades: 'Here we have horse to eat, and I have often found myself without anything. The climate is cold, but I have suffered still more on the burning sand of Africa. Patience and courage.'

On November 9th the army, by a forced march, arrived on the banks of the Wop, across which they made a bridge, but it was barely finished before it was broken by the floating ice, and could not be made again.

The Cossacks did not cease to harass us, and drove back our skirmishers, so were obliged to ford the river, through the ice, with water up to the waist. Many of the men, and part of the artillery, never did get across. Our carts, which followed, met the same fate, and in a few hours the river was encumbered with ammunition chests, cannon, etc. A little way off stood the Cossacks, who, seeing this confusion, laughed like madmen.

(*November 11th*). The weather became dull and cloudy; the sun never appeared, and a strong wind covered us with flakes of snow which froze on us. The snow soon covered the ground; rivers, lakes, and ditches disappeared from our view. We could not find our road, except by the corpses of the unfortunate wretches who had preceded us, for this cold increased the number of stragglers, who followed with difficulty, and a great number of whom, not having the strength to march, fell. They fell with their arms in the air, and died, frozen, in that position.

That there were so many stragglers arose from the fact that these poor fellows, having their hands frozen, could not hold their weapons, wandered about, and were driven from the bivouacs and the fires, because they did not contribute any food to the stock. They died behind the groups of those who were warming themselves, and who, seeing them 'playing the bear' (that was the expression used) stripped them, without ever thinking that their turn might come. Many of these stragglers took refuge also in the houses they found still standing, set fire to them, and often perished in the flames, not having the strength to get away.

I have seen this effect produced by the cold; soldiers whose hands were frozen, fell down, and the fingers and thumbs snapped like glass. One of my friends, Captain Chidor, of the 9th Regiment of the Line, had his feet frozen. When he arrived at Smolensk, and took off the bandages in which his foot was wrapped, three toes came off with it. He removed the rags from the other foot, and taking hold of the great toe, twisted it round and pulled it off, without feeling any pain. He went through the rest of the retreat thus mutilated, and died in Italy from the result of his wounds.

For my part I had my ears and chin frozen, and the hands slightly. The skin came off like that of a rabbit. One foot that was bare except for the shoe was not affected, but my wounded leg turned black, and I had no feeling in it. I did not have it dressed till I got to Gora; on removing the bandage, the skin, from the knee to the instep, came off, and the flesh under it was black and marbled. I felt no pain. Ever since then my left leg has been smaller than the other, but it is just as strong, and I never suffer from it.

The lot of the soldiers who were strong enough to keep their weapons was not less terrible. They were on the alert day and night to drive off the Cossacks who harassed us, but a few shots drove them off; though they came back it is true. So our poor fellows got no rest. At night they could not make a fire, because of the wind, and the scarcity of dry wood, and had to keep moving continually to escape the cold. Little by little they threw away their arms and increased the number of stragglers. Then they succumbed, like other brave fellows who had stood so many battles. Two hundred bivouacs presented a spectacle it is impossible to describe. Every house met with was burned down, and surrounded by corpses, half consumed and covered with snow. The soldiers crept under the snow into the smoking cinders, and died by the side of the corpses of their comrades.

Those who fell into the hands of the peasants or Cossacks— who would not always deign to take prisoners—met a not less horrible fate. They were stripped of their clothes, and driven by blows until they perished of ill-treatment or hunger.

Some days before we reached Smolensk, our cavalry had almost entirely disappeared. A good part of our artillery and baggage had been abandoned on the road. All our cavalry men left, who had looked so fine six months previously, were on foot with the stragglers. There was no discipline; all military rank was destroyed. Generals, superior officers, and subalterns no longer cared for the soldiers who had contributed to their glory. The men themselves asked nothing but death. Such a request was often made to me, and I had not the strength to recommend them to take courage, or even to weep for them.

Those who, like myself, had still a little strength, were tortured by hunger, and we ran after the horses, watching for them to fall; when we threw ourselves upon them like wolves, fighting for bits of flesh. To cook this miserable food, we had to seek everywhere for wood. Often it refused to light, or else the wind blew it out. This search for food took all the time we had for rest. Worn out for want of sleep and long marches, we had nothing but the snow to lie on. Generals, officers, and privates were mixed pell-mell, huddled against one another. There were some, who, nearly dead with fatigue, stood all night like spectres, round the faggots, when they had been able to light them,

(*November 12th.*) The army continued its march, and arrived this evening at Smolensk, where we found no resources, the guard having taken the little there was. And they sold us bits of bran or oatcake at five or six *francs* each.

I, with many others of my unfortunate brothers-in-arms, lodged in sheds or buildings outside the town; but none of us had the strength to drag ourselves about to seek for provisions, which were very rare, the Guards having seized everything.

They sold spirits, sugar and oat or bran bread at its weight in gold. I paid one of these egoists six *francs* for an ounce of oatbread, and a napoleon for a quarter of a bottle of spirits. These Guards, at Smolensk as at Moscow, were unworthy of their name, and disgusted the whole army.

Between Smolensk and the Beresina, the French were twice attacked by the Russians. In the latter of these, the regiment lost several officers, amongst them the officer who carried the "Eagle" and eighty-three rank and file. François, though he had received a bad bruise on the left arm from a splinter, was able to perform a brave action, which he thus describes:—

In this confusion no one thought of picking up the Eagle, which was by the side of the dead officer who had borne it. Although wounded, I hobbled back, and without caring for the danger, for the Russian sharpshooters were getting close, I picked up the Eagle and carried it off; hastening my steps to avoid the bullets that were fired at me, several of which passed through my cloak. The Russians also hurried forward, and kept up a constant heavy fire. Finally, I was hit by a round shot which took the skin off the back of my right hand, and made a bad graze on my side. Very luckily, I had sufficient strength and presence of mind to be able to withstand this cursed stroke of ill-fortune.

My left arm was in a sling, my crutch was broken, but I did not abandon the Eagle. When I got to Krasnoi, I asked a comrade to bind up my wounds, but he had neither linen nor water. I also asked him to break off the staff of the Eagle, and fasten the Eagle round my neck by its. cords and tassels. In the afternoon I rejoined the remainder of the regiment, which was to the rear of Krasnoi; and there I found my faithful soldier and my two horses. The brave fellow, on seeing me wounded, made haste to dress my wounds and wept over me. I told him about my feat, and he went and informed Colonel Ramaud, who related it to General Morand, who spoke about it to Marshal Davoust, who asked that a report should be sent in when we got to Thorn. There he gave me a certificate, signed by him, and assured me that application had been made to the emperor for the Officer's Cross of the Legion of Honour for me, the brevet for which was ultimately handed to me at Mayence, July 28th, 1813.

My commanding officers looked upon me as a dead man, but I never despaired. I had always had a good appetite, and I accustomed myself, little by little, to walk without a crutch, but I could not use my hands. From that day, my soldier never left me, and it is to him that I partly owe my safety in this terrible retreat. The Eagle of the regiment never quitted my shoulders till we arrived at Thorn.

At that time I still had my two horses. One I sold to a Captain of General Morand's staff for 180 *francs*, I kept the other, which stayed behind the column, and never lost sight of the regiment, which it rejoined at halts and bivouacs. This horse was taken by an officer of the artillery of the Guard at Gowno, who made me partake of his supper, that I paid very dearly for, as this officer carried away all my resources. I vowed vengeance on him, but from that day to this I never met him again—very luckily for him or me.

During our stay on the heights of Niemanitza and Borisow, where we bivouacked whilst waiting for all the army to assemble, I will describe our situation as it was before crossing the Beresina.

For a long time past, officers of all grades had been accoutred like the soldiers. Nothing could look more extraordinary than our clothing of skins, half-burnt, and smothered with grease. Our long beards had icicles on every hair. Everybody marched in a dazed state, with haggard eyes, and insensible to the sufferings of others. When a man fell, those who could speak, said, 'Hallo! another one "playing at bear!"' and a few instants later, one of those who had spoken played the bear in his turn. We marched anyhow. Our misfortunes had levelled all ranks. Some of the men bore on their shoulders a sack or nosebag containing a little flour, and had a pot hanging by their side by a cord; others dragged by the bridle ghosts of horses which carried a few provisions and cooking utensils. If one of these horses fell, it was quickly cut up, and the flesh packed on the backs of the other horses. The different corps of the army had almost ceased to exist, and their fragments were formed into small societies of six, eight or ten men, who marched together, had their stock of food in common, and drove away any person who did not belong to their gang.

All these poor wretches marched huddled together like sheep, and taking great care not to separate in the crowd, for fear of losing their own gang, and being ill-treated. If a man strayed away from one of these companies, another gang took his provisions, if he had any, or drove him without pity from the fires, when the wind permitted us to make any, and from any place where he tried to take refuge. He did not cease to be assailed till he had rejoined his own comrades. These men passed in front of generals, and even the Emperor himself, without taking any more notice of them than of the poorest wretch in the army. And the commanders saw all this without being able to say a word.

What could they say, in fact? Imagine 60,000 wretches, each carrying a sack, supporting himself with a stick, clothed in dirty rags, and eaten up with vermin. Our faces were hideous, yellow and smoked, smeared with earth, blackened by the greasy smoke of pine fires, the eyes hollow, the beard covered with snot and ice. We could not use our hands to button our trousers, and many fastened them with a cord. We were all indescribably filthy, and I journeyed several days without being able to wash myself, or still less change my clothes. Such was the spectacle presented by an army, which, eight months before, had been the finest in the world.

All the way along, could continually be heard the sound of dead bodies being crushed under the feet of horses, or under the wheels of carts. On all sides were heard the cries and groans of those who had fallen, and, struggling in terrible agony, were dying a thousand times whilst awaiting death.

More than common energy was needed to support so many calamities. Mental strength, however, increased as the situation became more and more terrible, and the man who allowed himself to be affected by the deplorable scenes he saw, condemned himself to death; but he who closed his heart against any sentiment of pity was able to resist these evils.

We marched as fast as we could during the day, in order to escape from these terrible scenes which were constantly occurring, and we never halted till nightfall in spite of fatigue, and even then we had to work hard to prevent being frozen to death.

When we were near a town or village, everybody rushed for the houses, and in a moment they were so crowded, that one could not get out again. Those who could not get shelter under a roof—for the more fortunate drove the others away—lighted fires outside, and often burned down the habitation and those who had taken refuge in it. Sometimes the houses were set on fire purposely, out of revenge.

This was not infrequently done, especially to houses in which generals were living. Or, sometimes, the houses, which were all built of wood, were pulled down bodily, carried away to the bivouacs, and used for making rough shelters. When these shelters were finished, a fire would be lighted, and everybody would set to work to prepare the meal. Flour and water were kneaded together, and these 'dampers' cooked on the ashes. Each gang took from its sacks the horse-flesh, and threw it on the embers to get cooked. I lived on this fare for twenty-three days, without salt or bread, though I occasionally had some barley, rye, or oat cake, which my soldier procured for me.

He had joined one of these gangs for the sole purpose of procuring me provisions. The dough was made of any sort of flour, mixed with snow water. It was a black mixture, and full of sand. Some gunpowder from the cartridges was mixed with it, for powder is salt, and, at all events, made the food prepared under such circumstances less insipid. The meal being finished, everybody crowded round the fire, and soon went to sleep, to get some strength to resist the morrow's sufferings. At daybreak, without drum or trumpet, the army resumed its march.

In spite of these terrible misfortuncs, the emperor did not cease to be considered as the *palladium*, which must be preserved at all hazards. His presence electrified our cast-down spirits, and gave us again a scrap of energy. The sight of our leader, marching on foot in the midst of us, and sharing our privations, sometimes produced the same enthusiasm we showed at the moment of victory.

Then came the terrible passage of the Beresina. The two bridges, which had been hastily constructed, often broke. The First Corps, to which François was attached, halted on a height from which they could look down on the bridges, and when they saw the terrible confusion, they lost all hope of being ever able to cross the river, and expected to have to lay down their arms. The horrible scene has been often described, but seldom so graphically as by François.

All night we of the First Corps were inexpressibly anxious, on seeing the unarmed troops pass the bridge. One of the bridges broke under the weight of the horses and waggons, and could not be repaired. Then the horses, baggage, and artillery, tried to cross by the other bridge, and a terrible struggle between desperate men ensued. A whole crowd of useless persons and women and children, who had followed the army from Moscow, rushed to the only bridge that was left. Besides which, a large number of stragglers, who had stopped to let the army pass, thought that their last moment had come, and crowded to the bridge, which was soon encumbered with corpses and waggons, and you could not get to it without climbing over the bodies of those who had been crushed. Those who fell tried to get up again by clinging to their comrades, who pushed them away violently, and trampled them under foot in their efforts to advance—efforts which often ended in their own fall a few yards further.

The difficulties increased; the men on horseback knocked down those on foot, and the vehicles crushed all those who were before them. On all sides were heard cries of pain, despair, and rage. . . .

The terrible disorder prevented us for several hours from even getting near the bridge, the approach to which was blocked for a distance of four or five hundred yards with broken carts, and horses and men killed by the enemy's artillery fire from the neighbouring heights. The division managed to pass. I, with my crutch and ray arm in a sling, was more than six hours trying to get on the bridge; and I tumbled more than fifty times between dead horses and men, but my courage never deserted me, and by dint of struggling amidst the dead and the dying, I ended by getting over the bridge, and rejoined my division; but my wounds had re-opened and were bleeding. My comrades made sure that I had not been crushed to death on the bridge. They made me partake of some of their 'baked dough,' which did me good after my fatigue, and the surgeon-major of the regiment dressed my wounds, for the first time since I left Moscow, He could not understand how I had hitherto borne so much fatigue, privation and misery.

Before reaching the bridge, I had, over my cloak, a broad collar of blue cloth, fastened with two silver hooks. It was torn off me, but I knew nothing about it till I rejoined my comrades. I thanked all my gods that I had got off so cheaply.

The only bridge which remained was so weak that often it broke under the weight of a four-pounder. Marshal Davoust remained some hours on the bridge to try and keep order; but neither he nor the other generals was listened to. The emperor himself would not have been; the soldiers were desperate, and the passion of self-preservation made some try to hew a passage through the crowd with their sabres.

The height of our misfortunes was reached when Marshal Victor and General Dombrowski were driven back; the carriages, the guns, and the chests were jumbled up together, and crushed men and horses. Some were pushed into the river, and others jumped in with the hope of swimming to the other side. All perished amidst the ice, and in the evening the bank to the right and left of the bridge was covered with horses and men. I love extraordinary sights, but I was horrified at this scene, and grieved to hear the shrieks which resounded from all sides, and were uttered by men, women and children. To all this noise were added the whistling of balls, and the explosion of shells and ammunition chests.

When all had crossed, the bridge was set on fire to prevent the pursuit of the Russians.

I cannot exactly say what our loss was, but it was enormous; it may be estimated at over 30,000, combatants and non-combatants, besides an immense number of guns, baggage waggons, and regimental chests—some of us knew, though, that the chest of the 30th was not lost—and the Russians regained all the trophies and riches that we had carried off from Moscow and other places. In fact, the Beresina was the grave of the remains of an army which, only eight months previously, had been so brave and so handsome. Those who escaped death were completely disbanded. My regiment numbered but 143 men, and the First Corps, 8,700; all the other corps were in the same situation.

During the night, my soldier, whom I had not seen tor thirty-six hours, arrived at the bivouac and embraced me, weeping for joy to see that I had escaped once more. '*Va, mon brave!*' I said; 'I was not meant to die.' Then I asked after my horses; he told me he had not been able to save them, and I was not surprised. But one of them carried twelve soup spoons, thirteen forks, a soup ladle, a sauce ladle, and a pair of spurs, all in silver, and an important sum in roubles that my soldier had given me at Moscow. The next morning a soldier brought me my valise, but it had been ransacked.

Some Russians had been taken prisoners at the crossing of the Beresina, and they were useful to the French in procuring provisions, but the cold increased to—31° C, or 56° F. below freezing, and fully half of the remainder of the army perished. The survivors were also discouraged at hearing that Napoleon had determined to hurry off to France, leaving the command to Murat.

On December 9th, the French entered Wilna, and enjoyed a brief rest and some comfort, but, as will be seen from the following extracts from the *Journal*, their troubles were not over.

The army quitted its position about seven in the morning, and entered Wilna at five in the afternoon, where it found the Bavarian Corps, commanded by General Wrede. It entered the town, driven in by the enemy's guns, and in the most fearful confusion. Other Russian corps were engaged with General Loison's division on the Olitta road, where that division was almost destroyed, along with a good number of the stragglers of the 5th Corps.

I did not get into Wilna till about 5 o'clock. I was worn out with fatigue. I lodged with a brave Pole, with six other officers of different regiments, two of whom belonged to the 30th. This worthy fellow received us well. He had been a soldier, and taken part in the first wars in Italy, so he spoke the language of that country a little. He made us a good fire and some soup, and got us some beer. Of the seven officers in his house, three were wounded, and the others frostbitten. Two of these latter got too near the fire, were attacked by rapid congestion, and died in the night. We passed the night at this house, not knowing that the army had precipitately hurried away the previous evening on the road to Kowno.

I cannot pass over in silence the following trait in the character of one of my fellow-officers, a captain of artillery. This officer, as soon as he reached the Pole's house, went with a soldier to fetch his trunk from the magazine (all the property of the officers was stored at Wilna). I also had a trunk there, but I had not the strength to go and look for it, and my soldier was not with me, so I asked this officer to sell me a boot, as one of my feet was bare. I paid him 20 *francs* for it. This officer had also been able to retain a horse. On returning, he filled a large portmanteau, gave me a pair of boots, and left several other pairs and many other effects in his room, without offering me or any of the other officers a shirt, or anything else, although we were nearly naked. I had given him my last napoleon. This abominable man died afterwards.

(*December 10th.*) We had hurried to get to Wilna, to find a little ease after the intense cold and hardships. The sudden change caused the death of many of the men. Soldiers, officers and generals crowded into the houses, and were suffocated there, like my two comrades. Those who slept outside, along the walls, were frozen to death. Many of these poor wretches were assassinated, especially those, it is said, who lodged with Jews. I left Wilna at six in the morning, and by out-of-the-way streets, and I saw thousands of dead bodies, completely stripped, and many of them had been stabbed with daggers. It was certainly not the Poles who committed these crimes, for they were much attached to us, and often exposed themselves to the daggers of the assassins to save us.

At the moment when I quitted Wilna the Russian advance guard entered it.

About 5 o'clock in the morning our host came to inform us that the army had left, and that there was no one in the streets but stragglers, and plenty of dead bodies. This brave Pole led us by bye-streets, to save us from the wrath of the populace, and principally of the Jews. He led us thus as far as the foot of Mount Vaka, where the army was collected.

From the Beresina to Wilna, more than 30,000 soldiers of all ranks—demoralised, stolid, wounded, frozen, sluggish, unarmed—marched in a troop, with their heads down, without saying a word. Many died on the road, and others, taken prisoner, died of want.

A thick snow darkened the air that day. We could hardly see the way, and the army had much difficulty in getting to the foot of the mountain, which is about a league from Wilna. We were surrounded by Cossacks, and, as many of their officers spoke French, they said to us, 'You will need frost-nails to climb that mountain. Wait a bit, and Tchitchagow and Platow will bring you some.' As a matter of fact, owing to the frost and the steepness of the path, we despaired of being able to follow it. The horses we had left were badly shod, slipped, fell, and had not the strength to rise again. We were obliged to abandon the remainder of our materials, the baggage, and the emperor's treasure, of which he had, it was said, fifteen millions and his gold and silver plate. The soldiers kicked away the dishes and jugs, or threw them far into the snow. The wardrobe was burned. When I was on the top of the mountain I saw the grenadiers of the Guard defending the last few chests against the Cossacks, who, however, finally carried them off.

The army had much difficulty in climbing this mountain. As for me, with my crutch, and my arm in a sling, I do not know how I managed to get to the summit. I fell more than a hundred times, and dragged myself along the ice. I cursed my fate, though I laughed sometimes at the oaths of those who, like me, kept falling down. When I got to the top, I was covered with bruises, my wounds had re-opened, and I was covered in blood; it was, I am sure, nothing but the intense desire to escape at all costs from so many misfortunes that sustained me.

(*December 11th, 12th and 13th.*) The army followed the road to Kowno. We found some provisions; many of the inhabitants not having had the time to fly.

(*December 14th.*) The army arrived at Kowno, and bivouacked in the squares and streets; others lodged in the houses, many of which were abandoned. I succeeded, after some difficulty, in getting a corner in a house which had been taken possession of by some officer of the light artillery of the Guard—a very insolent sort of gentleman.

During the night my soldier rejoined me with my horse. These scoundrelly officers left very early in the morning, and took away my horse, with the few provisions that my faithful soldier had brought me. The rascals had no regard for my position, and I vowed vengeance on them, but never to this day have I been able to come across a single one of them, luckily for them and for me, for I no longer have my arm in a sling.

In the course of the morning I borrowed 100 *francs*, and bought another horse for 60 *francs*. I kept it till I got to Thorn, where I sold it for 20 *francs*.

The French left Kowno that morning, before the Russians came up and bombarded the town; under the impression that the French were still in it. That, however, was the last of the troubles the army had to undergo, and a few days later some 25,000 men—all that remained of the magnificent army which had set out a few months earlier—reached Thorn. The First Corps numbered 1,385 men, or about the third part of the full strength of a single regiment. The division had taken 2,700 Russian prisoners at the crossing of the Beresina, but they also perished with the exception of some forty. One of them had attached himself to François, and proved very useful. He shared the amazing luck of our hero, survived the retreat, and was handed over to a Protestant minister at Combine to be sent home.

On December 30th, François was comfortably installed at an inn at Thorn, and the next day sent for a tailor, a bootmaker, and a haberdasher.

# CHAPTER 15

# 1813

It was quite characteristic of Captain François that he should send for these tradesmen before having his wounds seen to, though his leg was in a bad state, as will be seen from the following extracts from his *Journal*.

*(January 1st.)* The surgeon-major of the regiment came to see me, and took off the bandages and lint, which had rotted on my wound. The skin of the leg, from the knee to the top of the foot came off with the bandage which enveloped it—it was as black as ink. He bathed my leg with camphorated spirits and advised me to take care of myself—a regimen which did not suit my character. Then, my wound being properly dressed, I put on clean linen, trousers, coat, and the boot which was sold to me at Wilna, and with my left foot in a slipper, and my arm in a sling, I went to pay the customary visit to my colonel. Whilst he was waiting for the other officers, the colonel spoke of the retreat; but what pained him most was the loss of the Eagle of the regiment. I let him finish, and seeing that he had forgotten that I had had the Eagle ever since the fight at Krasnoi, I said: 'Colonel, I can excuse your forgetfulness. The Eagle is not lost. Ever since the fight at Krasnoi, it has been round my neck, and is now in my room.'

'Is it possible, brave Captain? Come here that I may embrace you.'

He said some very complimentary things about me. Afterwards the other officers came in, and we claimed our 'allowances' (every captain had 400 *francs*, and the lieutenants and ensigns 300 *francs*),—to which he replied that the regimental chest had been lost at the Beresina. 'Yes,' we said—'but not the money that was in it—*that* we know for a fact, so pay us our allowances, or we shall complain to the proper authorities.' Thereupon he decided to give orders to the paymaster to settle with us, and we received the money the same day. We continued our visits, and called on Marshal Davoust, General Morand, and others. During this visit, the colonel told the marshal and the general that it was I who had saved the Eagle of the regiment. They shook hands with me, complimented me, and the marshal invited me to dine with him that night. (January 2nd.) After having my wounds dressed by the surgeon-major, I took the Eagle to the colonel, who embraced me with tears in his eyes, and promised me a lot of things.

The same evening he called upon me, and gave me a certificate signed by the Councils of General Morand and Marshal Davoust, and told me I might rely on those officers and himself doing everything for me; he also invited me to dine with him the following evening. As will be seen, I obtained some very highly flattering testimonials for my feat, but they were never of the least use to me. However, I am not at all ambitious, and it is all the same to me. I am satisfied with my own esteem.

(*January 3rd.*) The paymaster of the regiment died, and there was found in his belt 7,000 *francs* in gold, and 175,000 in bills. It is easy to understand where those sums came from.

There was not much rest for the soldiers of Napoleon's army and, on January 13th, François was ordered to Bromberg, where he saw his old friend Captain Chidor, of the 9th, who pulled off his big toe, as has been already related; and the next day to Posen, where he received orders to proceed to the depot of the regiment, which was at Mayence. They passed through Leipzic, and other towns, and found the Prussians inclined to gloat over their misfortunes. He says:

I will not speak of the nice reception, which the Prussians gave us, when we passed through a part of their country. Those boasters of the North insulted us in a most abominable manner, telling us to go back to Moscow, and to the devil. To them, as to the English, I swear an eternal hate!

By the middle of February François was in Mayence, where, being:

A friend to joy and pleasure, I had some intrigues and bits of luck, for my motto has always been, *forget the past, live in the present without thinking of the future.* And, considering my state of health, I reflected that a day might soon come when I should not be able to enjoy myself.

He seems to have trusted to his cast-iron constitution, which, indeed, never failed him. He writes under date of February 15th:—

The surgeon-major of the regiment came to dress my wounds, which he found in rather a bad state. He prescribed a regime and rest, which I followed—more or less—not being ill either in body or mind.

He afterwards, perhaps, regretted this inattention to medical advice, for, in April, the emperor arrived at Mayence, reviewed the troops and bestowed some decorations and promotions. By his usual bad luck, François was not present at these reviews, being unable to walk, his wound being in a very bad state; and the emperor having "the noble habit of only rewarding those who appeared before him." To make up for this disappointment, he had a love affair, his latest mistress being:

The daughter of a Dutch colonel, a very pretty woman, *coquettish*, and extremely prudish. This young woman had remained at Mayence, with other ladies whose fathers and husbands were the other side of the Rhine, and they procured each other substitutes,—the old ones finding lovers for the young married women, and these latter finding them for the girls. It was by this means that I made the acquaintance of the fair Amaranta, who rather acted the novice, though she was a bit of an old stager.

His wounds, however, were healed by the end of May, and he was able to be present at the review, when the emperor again passed through the city on July 28th.

The emperor reviewed the 3rd Battalion, and the depot of the regiment. Major Hervé presented to the emperor the list of officers for promotion and reward. The emperor wished to see us. The major presented me, and said: 'Sire, this is one of your old Dromedaries.'
The emperor looked at me, and said, 'What do you wish?' The major, without giving me time to answer, replied for me, 'Sire, the officer's cross.' 'Granted!' replied the emperor.

Major Hervé did me a bad turn, for as the emperor was granting everything that day, I had intended to ask, in addition to the cross, for my nephew's admittance into a *lycée* as a free scholar. The review being ended, the emperor ordered the 3rd Battalion to be ready to march at 10 a.m. the next day. I belonged to that battalion, so I got ready, and as the depot and my Amaranta both bored me, I found legs enough to go and join the 1st Battalion at Hamburg, which was all the more easy as we made part of the journey on the Rhine.

François enjoyed a little desultory fighting during the autumn, but he was not at "the Battle of Nations," which ruined Napoleon's hopes, and makes no mention of it. But, two months before that battle, he states that there was a rumour amongst the soldiers—"and such rumours often prove true"—that various divisions of the army had been beaten, and the emperor must retreat to the Rhine. At the end of the year, François and his division were at Hamburg, where 42,000 men, French and foreign, were blockaded by the allied armies.

# CHAPTER 16

# 1814

Concerning the siege of Hamburg by the Russians, François has few details to give us, for he carried his note-book inside his *shako*, and both fell into the Elbe in the course of a sortie and could not be recovered. But some of the incidents were in the inside of his head, and we get a curious glimpse of the life of a beleaguered city. The hardships were trifling—at all events, to one who had been through the retreat from Moscow. The officers—in addition to their ordinary rations—had two or three bottles of rum every month, several pounds of coffee, sugar, rice, and white bread. Nor was there much distress in the city, for everybody who could not prove that he had six months' provision stored away was turned out of the town. It is said that more than 30,000 of these poor wretches perished, but François makes no mention of their fate. Great events happened, for this was the year of Napoleon's downfall—but they affected François only indirectly, and he says little about them, but the little he has to say he had, perhaps, better relate in his own brisk, forcible, old soldier's style.

(*January*.) During this month frequent sorties took place without much success. The weather became excessively cold. More than 20,000 of the inhabitants, and 5,000 or 6,000 soldiers, were employed day and night in breaking the ice on the Elbe, to prevent the enemy from attempting any surprises. The officers and soldiers had frost-nails on their boots, to prevent slipping. These workmen were paid, which cost a great expense. To meet that. Marshal Davoust afterwards seized the money in the bank, and has been much blamed for that, and called an egoist. He has been accused of having taken large sums for himself. The marshal was a man of honour, and incapable of such a crime, and the money that he appropriated at different times in Germany he gave to his soldiers. He was the poorest general in the army, although he had the most opportunities of enriching himself; and by his good management endeared himself to all the officers and soldiers. When, at the end of the siege, horse-flesh was distributed to the troops, the marshal was the first to eat it.

(*February 9th.*) The enemy attacked several points. At the island of Wilhemsburg, the 2nd Battalion lost 200 men; Colonel Pierre, of the 29th, was killed, and General Holstein mortally wounded. The fight was obstinate on both sides. The enemy was repulsed at all points, could not cross the Elbe, and lost many men. When the affair was over, the troops returned to their quarters. I, like many of my comrades, went to balls and other festivities. The town did not look as if it were blockaded. We had theatrical performances in French and German every day. We often left a ballroom to go and fight, and, when that was over, resumed the dancing. One officer would ask another, 'Where is A——?' 'With the outposts.' 'And B——?' 'Gone to his Maker!' And the dance continued.

(*May.*) In the beginning of this month the enemy told us what had happened in France—that Louis XVIII. had returned, and the Emperor had fled to Elba. We were incredulous. The enemy teased us by showing white flags, upon which we fired. We also fired at the ships in the Elbe, which were decked out with white flags with the *fleur-de-lys* on them. It was not till the 20th that General Gerard arrived at Hamburg and confirmed the news. He wore a white cockade. He took command of Marshal Davoust's division, and gave orders for the garrison to be in readiness to leave for France, in several columns.

The army started early in June, taking with it 101 guns, but nearly all the powder, and some of the other material, was thrown into the Elbe. François' regiment—with three regiments of *cuirassiers*—was quartered at Thionville (Didenhoffen). He lodged with a young widow of twenty-eight, who was rather *too* fast, and very fond of parties. A lieutenant of cuirassiers was one of her adorers, and François shared with him the task of providing amusement for this very frisky widow; but "it suited his character," and he enjoyed himself much more than he had expected in this little town.

In July, the regiment was re-organised, and then reviewed by Lieu-tenant-General Lorencey, who said:

Thirtieth Regiment, in the name of the king I declare you dis-banded; in the name of the king I now declare that you are the 30th Regiment of the Line.

The Duc de Berry came to review the troops in September, and the officers clubbed together to give him a dinner and a ball, which cost François 63 *francs*. General Hugo commanded the garrison, and, no doubt, François may have seen and spoken to little Victor Hugo, for he often dined with the poet's father. But, in September, General Hugo was replaced by General Curto—"the handsomest man in the world," François says—but with whom he refused to dine, for fear of being suspected by his comrades. François sums up the general's char-acter in one line, but what that line contains we cannot say, as it is the only one in the *Journal* written in cipher.

The entry under the date of October is strictly personal, but is not uninteresting, as it throws some light on the military matters and manners of that day.

(*October*.) The 3rd instant, a man named Duchateau, a corpo-ral in my company, came and told me a lady was at the Hôtel de Malines asking for me. I went there, and saw a young and pretty woman I did not know. The lady began to laugh, and I was not sure whether I ought to follow her example or not. She put an end to my surprise by stating she was the corpo-ral's wife. She invited me to lunch with her, and archly asked me to procure her husband's discharge. I replied that was not within my power, but that I would send her husband to the surgeon-major. I saw the surgeon-major, and introduced him to the lady. He found her amiable, and succeeded in procuring her husband's discharge the following month. Meanwhile, the lady took an apartment in the town, and though I do not like married women, I paid her some visits, which she returned.
The husband, having obtained his discharge, started on a jour-ney of several months, and asked me to look after his better half, of whom I took the greatest care. I presented her to my hostess, who thought her pretty and amiable. The two women became close friends, and my *protégée* lodged with my host-ess. They made up pleasure parties, and invited other persons. My apartment was clean and convenient, and had a side door.

I sometimes provided the refreshments. We had some music. The orchestra was conducted by M. Etienne, the bandmaster of the regiment, who had married a Prussian woman, and who brought his wife with him. My hostess had a lot of female friends—amongst others, one who had a daughter named Eugenie, who' was my shepherdess in a fancy-dress *quadrille* afterwards. She ended by falling in love with me—if girls ever do fall in love with a man of thirty-six. The corporal's wife looked upon herself as my sovereign; she did the honours, and, though my guests often stayed very late, she—stayed longer still. After this princess left, my hostess wanted me to marry, but the young women she proposed did not please me.

(*November 3rd.*) M. Etienne, my music-master (for I played the flute), sent for me. The wife of the assistant surgeon-major had given birth to a fine boy, and he wanted me and the bandmaster's wife to be godfather and godmother. I accepted, and the ceremony took place next day. I was generous, and there was some dancing; but people gossiped, and the music-master got jealous. He was mistaken, for I always respected his Berliner—she was from Berlin.

This month, the officers and some amateurs of the townsfolk, male and female, had private theatricals. I took part. Then we subscribed for winter balls, and danced twice a week.

(*November 25th.*) The officers subscribed to the statue of Henri IV. I gave 24 *francs*.

(*December.*) In the course of this month, I noticed that, in the society I frequented, there was a great diversity of opinion, and no real confidence anywhere. Many of the laws caused dissatisfaction. The soldiers were dull and moody. They thought their services would not be reckoned, because they had fought for Napoleon Bonaparte. The oaths—demanded by the Allies more than by the Royal Government—humiliated them, and so did the addresses which they were compelled to sign. The regulations for the military reorganisation of the king's household on the old footing were heartily cursed. It was thought—perhaps with some reason—that the victorious nation was to be brought back to the *ancien régime*.

# CHAPTER 17

# 1815

The year 1815 was the year of the escape from Elba, the last effort of Napoleon, and the fatal day of Waterloo. At that great battle, François was not, strictly speaking, present, but he could and would have been had Marshal Grouchy interpreted his orders more intelligently and less literally, for the division was within marching distance of the historic field. The most interesting portions of the Journal are those which show with what enthusiasm the reappearance of Napoleon was greeted by the troops.

François was still in garrison at Thionville at the beginning of the year. There was a good deal of discontent amongst the men, and the commanding officers did nothing to lessen it. Colonel Ramaud made the men and officers of the 30th drill several hours in bitterly cold weather, when the snow was up to their ankles. In fact, they were treated as recruits, though most of them had seen from ten to twenty years' service, and François counted "twenty-three years and as many campaigns." It is hardly to be wondered at that the men thought that their past services were not to be reckoned, and that the grizzled veterans of Napoleon were the fresh recruits of the Restoration.

Except for drilling, François had, personally, little to complain about, and seems to have enjoyed himself as usual. He was a member of a small society of "friends of joy." They indulged in the rather mild dissipation of dressing up as shepherds and shepherdesses—"some in silk, the others in sky-blue" is François' rather vague description of the costumes—and dancing *quadrilles* together during Carnival. He notes also that his costume cost 117 *francs*, and that a young woman named Eugenie was his partner.

He found a more intellectual amusement, however, in the society of the new major, an officer named Verdier, who had been some years in Persia, and spoke Persian, Latin, Spanish, German, Turkish, and Arabic. He took a liking to François, with whom he conversed in Turkish.

Towards the end of February, rumours began to circulate that "a certain personage" would soon reappear on the world's stage. Citizens and officers possessed a medal, in gold, silver, or bronze, representing an eagle asleep with its head under its wing, but appearing just about to wake. "It was easy to guess the allusion," says François. The rumours took definite shape, when, on March 1st, a Bonapartist agent said aloud in the *café* that he had just arrived from Paris, and that the emperor had sailed from Elba on February 26th and landed at Fréjus; and that Generals Bertrand, Drouot, Cambronne, with other officers, had already joined him, and they were marching on Paris, where he had a strong party, and all the army would flock to his standard.

As Napoleon landed that same day, the person who made this remarkable statement must have been aware that the escape had been planned for a certain hour—unless he was a clairvoyant, or François has got the date wrong. At any rate, the Bonapartist agent was regarded as a madman, and clapped into prison—but let out a few days later, when the news proved true. For, three days later, other rumours began to circulate that the emperor had really landed, and though General Curto officially contradicted them:

> Nearly all the officers rubbed their hands. They were ordered to be constantly amongst the soldiers, who, despite our presence, did not conceal their joy. Many showed tricolour cockades that they had kept hidden away. They were sent to prison, but they cried '*Vive l'Empereur!*'

When the news was confirmed, General Curto remained shut up in his house; whilst the soldiers "played the devil," and laughed openly at any officer who reminded them of their duty. On March 14th, a proclamation was posted up declaring Napoleon a traitor and rebel, who was to be arrested and tried by court-martial, but it came too late. The Bonapartist agents were all over France; they spread the news that Napoleon had found at Grenoble 6,000 men, who all donned the tricolour cockade "without having bought it." At Lyon, the Comte d'Artois had tried, by money and promises, to make a regiment shout "*Vive le Roi!*" but the men were silent till one of the dragoons made himself their spokesman, and said, "No, we will not fight against the man who has so often led us to victory; our hearts and lips are accustomed to utter another cry!"

François and his battalion were ordered to Metz. On the road, they learned that Marshal Oudinot,[1] who commanded there, had told the officers and men that, "The King and Honour were the compass by which they had to steer!" but they all deserted that night. The marshal's son, who commanded the 1st Hussars at Pont-a-Mousson, saw that all his men were determined to join Napoleon.

> He fired a pistol at the first hussar who cried "*Vive l'Empereur!*" then snatched the guidon from the officer who carried it, and went away with it. When the 30th regiment arrived near Pont-a-Mousson, agents passed through the ranks, wearing the tricoloured cockade, crying "*Vive l'Empereur,*" and telling us he was at Lyon, and in four days would be at Paris. They were not arrested, and they dropped proclamations along the road; the soldiers did not pick them up, but could not conceal their joy.

At Metz, François heard particulars of Napoleon's entrance into Paris from travellers who had come from the capital. It seems strange that the 30th regiment should have waited so long before it declared for Napoleon, into which it was practically forced by the action of another regiment, as François relates:

> (*March 26th.*) The regiment left Metz and returned to Thionville, where it was received with pleasure by the inhabitants. I went back to my old lodgings with Widow Vatry.
> The night of the 26th, the captain commanding the 1st company of *voltigeurs* of the 96th regiment, assembled his company silently, about midnight, and drew them up in battle array opposite the door of the general's house. Then he rang, and, when the door was opened, he asked to speak privately to General Curto, who was not much liked either by the garrison or the townsfolk. Somebody went to his room, but he was not there. Then Captain Duplessis, an officer, and some sergeants searched everywhere.
> One of the sergeants ascended to the garrets, and there found the general, in a nightcap and a great-coat, hidden in a box of hay. The poor general, who was more handsome than brave, begged for his life. He was told he had nothing to fear, and was taken to the captain, who re-assured him, and advised him to disguise himself and leave the town at once, or he would

1. *Memoirs of Marshal Oudinot* by Eugénie de Coucy & Gaston Stiegler is also published by Leonaur.

be thrown into the Moselle. The general thanked him, dressed, and left the town without speaking to anyone, and passed the night near one of the gates. In the morning, he asked for his personal effects, and then went to Metz. Captain Duplessis, his expedition being terminated, led his company back to quarters, and on the morrow we learned what I have just narrated. Some laughed, and others were grieved at such an act of insubordination. No proceedings were taken against the captain. Colonel Ramaud, of the 30th, took command in the place of the poor devil, Curto.

All the inhabitants wore the tricolour cockade. The soldiers tore off their white cockades, and went about the streets in squads, with swords drawn, singing and crying '*Vive l'Empereur*,' but not insulting anybody, and obedient to their officer's orders. Many of the officers secretly shared their joy.

(*March 27th.*) Marshal Ney passed through the town, and paid the usual visits. He spoke of the emperor with enthusiasm, ordered us to wear the tricolour cockade, and asked if there were no intruders amongst us. He said the king was unworthy to govern a brave people, and that he and his family spoke Chinese. He added that the Emperor Napoleon was the only man fit to command us and lead us to victory. Today, our regiment, and all the regiments of the garrison, assumed the tricolour cockade.

(*March 28th.*) General Hugo assumed temporary command. He had commanded Thionville during the blockade of 1814, and was much esteemed by all the inhabitants.

Today the soldiers were drunk; they went through the streets singing. Some grenadiers of the 30th went to Colonel Ramaud, and demanded the white flag. The colonel refused to give it. The soldiers replied, 'It must be burned,' 'No!' said the colonel, and requested them to leave, which they did, without any further remark. In the afternoon, the colonel went to the men's quarters, assembled the grenadiers, and said to them, 'You asked me for the flag which the king confided to you. I no longer have it; I have sent it to the person entitled to it.' The grenadiers were silent on hearing this, and then cried, '*Vive l'Empereur!*' I, as a member of the administrative council, knew that the colonel had sent the flag to M. Chevalier, a braid-maker at Metz. He told us afterwards he had hidden it, then that it had been taken from him, and with that we had to be satisfied; but this clumsy put-off made us think that the price of the white flag was with the money of the regimental chest, which was supposed to have been lost at Beresina.

Then follows an account of Napoleon's return to the Tuileries and his various enactments and regulations, which, as they are included in scores of histories, and are only "hearsay evidence" in François' pages, may be omitted. Colonel Ramaud pleaded ill-health when the regiment was ordered to join Napoleon's forces, and handed over the command to Major Verdier. This convenient illness caused some sarcastic comments amongst the soldiers, who are pretty good judges; but they were glad to see the regiment commanded by a man they liked.

The regiment changed camp several times between April 16th and June 3rd, when it was at Kange, near Thionville, where François was glad to meet old acquaintances, though one of his many lady friends made him very sad. She gave him a lock of her hair, and a wedding-ring engraved with his and her initials, and said:

Farewell, Charles, forever, for I shall not see you again. We shall have war with all the powers of Europe, and you will perish, as well as the army; and France will be invaded by the allies, for you will be betrayed.

In after days he often thought of this prophecy.

Whilst Marshal Ney was engaged with Wellington at Quatre Bras—Quatre Chemins, François calls it—another portion of Napoleon's forces attacked the Prussians at Ligny. The 30th and 96th Regiments were ordered to storm the village. They did enter, but came to a brook they could not cross, and exposed to a galling front and flank fire, were obliged to retreat with a loss of thirty officers and 700 men.

François writes:

Not for many a day had I fought with so much intrepidity, but I got no harm but a few slight bruises on the thighs and right leg. The disorder into which the enemy threw us made me curse my existence. I wanted to get killed, so angry was I to see a battle so badly ordered. There was no commander. We saw neither generals, nor staff-officers, nor *aides-de-camp*. The regiment was two-thirds destroyed, without receiving either supports or orders, and we were obliged to retreat in disorder, leaving our wounded comrades, and try to rally near our batteries, which were pounding those of the enemy.

Captain Christophe and I rallied the remains of the regiment, and, I can say to my glory, the soldiers were glad to see me again amongst them; and asked me to lead them into the fight once more. In spite of the check we had received, we had taken about 500 prisoners. Just as we were trying to get the regiment together, General Rôme arrived, and ordered us to re-enter the village of Ligny. The soldiers, not at all disturbed by their failure, nor alarmed at the loss of nearly two-thirds of their comrades, cried '*Vive l'Empereur!*' and marched forward. Captain Christophe sounded the charge; the battalion entered the village and was repulsed. He rallied the men and tried three times with the like result.

Then General Rôme ordered Captain Christophe and me to assemble the men behind the batteries of the division, which had not ceased firing; about 200 men assembled. General Rôme, seeing their courage, ordered me to take 100 men (they all wanted to follow me) and make a fresh attempt. These 100 soldiers, glad to see me at their head, cried, 'Long live the Emperor and Captain François!' I was proud of their confidence, and General Rôme said some very flattering things to me on the subject. We arrived at the hollow road which led to the village. The enemy's fire had greatly diminished. I ordered silence. Just as we were about to enter the village, we met a company of Prussians commanded by an officer; we were both surprised at finding ourselves so close to each other. I hit General Rôme's horse on the nose with my sword, for he was right in front of my men, and the general squeezed as close to the bank as he could.

I stooped down, and gave the command, 'Ready, Present, Fire!' The Prussians did the same, and though I was in front I was not hit. But there were dead and wounded on both sides. I was hit by a bullet, but it was stopped by my cloak, which was in a tight roll over one shoulder and across my body. I found the bullet afterwards in my cloak. All it had done was to give me a bruise on the left breast; but that made me spit blood for several days. I ordered my men to charge with the bayonet; the enemy defended himself, and for some minutes the carnage was terrible. In parrying the thrusts that were made at me, my sword broke.

At last I was knocked down by the crowd, and trampled under foot by my own men and the enemy. At that moment. General Rôme ordered the 96th Regiment to advance. The enemy fled. I was picked up, along with several of my wounded soldiers, who had not abandoned me.

I was badly bruised in many places by being trampled under foot, but I rejoined the regiment, which was posted behind our batteries. I had seven men killed and eleven wounded, but most of them slightly. I was only stunned, and was able to get back to the regiment, upon which the enemy was still firing.

A little later, the village was taken, the centre of the enemy's army thrown into disorder, and the Duke of Brunswick killed. During the night I learned that we had gained the battle, taken forty guns and eight flags, and done prodigies of valour. So, in spite of the want of unison and order, the troops of all sorts had done their duty, and, for my part, I had done mine.

The regiment consisted of 467 men, officers included, and was commanded by Captain Christophe and myself. General Rôme brought us our orders that evening. On seeing me, he said:

'Is that you, my brave captain? I am glad to see you again.' He shook hands with me, and asked—'How are you?'

'All right, General, barring a few kicks and bruises.'

'Rest yourself,' he said.

'No, General! The emperor has need of all his soldiers, and I can still lend a helping hand.'

The general shook hands with me, and promised that he would stand my friend. As a matter of fact, the next day, on the march, he handed me a certificate signed by him and General Pécheux, and advised me to present it to the emperor on the first occasion. But I never saw Napoleon again, and during the retreat I lost the certificate, my portmanteau, and my orderly; who deserted, and carried off all my property.

In our first attack on Ligny, the regiment took about 500 prisoners in the yards and houses round the church. Some of the cowards, of whom there are plenty in every regiment, offered to guard these prisoners—really, to get out of danger themselves. A captain of grenadiers, about as brave as his soldiers—a garrison dandy, who had hidden himself during the attack, and pretended he was wounded—took charge of these prisoners. He conducted them to headquarters, and declared they had been taken by him and his company, and was given a receipt, which, no doubt, he would have made use of if things had turned out differently. He was sent to the depot of the regiment, then at Metz, and some of the stragglers and wounded, who had rejoined the regiment, recognised him, and stated that he had run away during the battle.

The rumour spread abroad, and some of the officers tried to provoke this fine gentleman to a duel, but he did not reply to any of these provocations. But he related stories to his own advantage, and spoke against his comrades, and even against me, whom he believed to be dead—a rumour to that effect having got abroad. When his scoundrelly conduct became known, everybody turned their backs on him, and he was recommended not to show himself in any public place frequented by the officers. He took the hint. I mention him here because he was the first officer I ever knew who was unworthy to be in the army.

About 9 o'clock that night, 100 men were asked for to support the cavalry, which was attacking the enemy's sharpshooters in a ravine to the right of Ligny. I volunteered, and took the command, along with Lieutenant Dodet, in spite of the advice of my comrades. Although we had almost won, I foresaw misfortunes, and I almost envied those who had fallen. I said to myself, 'Let the end come!' We skirted the brook, and had not gone 200 yards when we received a volley which killed three men and wounded seven. Lieutenant Dodet was wounded by a ball through the leg. Most of my men were seized with a panic, and wanted to fly. I rushed amongst them, and compelled them to face the enemy. We went on, and lost four more men, and then were ordered back by Marshal Grouchy.[2]

(*June 17th.*) At daybreak the army started on a forced march. The roads were bad. Exelmans' and Grouchy's cavalry, and the divisions of Vandamme and Gerard marched on the Wavre, the Arneau, and the Beyle, by the Gembloux and Mont Guibert roads. The other divisions of the army marched on different points, that of Marshal Ney on Quatre Chemins, to attack it again. We, of Marshal Grouchy's division, marched on Blücher, who was believed to be on the Wavre, to prevent him from ef-

---

2. *The Battle of Wavre and Grouchy's Retreat* by W. Hyde Kelly and *The Sound of the Guns*, (Marshal Grouchy and the Campaign of 1815—an Anthology of Writings) by Frederick Llewellyn are also published by Leonaur.

fecting a junction with Wellington.

The emperor, we learned afterwards, after having manoeuvred all day, had established his headquarters at a farm, a league from the village of Mont Saint Jean.

We made very little headway, despite our forced march, owing to our useless manoeuvres in the direction of Liege to discover the movements of Blücher, who had, it was said, 75,000 men marching towards the Wavre. Towards 6 o'clock in the evening, we came to Gembloux, where we found General Maurice's cavalry, and Exelman's dragoons.

The division bivouacked round this town, unfortunately, instead of following Blücher, of whom we lost sight—a mistake that was fatal to the army the emperor commanded. Napoleon supposed Grouchy to be at Wavre and had sent word that he intended to fight on the 18th, and Grouchy was to send him 7,000 or 8,000 men by the Saint Lambert road.

But Grouchy, who was at the place assigned to him, did not receive this order, nor the others relating to the battle. As will be seen, he was the cause of all the misfortunes of the 18th.

On the 17th and 18th, I was orderly officer to General Pécheux. I even ate a bit with him and his staff. The general spoke little, and seemed sad and anxious when he talked about the slow march, and the position of the troops. He said that Marshal Grouchy must have learned from the country people that the Prussian Army had taken up a position at Wavre; and, if so, the marshal must be making a great mistake, and he could not understand his conduct. That night, Generals Exelmans, Vandamme, Gerard, Pécheux, etc., met at General Vandamme's quarters (I accompanied General Pécheux), studied the map, and discussed our position and that of the enemy. Generals Walmé and Milhaut, they said, were encamped in, the front and rear of Planchenois, on the road to, and about five leagues from, Brussels.

In front of them was the Anglo-Dutch Army, 80,000 strong, commanded by Wellington, whose headquarters were at Waterloo. General Exelmans' opinion was that the emperor's position was ticklish, for the enemy might receive reinforcements, and it would be risky to cross the forest of Soignes to fight forces more than double his own; and supposing even he did beat the enemy, the Russians, Austrians, and Bavarians might afterwards cross the Rhine, and enter France through Alsace, where there were only 26,000 men to oppose them. General Vandamme said that he distrusted the chief officer of his staff, General Maurice. He was right, for Maurice afterwards turned out to be a traitor. General Exelmans also grumbled at the slow movements of Grouchy.

(*June 18th.*) General Gerard's division (to which I belonged), under the orders of Marshal Grouchy, left Gembloux, with the other divisions, at 10. o a.m. The soldiers were impatient to engage the enemy. About 1 o'clock in the afternoon, we arrived at Walhain, a village situated about halfway between Gembloux and Wavre, where we heard a brisk cannonade on our left, in the direction of Mont Saint Jean and Waterloo, and we felt certain that the emperor was engaged with the enemy. Marshal Grouchy called a halt (we of the 30th were at the head of the column). He seemed anxious, and did not know what to do, whether to cross the Dyle, or march in the direction of the cannon, leaving one or two divisions on the left bank of the river, which they could cross, the bridge not having been cut, and the neighbouring positions of no importance, or the town itself either, which was surrounded by mud.

Marshal Grouchy called a Council of War. General Gerard voted for marching at once in the direction of the cannon; leaving a corps of observation on the right bank of the Dyle. This opinion did not prevail. General Exelmans, who was much excited, said to the marshal:

'The emperor is fighting the English Army, there can be no doubt about that. Marshal, we must march towards the firing. I am an old soldier of the army of Italy, and I have heard Bonaparte lay down that principle a hundred times. If we keep to the left, we shall be on the field of battle in an hour.'

'I believe you are right,' replied the marshal; 'but if Blücher comes out of Wavre and takes me in flank, I shall be blamed for not having obeyed my orders, which are to march against Blücher.'

General Gerard, who was glad to find General Exelmans of his opinion, said to the marshal:

'Your orders state you are to be on the field of battle. Blücher has gained a march on you. He was yesterday at Wavre when you were at Gembloux; and who knows where he is now? If he has joined Wellington, we shall find him on the battlefield, and then you have executed your orders to the letter. If he is not there, your arrival will decide the battle. In two hours we can be taking part in the fight, and if we have destroyed the English Army, what can Blücher, who is already beaten, do?'

If Marshal Grouchy had followed the advice of these two brave men, the battle would have been won. I attribute the disaster of this unfortunate day to him.

General Vandamme's opinion prevailed. We marched forward at 3 p.m. crossed the three bridges and attacked Wavre. Horse and foot performed prodigies of valour. General Vandamme finally made himself master of the position. The battle was of little use to us, and made us lose 1,100 men. It did little honour to our generals, who seemed to be groping in the dark; and all day long we heard the cannon on our left, in the direction of Waterloo. We ceased to hear it about 10 p.m. Nothing can describe the uneasiness this cannonade caused us.

The soldiers were melancholy, and had the presentiment of a misfortune. They boldly declared that the emperor was beaten, because the sound of the cannon was always in the same direction. Contrary to my custom, I was sad also, but inwardly I was raging.

(*June 19th.*) We, of the 30th at the outposts, were attacked at three in the morning by the troops of the Prussian General Thielmann.

General Pécheux sent us forward, and we surprised a Prussian guard of about 300 men, some of whom we bayoneted, and the rest we took prisoners. I was the last to cut and slash in the enemy's ranks, being enraged, and wanting to avenge myself, I did not know on whom, whilst cursing most of our generals, whom I considered traitors. This affair being over, we advanced noiselessly, and, when daylight came, formed a line of skirmishers; then we fired on *Messieurs* the Prussians, who retired without making great resistance, towards Wavre and the woods, to draw us on. These boasters seemed to know of the disaster of Waterloo. Many of them, after having fired, retired, crying in German; 'Come along with us, brave Frenchmen. You have no army left; Napoleon is dead.' I, and several of my comrades who understood German, did not know what to think of these rumours.

Our generals gave few orders, and let the men shoot if they liked. Their conduct puzzled us. We took and retook Wavre several times, without being able to keep it. The Prussians came out of the woods, and our sharpshooters fell back. Many of the officers had retired to the divisions, and the men were fighting without any leaders. About 1 o'clock in the afternoon, the generals sent for the superior officers, for the soldiers were grumbling, saying they had been betrayed, for they had noticed that, since the previous evening, no cannon had been heard in the direction of Brussels. Was the emperor beaten?

At 2.30 p.m. orders were given to cease firing. The enemy's fire also ceased. A minute later, the generals sent for the superior officers of our regiment, Captain Christophe and myself. They said that as they were ignorant of the result of the battle on the 18th, we must call in our sharpshooters and retire, but conceal from the soldiers that we were retreating. It was easy to see our generals were hiding something from us.

The soldiers grumbled about all this mystery which environed them. They were ordered to march in close ranks, and in silence. Some of the more wide-awake ones saw that we were retrograding, and did not hesitate to express their opinion about it.

The retreat was made with some difficulty, for the allies were close on their heels. Near Namur they were worn out with fatigue, and very hungry. The sappers of the 30th found three oxen, which they killed and were cooking, when news arrived that the enemy were close at hand, and the saucepans had to be abandoned. At Rheims the inhabitants were astonished to see a French force in good order; the runaways having announced that the whole army was dispersed. At Villers-Cotterets, a battery of twelve guns was seized by the allies. It was General Maurice, the chief of General Vandamme's staff, who had treacherously revealed to the enemy the whereabouts of these guns. Vandamme tore off the traitor's epaulettes, and sent him to Paris, closely guarded by gendarmes.

On June 31st, Marshal Grouchy's forces entered Paris by the *barrière du Trône*, crossed the Seine, and camped at Grenelle. The soldiers were not allowed to enter Paris, nor the citizens to come out to them; but François obtained permission to visit his brother and sister, who told him he had passed through dangers enough, and had better come and live with them in Paris, to which François replied that honour called him to his post, and the blacker things looked the more energy and courage a soldier felt.

The fighting was not all done, for there was a little skirmishing with the Prussians on July 3rd; but that same day a Prussian officer came to François with a flag of truce. He was sent to General Pécheux with his eyes bandaged, and half an hour afterwards orders came to cease firing. So far as François was concerned, that was the end of the campaign, though, after that, Blücher lost 1,000 men in a fight with Exelmans at Versailles, and François thinks that if his division had followed that general's example, Blücher would have been "done for."

Then followed, the capitulation. Some of the soldiers were much excited about it; broke their swords, and swore they would perish rather than submit to a convention signed by traitors. François seems to have been more concerned at the loss of his portmanteau (containing "a pair of blue cloth trousers, two shirts, four cravats, a razor and various papers, etc.") which was stolen out of the canteen-woman's cart. To make matters worse, his trunk, which he had left at Thionville, fell into the hands of the enemy. Even when he got his back pay, a few days later, it was in bills, which could only be discounted at a loss of ten *per cent*.

The army was ordered to the other side of the Loire, and started to march down the Orleans road on July 7th, closely followed by a "corps of observation" of the allied armies. On July 20th, the soldiers were ordered to wear the white cockade, and obeyed without murmuring. The 30th was ordered to Saint Flour, where, being regarded as partisans of the ex-emperor, they were not well received, but François managed, as usual, to fall on his feet. He says:

I lodged with the Comtesse d'Autil de la Roche, where the old canonesses, ultra in the extreme, received me, but getting acquainted with me they granted me their esteem, and offered me their table which I refused, though as poor as Job. However, I accepted several dinners, and became the friend of one of these priestesses. I went out for walks with her, and she introduced me to several families. Sometimes when my hostesses gave an evening, I brought the band of the regiment, which performed appropriate and other pieces.

At last the old dowager took such a liking to me (she was fifty to fifty-five years old) that she proposed I should stay with her till matters were arranged or I was fixed (there was some talk of the regiment being disbanded).

I thanked her and said I would 'dree my weird.' As I had already told her I had lost my portmanteau and my trunk in this unfortunate campaign, she offered me money, and even that I refused.

When he left Saint Flour, the "priestesses" gave him their blessing, and he went to Langeac, where he lodged with M. Bonhomme, a former deputy.

I ended by being beloved by Mile. Julie, my host's daughter, aged about twenty, who wanted me to ask her father for her hand; but I did nothing of the kind, although the match would have been advantageous. I believe I should have obtained papa's consent, for he liked me very much. But the moment had not yet come; I was too fond of liberty.

The men were disbanded, and a little later (September 18th) the officers were called to Saint Flour to be dismissed. François, of course, lodged with the countess, who renewed her offers, and was prodigal of her old charms and caresses, apparently to no purpose.

The final separation of old comrades took place at a dinner given by the officers of the two regiments—the 30th and 96th—at which "the generals did us the honour to be present." Never was there such a melancholy repast. Some, when they embraced the worthy and brave General Rôme, were taken ill, others broke their swords; all wept.

François seems to have wished to enter the king's service, and (for some reason not very clearly stated in the *journal*) was shortly afterwards sent to Angoulême in command of the remains of the regiment—one of the queerest regiments with which man ever marched through Coventry or any other town. His account of it is worth reproducing:—

Before going to Angoulême, I procured a third shirt, two pocket handkerchiefs, and a pair of boots; tied them all in a handkerchief and was ready to start with the remains of the regiment, which was composed of a sergeant (German), a drummer, four children, of whom two were girls, one of sixteen, the other of eighteen; M. Etienne, the bandmaster, and his wife, a pretty Prussian; my cousin, as faithful to her husband as one is at Paris; also MM. Henry and Prévot, musicians, the latter married, having a daughter of seventeen; and the canteen-woman of the staff (Mme. Tulary) who had a boy of thirteen and a girl of sixteen. Commandant Blain charged me to look after this joyous band.

The 23rd, after having said farewell to my countess, I went to the starting-place of our departure. There I found two carts laden with the archives of the battalion, musical instruments, a big drum and seven side drums, the flag, and the sappers' axes; and the women, girls and children mounted on the top of all these military paraphernalia. Many of these troopers had dogs with them, and these animals collected together looked both melancholy and comic at the same time, and made me laugh to myself. On the march, all these females sang, quarrelled, wept, scolded. I recommended them to keep quiet, and took advantage of the occasion to amuse myself. I appropriated to myself the two nicest troopers, with whom I lodged and fed. I lived in this military style the whole of my journey from Saint Flour to Angoulême.

The standard of morals in the army was not high in those days, and we are not surprised to learn that the quartermaster of the regiment had made £10,000 in fifteen years, though he could hardly have saved that sum out of his pay. How he had amassed the property is amusingly told by François.

Quartermaster Fremont lodged in a house opposite the *prefecture*, where we went on the 5th to examine the accounts of this honest fellow; who had property to the amount of 250,000 *frs.*, which the poor man had legitimately gained in fifteen years. We saw: *primo*, the money chest—but it was empty; afterwards the cash books—everything was in disorder. The signatures of the men on the monthly pay-sheets were forged more or less neatly, and the sums debited to my account as having been paid to me. I complained, but there was no money in the chest; however, the honest man afterwards paid me. All the accounts had been examined and signed by the Council of Administration, and audited by the sub-inspector, but all these signatures were forged; mine as well, for the honest fellow believed I had been killed at Ligny, a rumour to that effect having been current. He had marked down that he had given me my pay up to the day of my death—I suppose, to provide me with travelling expenses on my journey to the other world, but my resurrection, and that of many others he had struck out of the list of the living, quite knocked him over: he promised to pay me.

The *peccant* quartermaster died a month later—probably he had preferred poison to the hulks, François thinks—and "was buried like a dog." François had a busy time trying to get the accounts straight; and the colonel, finding he was a good fencer, asked him to manage the fencing and dancing (!) schools, and also to superintend the decoration of the barracks; which he accomplished so well that the doors of the barracks looked like triumphal arches.

However, he found leisure for a little love making. The daughter of his landlady fell in love with him, but he only returned her passion "in soldier fashion"; and he also had a neighbour, a fine woman, who was fond of the military in general and François -in particular, but "being always inconstant, I was not very faithful to her." The first-named young woman was married a few months later, by her ambitious *parvenue* mother, to a "foolish and ridiculous sprig of nobility." The poor girl told François she loved him, and gave him a pledge of her affection, which he kept, for he believed that he loved her—a little. He heard afterwards she was wretchedly unhappy.

# Chapter 18

# 1816—1853

Though the curtain had been rung down on the great drama in the world's history in which François had played a part, and he was never more to draw his sword for king or country, he still continued for some years to come to jot down in his *Journal* racy comments on political and social events, and ingenuously frank histories of his love affairs. If his narrative no longer reeks of slaughter, it is still not devoid of interest of another kind, which may amuse the reader, or, perhaps, slightly shock him. I have therefore given translations of those passages in which mention is made of historical events and personages, or which serve to illustrate the writer's character, or throw some light on the social condition of the time.

(*January 23rd*, 1816.) The colonel called the officers, and proposed that we should present the king with two years' of our Legion of Honour pension, back pay, campaign money, etc. I was fool enough to give up my pension for 1814 and 1815, and in all I was asked, and thus paid 2,700 *francs* for the honour of serving the king, at a time when he owed me a retiring pension of 1,200 *francs*. The best part of the joke was that many of our egotistical chiefs never gave anything at all.

(*April 12th*.) We received the 9th Chasseurs. After dinner we went to the Café de Plaisance, where we did a lot of sillinesses. We broke the silver cups and the glasses, cut the cloth of the billiard table, and—amused ourselves. But we officers have to pay (the captains 83 *francs* each) for the honour of amusing these braggarts, who did not care a d—n about us. Our colonel liked these affairs, which cost him little but ruined us.

(*April 17th.*) The captain and treasurer of the old 30th died, and was buried without drum or trumpet, the priest having refused to receive him into the church, because this honest man, who had made 300,000 *francs* in nine years, had not confessed, and had left nothing to the priests to save his soul from purgatory.

In June, there were grand rejoicings to celebrate the reception of a stand of colours sent by the king. In making the preparations, François caught a chill which nearly killed him, but got well in time for the ceremony. All the poor in the town had three pounds of bread and 50 *centimes* each, and the soldiers a bottle of wine apiece, and something to grease the saucepan. There was a ball for the upper classes, dancing was kept up till 4 a.m. and refreshments were in profusion. François enjoyed himself, but it cost him a lot of trouble—and 120 *francs*.

Marshal Roucherville reviewed the regiment in September, and asked the colonel if any of the officers were "scum"—*i.e.* old soldiers of Bonaparte. As the colonel had, very wisely, got together as much of this "scum" as he could, he was greatly shocked and told the officers of the marshal's question. They wrote to the Minister of War, and the marshal was recalled. The regiment was ordered to Toulouse in December. There was a lot of leave-taking, and a "princess" who was one of the prettiest women in Angoulême, gave François a bracelet with her hair in it,—and other proofs of her affection which need not be particularised.

At Toulouse there were many English families "ridiculously dressed and aping our *coquettes*." The colonel introduced his officers to some of these families. François says "We drank their punch and made fun of them."

(*June 17th*, 1817.) The legion went, in full parade order, to assist at the baptism of a soldier,—the colonel stood godfather—and the first communion of thirty non-commissioned officers and soldiers; a ceremony which took place at the parish church of la Dorade. After the ceremony, the cure took his thirty sheep to his house, and gave them a dinner. These soldiers afterwards told their comrades what a good dinner they had had. Then a great number of the soldiers suddenly discovered that they also had never taken their first Communion. They took it, but there was no ceremony, and they did not dine with the *curé* whom they sent to the devil, and they lost all taste for these mummeries.

(*July 24th.*) I received an anonymous letter, by the hands of a jockey, and, afterwards, several others through the post. The letters were signed B——, married woman. She gave me a *rendezvous* at the church of la Dorade, at the hour of Mass, to which she would go with her maid. I should recognize her by her dress, a description of which was given. I told my comrades of my good luck. Several of them accompanied me to the church, where they left me. I recognized a lady with whom I had waltzed, and I thought was unmarried. She was a nice-looking woman, twenty-three years old, married to a man of sixty, very rich, and as jealous as a Spaniard. I followed her out of the church. She left the town and walked along by the canal, where I accosted her. After a little talk, she made an appointment with me at her house, rue de Nazareth. At 8 o'clock I went there and had *bon souper, bon gite et—le reste*. My intrigue lasted six months. I did not learn till several weeks later that she was married. I have stated already that I do not like married women, because I respect husbands; a man never knows what may happen to himself.

The mystery and precautions that had to be observed decided my conquest—of whom I was very proud—to take a room in the town. She occasionally sent me Strasburg pies, truffled ducks, and hampers of Bordeaux wine, which I drank to her health with Captain Gaillard and some others.

The 30th December I went to see my mistress about 11 o'clock at night, but the husband, who was in the country, returned about midnight to finish the year with his better half. The lady, surprised by this sudden return, pushed me into a closet, where I began to dress. The husband caught sight of one of my boots, which I had forgotten, began to swear, picked up a pistol, ran into several rooms, and met me, bare-footed, at the top of the staircase that I was groping for in the dark in order to escape. At last I found the door, opened it and fled home; where I arrived at half-past one, muddy as a water-spaniel, and my feet bleeding.

My comrades, who lodged in the same house, were surprised to see me return in that state, and asked me to recount my adventure, which I did, and swore I would never have another intrigue with a married woman. The next day, the lady wrote to me making an appointment for January 2nd, at the room I have mentioned. I went there and tried to break off with her. I ended by leaving her, being tired of her charms and her love. I came out of the business with the loss of a boot; which was sent to the police station, and I never went there to claim it.

(*September 28th.*) I made the acquaintance of a young and pretty Spanish girl. I was tired of Frenchwomen. The young Spaniard was named Josephine Rodriguez; her father had been chamberlain to King Joseph. He had left his country in 1814, and was pensioned by the Government. It was thanks to the papa, with whom I talked Spanish, that I knew the daughter who was a musician, and sang fairly well. She loved me; I returned her love, and was happy with her till the drum beat for us to leave Toulouse. She was seventeen or eighteen. Iloved her a bit, and made a fool of myself for her sake; but that devilish *amour-propre* had a good deal to do with it.

(*November.*) The celebrated tragedian, Talma, gave several performances at the theatre. The crowd was so great that, the first night, the guard of 150 men under my command, was insufficient to keep order. Many persons were nearly smothered; coats were torn, shawls lost, and even shoes. In the crush, my tunic was torn from the waist to the collar. One woman was suffocated, and another gave birth to a child and died. My men suffered a good deal, so I rewarded them with bread and cheese, brandy, and half a bottle of wine a-piece. I got off with a torn tunic.

Early in January, 1818, François was notified that he had been created a Knight of the Order of St. Louis, and a month later received the accolade at the hands of the colonel. In the evening there was a reception given by the colonel to all the Knights of the Order in the neighbourhood. They drank mulled wine, and the band of the regiment played appropriate tunes. Some of the old knights grumbled that the Order should have been given to one who was a plebeian, and a soldier of the Revolution to boot, but François was not greatly concerned thereat, for he sensibly considered it better to be the first of one's family than the last, like them.

The same month, one of his comrades married a Mlle. Lafon, whose father was "director of military bedding." The young lady was one of the many who had nursed a hopeless passion for François, and as he was best man, he was in rather an awkward position. He writes:

After the ceremony, which took place at eleven at night, there was a splendid supper for the family and friends. I, as representing a member of my friend's family, was placed at the right of the bride, who did nothing but weep, and squeeze my hand under the table. I was on thorns, on account of my friend and her relatives, who knew that the girl loved me. At last the supper finished, and I thanked all my gods, for I felt deeply for my friend, and was afraid he would suspect me, but he afterwards showed that he was not offended, and he did me justice, for I never betrayed his friendship. The bride said to me at the church: 'Charles, it was you who wished this. I obey my father and sacrifice myself. Do not forget that I love you. I repeat it for the last time. Kiss me.' Which I did, weeping. This young lady had 25,000 *francs* cash down, and as much more after the death of her parents. It was a good match, but I could not betray friendship. May the Supreme Being grant that I may one day find a wife like Augustine.

The young Spanish woman did her best, not unsuccessfully, to console him for his matrimonial disappointment.

In May, a captain of *gendarmes* carried off this young person, but her father brought her back, and François vowed he would be revenged on the *gendarme* if ever he met him. The regiment was ordered to Bourbon-Vendée in June, much to the chagrin of officers and men, especially François; who says he had enjoyed himself like a king in Toulouse—if crowned heads ever do enjoy themselves—which the old Republican seems inclined to doubt. The Spanish girl was inconsolable at his departure, and her father said he would never make friends with an officer again, because it pained him too much when they had to leave.

At Bourbon, he lodged in the house of an old milliner, who had a "first-hand" who thought herself the prettiest of all the pretty women in the town, but she was no longer young, and François calls her "stupid, wicked, insolent, and proud,"—apparently because she did not like being chaffed about her age.

But she had not attained her thirty-sixth year without having acquired some experience, and she knew that François only pretended to make love to her to cover his intentions towards one of the apprentices, a girl of sixteen, and the daughter of one of the Vendean leaders. The girl was sent to live in an adjoining house, and François was locked in at night. But love notoriously laughs at locksmiths, and François had not been an old campaigner for a quarter of a century without having learned a trick or two. A rope ladder from his window enabled him to see the little milliner as often as he wished. At last one night he missed his footing, and was left dangling in space for three-quarters of an hour. Luckily for him, a carter came out to feed his horses, and released the gay Lothario. But in the morning the rope ladder was found hanging from the window, and caused a good deal of excitement in the town. The poor girl was called a hussy and turned out of doors; but François provided for her, and finally sent her home, "less of a novice than when she left, but not knowing much about fashions."

Nothing much happened during 1819 except that the regiment moved to Nantes, where François had the honour of seeing the "first Grenadier of France, the brave Cambronne," who was a native of that town. On September 25th, five guns announced that the Duchesse de Berry had given birth to a daughter.

In the following February (1820) François' "chum," Captain Gaillard, married a Mlle. Pauline Guibert—"an epitome of a woman, only four feet seven inches, but rather pretty and *coquettish*"—but there was no ball after the wedding, on account of the assassination of the Duc de Berry. The regiment went into mourning for twenty-one days. The only other items noted are that General Cambronne left for Lille—("He had married an Englishwoman, out of gratitude for the services she had rendered him and his family")—and that when a legion passed through the town on its way to Dijon, the officers of the garrison refused to give it the usual "reception." François says:

> The fact of the matter is, that these receptions ruin us, and henceforth we do not intend to give a reception except to those who have received us, and, up till now, very few have done us this honour, but they are quite right, for in our own case, these receptions cost the captains 800 *francs* each in five years, and we were as poor as Job.

François, Captain Gaillard, his wife, and a notary named Desgages were invited to a country house for a week in June. On the road they dined with "an original"—an old bachelor of sixty, who thought he was a woman and dressed accordingly.

At this country house, a determined attempt was made to marry François to a Mlle. Manette, but as he fought shy of her and her parents during the last days of his stay, he convinced them he did not mean business.

He was, however, destined to fall a prey to a young woman only two months later. The regiment was ordered to Rennes, and arrived there June 8th. The next day, news arrived of the execution of the assassin of the Duc de Berry, and a few "hooligans" took the opportunity to get up a small riot. François and his company were sent to keep order, and the local authorities wanted him to fire on the mob, but the caustic, old soldier replied "there were better ways of showing loyalty to the king than killing as many as possible of his subjects." He also made sarcastic remarks about calling him and his men, when a corporal's guard would have amply sufficed.

We now come to the story of our hero's last "engagement," which, if a victory, was hardly a success. On July 3rd, he called to see one of his colleagues, who, with his wife, lodged with a Mme, Posselin, a widow, "in a nice house with a pleasant garden, and an arbour overlooking the Champ de Mars, the favourite promenade of all classes." With his friend's wife was a girl—the daughter of the house, he was told.

> Without troubling about etiquette, I spoke to her, thinking to myself, That is the sort to suit you; so now, Charles, my friend, if that little girl will love you, you ought to marry her, and learn what a woman's first kiss is. The same day I spoke to Dupayron (the colleague abovementioned), who said there were four children, and he did not think they were rich. That did not interest me, and though I myself had but my campaigns and my laurels, I added that two nothings might, perhaps, make something. To-morrow I will come to see you and your wife, the girl, and the garden, which greatly pleases me.

Every woman is at heart a match-maker, and, of course, his friend's wife assured him that the girl was as much struck with him as he was with her. His war experience having taught him the value of a sudden attack, he proposed to her at once, and she, as is the rule in such cases, asked for a few days to make up her mind. Then she said "Yes," and told him to speak to her mother. He was not greatly impressed with the mother, who appeared wanting in frankness; and he rather resented the masterful ways of his *fiancée's* brother, who said he would compel his sister to have François if she tried to back out of her engagement.

François informed his colonel of his intention to get married, and the colonel made some fatherly observations, which, of course, had no effect on a man in love, though the captain was shrewd enough to see that he was making a fool of himself, and that Emilie's mother was shifty and untruthful, and her brother and sisters were only too glad to have found an idiot to take off their hands a sister they did not like, because she was too amiable.

But, in spite of all this, he wrote to the Minister of War to ask permission to marry. In reference to this demand, the Prefect of the Department sent for him, and said that the girl's brother had bad notes in the police records, and that all the family, though honest, were Liberals, and therefore enemies to the king, and therefore a marriage into such a family might spoil François' prospects of promotion. The blunt, honest soldier replied that he was not marrying the political opinions of the family, but a sensible and modest young woman, who would be hated by all her family if he deserted her, and that consideration alone was sufficient to make him carry out his intention. The *prefect*, pleased at this frankness, promised he should receive the necessary permission—which he did, three weeks later. The banns were duly published, and there were some religious formalities to be observed, which François amusingly describes:—

(*November 3rd.*) Being a Knight of St. Louis, and consequently a Catholic and all that is connected therewith, I called on M. de Pensé, chaplain of an artillery regiment at Toulouse, and a man with whom I could make arrangements to obtain a certificate of confession—a very necessary document for those who enter the brotherhood. He lodged in the Faubourg de Brest, with a niece. I went and saw the worthy man; he made me sit down, spoke of my services, campaigns, and decorations; then he asked me if it was long since I had confessed? I replied, 'Thirty odd years.' 'Very good,' said he. Next he asked me if I had—well, frequented the society of certain ladies? 'Yes,' I replied. 'Very good,' he said again. Then he asked me if I had fought a duel? I replied, 'Often.' Then, if I had robbed or shared stolen goods? 'Yes, I had often shared in the spoils of marauding expeditions.' 'Very good,' he replied for the last time.

Then turning to his niece—who was not extraordinarily pretty, and who was present at our interview—he asked for a bit of paper, about as long as my little finger and the same width, and wrote on it his *audivi*, which absolved me from all sins, past and future. I thanked him, and left six *francs* on the mantelpiece for the poor.

The wedding took place a few days later, François writes:—

> About ten o'clock we had a family lunch, with the witnesses. Never was a marriage more modest. There were only two relations of my wife—a talkative old woman, and another quite as old, unmarried and devout. They are the only relatives of my wife that I know. May *Allah* preserve them!
>
> The ceremony took place at six in the evening. After my marriage I continued to live with the family, and soon saw there was no harmony between them. My wife's mother was sulky, and incessantly reminded us of her former condition and her misfortunes. The children quarrelled, and had no respect for the mother. My stay there was almost insupportable; but I bore it because my situation made it necessary I should. My wife herself had no esteem for her mother. I observed to her that we ought to respect the authors of our days, but that young person had a Breton head. I was present at some scenes, and was obliged to restore order. I showed them what a Picard and a soldier, who has no ambition but to live in peace, is capable of, and I ended by being more feared than loved, but I think I managed to acquire the esteem of the mother, the friendship of my brothers-in-law and my little fool of a sister-in-law, and the confidence of my better-half.

The brothers-in-law squabbled with each other, and would have come to fisticuffs once (July, 1821) if François had not kept order. His wife, too, was sometimes ill-behaved, but she had a good heart, and was amenable to reason. The only other items worth noting this year are that the officers subscribed a day's pay towards purchasing the Château of Chambord for the Duc de Bordeaux; and that, on July 9th, François heard of the death of Napoleon at St. Helena.

> This great captain died May 5th, at six in the morning. His last words were, 'head . . . army.' He died with his eyes fixed on the bust of his son, now living with his grandfather at Vienna. Napoleon was ill forty days, suffering from a cancer in the breast. His will was sent to Beauharnais, viceroy of Italy, his adopted son.

François' only comment on the death of his old leader is that:

This great man did good and evil, but more good than evil.

In February, 1822, François was charged to conduct a draft of recruits to a regiment at Bethune. He came back through Paris, and brought some presents for his wife from his brother. His wife's family said they were glad to see him back, but he doubted their sincerity. The usual bickerings continued. His wife turned her mother out of the house, and refused to apologise for this unfilial conduct, so François assumed his marital authority, and was obeyed. But he swore that if such scenes were renewed he would quit the cursed family. He was not at all sorry when, in June, the regiment was ordered to Dunkirk, and he sent his wife to Paris, to be kept there till he asked for her.

At Dunkirk he made many friends, amongst others a Mr. and Mrs. Weston, who were English, and *bien braves gens*—a wonderful concession for François to make. In March, 1823, the regiment went to Metz. There François and his wife lodged with a grocer for 48 *francs* a month, "which was too much for a poor captain to pay, but I was one of the best lodged officers in the garrison."

Whilst at Metz, François underwent a surgical operation, which he describes at some length:—

> (*April 24th*, 1824.) I was operated on for a kind of tumour, which had grown at the back of the neck, between the flesh and the skin. For many years past it had grown in size, and I had at various towns, and even at Paris, consulted many surgeons and doctors; all advised me to have it taken out before it grew larger, but not one was willing to undertake the job. At Metz, there is a School of Surgery. I consulted M. Gauthier, the surgeon-major of the regiment, who advised me to go and see M. Villemain, his colleague, at the hospital, to whom we both went. By the advice of these gentlemen, I went again, two days later, at seven in the morning, accompanied by M. Gauthier. We went into the amphitheatre, where more than eighty students had collected, who had come to see the operation, this being an extraordinary case. They did not know I was the patient. 'Is this a difficult operation?' I asked. 'Yes,' they replied; 'an operation of that kind is long, painful, and sometimes fatal, but our professor is very skilful.

When the surgeon came, and the students saw François begin to take off his coat, they were much surprised. Two of them were going to hold his head—anaesthetics were not used in those days—but

201

François told them not to trouble, though he owns the pain was "insupportable." After the cyst had been successfully extracted, François asked for a pinch of snuff, which the regimental surgeon handed him, with tears in his eyes. Dressing the wound took twenty-seven minutes, and then François walked home! The wife was surprised to see him with his head and neck enveloped in bandages, but she guessed what had happened. He was put to bed, with strict orders not to talk or move his head. His comrades came to see him. Some said, "It's a stupid trick at his age;" others said, "He's a goner!" They did not use that exact expression, but another—which also is not in the dictionary.

He had a fever for three days, but, on the sixth, he could not resist the temptation of going to see his company. In eighteen days he was quite well, and resumed his duties; much to the joy of some of his comrades, and the chagrin of others, who thought they had lost a good chance of promotion. He celebrated his recovery by a dinner to the surgeons and his fellow-officers. He wanted to pay M. Villemain for having relieved him of this unpleasant companion, but the surgeon replied he was sufficiently repaid by the confidence François had in him, and the courage he had shown.

On July 17th, François was much astonished to receive a letter from an army-agent in Paris, informing him that he had been pensioned off, and offering his services. The bad news was, unhappily confirmed by the colonel a week later, who, in a touching, manly letter, informed François of the decision of the Minister of War, and assured him that when he left the army, he would carry with him the esteem, friendship, and regrets of his commanding officers and comrades.

On August 7th a farewell lunch was given him by the colonel and officers, but poor François could hardly eat a morsel, and nearly the whole regiment, from the colonel to the drummer boys, came to see him off when he started in the *diligence* for Paris. His object there was to try and get the minister to alter his decision;—a hopeless task. Of course, he failed, and he writes, bitterly:

I find myself condemned to go and plant cabbages. Alas! in spite of my thirty-two years' service and my campaigns, I have not the wherewithal to buy an inch of ground, so if I do plant cabbages, it will be in another man's field.

He went about Paris with his brother's clerks, and saw:

The *greatest* of Frenchmen, Louis XVIII., surnamed the Desired, who was rolled in a wheeled-chair from one window of the

Tuileries to another, to hear the cheers of his chuckle-headed people, some of whom were base enough to cry, '*Vive le Roi!*'

His enforced retirement before he attained the age of fifty, was probably due to his political opinions, which were Republican, as is shown by the following extract from the diary for the same year.

I often saw General Joubert. Having become a general, he acquired the title of baron; at the time of which I speak, he was a viscount. His wife was very proud of this title. As I never called her anything but *madame*, she thought me a rude soldier. She made this remark to her husband, who repeated it to me. I replied that I never gave titles to anyone, not even a prince. 'Then, my friend,' said the general, 'you are still a Republican?' 'Liberal, yes. General.' It ended by my no longer visiting there, and not even saluting the viscountess when I met her. Annoyed at this, she again spoke to her husband, who informed me about it. I said, 'General, I am sorry you should consider me badly brought up, but it is impossible for me to pronounce feudal titles.'

He selected Rennes as his place of residence—rather a dull town, but his wife's family obligingly undertook to provide him with excitement. His brother-in-law had, by his extravagance, ruined his mother, and even compelled her to sell the orange-trees out of the garden François had so much admired. His mother and sisters were frightened of him, but he failed to impress any dread on a man who had followed Napoleon across Europe.

(*November 5th*). Another scene took place. The eldest son, not content with ill-treating his mother, after having ruined her, struck his younger sister, and threatened to turn my wife out of the house. I was absent, very luckily, but on my return, I was informed of what had happened. I went and saw the rascal, challenged him to a duel, but the coward refused, and I forbade him to put his foot in his mother's house. As he feared me more than he loved me, he went away and I never saw him again.

(*November 25th to 30th.*) This jewel of a brother, taking advantage of my absence, came several times to plot with his little slut of a sister to make us leave the house. This little fool insulted the people who came to see me and my wife. I threatened her. She declared that her mother and brother forced her to act thus, in order to make us leave the sooner. I thanked the mother, who

203

denied it, and said she loved me like her own child. I knew which to believe.

Today, on returning home, I heard my sister-in-law insult my wife, who was in our bedroom. I entered, took the little fool by the arm and put her out of the room. I do not turn nasty as a rule, but I made the house shake. I married to have a family, and it may be truthfully said I have succeeded! Those who read these pages will see that if I liked extraordinary things, my marriage was not the least curious of all my adventures.

An opportunity soon occurred of getting away from this charming family. Just before Christmas, he received an invitation from his old friend Gaillard to visit him at Nantes, stay several weeks, and stand godfather to the baby. He and wife started the next day, and enjoyed themselves thoroughly at Nantes. François did things so lavishly at the christening that he reckons he spent five months' pension on that occasion. His friend's relations made much of him, and as selections from his *Journal* had appeared in a local magazine, he found himself a popular author on a small scale. He was elected a member of the Academy of Sciences (local), put on the free list of the theatre, and, in fact, was quite a lion. His portrait was painted and shown at an exhibition of industrial products of the department. It was, or ought to have been lithographed, but no copies appear to exist now.

The upshot of all this was that he determined to quit Rennes and establish himself at Nantes, which he did, in April, 1825. A French-American firm was building a couple of steamboats for passenger and goods service on the lower Loire. François was offered 1,200 *francs* a year to superintend the building of these boats, and, when they were completed, act as clerk or purser fifteen days a month. The boats ran from Nantes to St. Nazaire, and François found his duties pleasant but monotonous. He studied the construction of the engines, and was able to teach the stokers how to drive them. By this means he was able to get rid of the engineers, who were English, by which he saved money to the company and did a bad turn to his old enemies.

One of his engineers, however, came to a sad end. He had lunched too freely on the down trip; for which François scolded him and told him to go to bed. He insisted on performing his duties, fell asleep, and his head was cracked like a walnut-shell by the engine-beam. The accident created a panic amongst the 140 passengers, but the imperturbable coolness of the old soldier reassured them, and he brought them safely to Nantes.

★★★★★★

There are a few unimportant entries in the *Journal* during the next three or four years, and the diary stops with a brief mention of the Revolution of July 30th, 1830. Of the rest of his long life we know little. He continued to live in Nantes, where he was popularly known as "the Egyptian Dromedary," and was universally respected. The National Guard elected him their commandant in 1832, and re-elected him every year till 1846, when his age and infirmities prevented him from accepting the post for another year.

Captain Charles-François François died April 3rd, 1853, in his 78th year. There were highly laudatory obituary notices of him in the local papers, and the last honours were rendered to his remains by a company of the 59th Regiment. The Municipality of Nantes granted a free concession of the ground in which the old hero's bones rested, and also subscribed, with many of his old friends, to erect over his grave a stone on which was inscribed a record of his long services. That stone still stands, but is time-eaten and neglected.

The voluminous MS. of the *Journal* he had kept so many years, was bought from the widow, in 1869, by an old friend of her late husband, Dr. Foulon. The MS. passed to his son, by whom it was sold to the French publisher, under circumstances which have been already related by M. Jules Claretie in his preface.

★★★★★★

Here, my task as translator ends. It is (happily, I think) almost impossible to write a life or transcribe the autobiography of any man without feeling a sympathy with the subject, but I do not put forward Charles François as the noblest type of soldier. By the very nature of the case, such a man is rarely found in the army of a leader who fights for lust of conquest. Moreover, it is not the man but the events—*quarum pars minima fuit*—which make the interest of his book. But, with all his faults, he had the bull-dog pluck and determination which Englishmen admire in friend or foe. He was—in Mr. Rudyard Kipling's words—"*a first-rate fighting man*," who never willingly turned his back on a foe. As I close the book, and am about to lay down the pen, there comes into my mind the epitaph, uttered by an old soldier, which would not have been inappropriate on the grave of François.—

*Had he his hurts before?*
*Ay, on the front.*
*Why then, God's soldier be he!*

.

www.ingramcontent.com/pod-product-compliance
Lightning Source LLC
Chambersburg PA
CBHW032032090426
42733CB00029B/309